Research Methods in Information

Research Methods in Information

Alison Jane Pickard

facet publishing

Published by
Facet Publishing
7 Ridgmount Street
London WC1E 7AE
www.facetpublishing.co.uk

Facet Publishing is wholly owned by CILIP: the Chartered Institute of Library and Information Professionals.

First published 2007

British Library Cataloguing in Publication Data
A catalogue record for this book is available from the British Library.

ISBN 978-1-85604-545-2

Typeset from author's disk in 9.5/12.5 pt University Old Style and Zurich Expanded by Facet Publishing.
Printed and made in Great Britain by Cromwell Press, Trowbridge, Wiltshire.

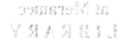

Contents

Acknowledgements

It would be impossible to produce a work such as this without contributions from many and varied sources.

My greatest source of inspiration in beginning it was Pat Dixon; the seed was planted a decade ago when she handed me a research methods text I had never seen and sent me down 'the road less travelled'. She taught me that research isn't just about the end product, the discovery – it's also about the journey. Pat is a born teacher; she instinctively knows how to get the best out of people and how to urge them on to reach their full potential, even when they doubt themselves. As a teacher, and as a friend, I owe her a great deal.

Creating this work has been aided and abetted by the many students, past and present, who I have had the great privilege to guide through their dissertations. I thank them all for the contribution they have made and the research experiences they have shared with me, many of which I'm sharing with you in this book. The practical exercises in the book are based on the learning experiences of my students, and have gone through many and varied adjustments based on their experience of actually engaging in them. In particular I want to thank one PhD student, Wendy Beautyman, for her meticulous attention to detail and constant nagging to get this work finished. Shona McTavish has that extraordinary quality that allows her to be a friend, a mentor and a boss, all in the right proportions and at the right time. Her new life will mean her role as my boss will disappear; the other two roles I hope will go on for ever.

I think I have been extremely fortunate in having the best editorial team there is – only they could have got this out of me! Helen Carley and Lin Franklin are possibly the most professional and accessible editors a person could have; thank you both for your faith, patience and guidance. I have to thank Elspeth Hyams for introducing us.

When people have faith in you anything is possible, and I'm lucky to have a lot of people around me who have had that faith: Pat, Shona, Matt Pointon, Genevieve Inkster, Linda Banwell, Colin Creasy, Margaret Graham, Alastair Irons, Rita Marcella and Alistair Sambell have not only tolerated my exuberance and passion, they have actually encouraged it! Thank you all.

I must acknowledge my gratitude to the authors of all the books and articles that have influenced my thinking, especially to all of those I have had the great fortune to meet and discuss my work with, receiving invaluable comments and suggestions.

My family are responsible for giving me the security, confidence and love we all need on a scary journey. My parents always have the same answer when a new challenge comes along and I'm unsure of my ability to rise to it: 'Yes, you can', they say, and after a while you have to believe them! This book is dedicated to my family: my daughter Zoë (it was because of her all of this began); my parents, Muriel and Bart, for not only saying 'yes, you can', but for providing the support I needed to make it happen; my partner Ian for being there and never shrinking under the weight of my more stressful moments; and my best friend, Dawn, for always loving me and never giving up on me. My family has been tolerant beyond the bounds of reasonable expectation and for this I am eternally grateful.

Alison Jane Pickard

Introduction

The purpose of this handbook is to provide a reference guide to the research process for students and practitioners in the fields of information studies, communications, records management, knowledge management and related disciplines. The importance of research within these disciplines should not be underestimated, as 'research skills are a prerequisite for those who want to work successfully in information environments, an essential set of tools which enable information *workers* to become information *professionals*' (Harvey, 2000, xiv). Knowledge and experience of research is a fundamental part of what makes the 'information professional'.

Harvey provides a number of reasons why research is so important in the workplace; not least of them is the need to meet the ever-increasing requirements of accountability of services. In order to maintain dynamic and appropriate services we need to be constantly examining what we do and how we do it. When attempting to improve these services, research often offers the answer; research can help us identify problems in the workplace and very often provide solutions to those problems (Harvey, 2000).

These are very practical, 'real' benefits of research but there is also the need to increase the body of knowledge that makes up the profession, to continue to engage in the questioning process that allows the professional to grow. This should never be underestimated. Even if information professionals are not active researchers all of the time, it is an inescapable fact that they must certainly be intelligent and informed consumers of research. In a recent survey, which scoped practitioner research in the library and information profession within the UK, McNicol (2004) highlighted the ways in which research is used by practitioners to enhance service delivery and provision. These include benchmarking exercises, service planning, strategic development, refining existing services, improving effectiveness of service delivery, demonstrating value to stakeholders, marketing, publicity, mapping user behaviour, planning accommodation, making operational changes such as altering opening hours, collection development, and more.

This handbook is designed to be of continuing use throughout the student and professional lives of its readers. In this book I aim to provide insight into the research process and lay before you the choices and opportunities available to you in your research endeavour. The book draws on established research practice in a number of disciplines. Because of the diversity of information and communication related subjects, it is necessary to have some understanding of research in sociology, psychology, education and computing. From the variety of research methods, data collection techniques and methods of analysis discussed in this book it is hoped you will be in a position to make an informed choice on the approach best suited to your own context, goals and experience. Once these choices have been made you can go on, using the recommended texts in each of the chapters, to develop your understanding of the particular approach you have designed, based on the choices placed before you here. You may well establish your own preferred approach to carrying out research, but always try to stay open to other possibilities, depending on the questions being asked.

A second purpose of this book is to share with potential and practising researchers the sheer joy of exploring the world around us by whatever means is appropriate to the subject under investigation. I see research as a grand adventure and researchers as intrepid explorers seeking out their own truth, however small the question may be. Always remember that producing research of a high standard will inevitably be more difficult and problematic than you first envisage. One thing I would emphasize above all else is to keep it as simple as you possibly can. In research you usually achieve much more by attempting less; research is not about changing the world, it is about making your own discovery that can inform others in some way.

Although many of you will be students reading this as part of your, in most cases, compulsory research project, it is still hoped that the experience will be a good one, if not a splendid one. The joy of research cannot be bestowed on an individual but it is sincerely hoped that this book will go some way to planting the seed and encouraging at best that joy, at least the inquisitive nature that defines the researcher. I was once told that the greatest quality of a good researcher was to have infinite curiosity and constant desire to discover the as yet unknown. This book cannot create that curiosity, (although I would love to think that it might) but it can provide direction in designing ways to satisfy it and I hope it will encourage you to question how we question the world around us. Although there are tried and tested research strategies laid out before you there is always more to know and more ways to know it. Here are some options, but our knowledge of investigative strategies continues to expand; this is not a definitive collection of those strategies, it is a guide to what we already know and what has already been done. Continuing to explore potential methods can only increase our ability to understand our environment. I would encourage you to take a critical approach to this text and, if the desire is there, to experiment with these ideas in whatever way you see fit within your own research context.

This handbook is based on my own experience of the research process and teaching that process to undergraduate, postgraduate and doctoral students over a number of years. One of the greatest frustrations faced by those students, and myself, is the level of disparity in the use of terminology within the research methods literature. Terms such as 'method', 'technique', 'strategy', 'approach' and so on are applied by different authors in a multitude of ways, discussing very different things. Much of this inconsistency in use of terminology is the result of the multidisciplinary nature of the research approaches which have been applied to our own discipline. (See Budd, 2001, for a detailed discussion on the philosophical background to research in information and communication disciplines.) Like all researchers, I have my own view of the 'best' type of research but I hope there will be no hint of that preference in this book. There are two reasons for this: first, I have no desire to 'push' you down a particular road against your natural instinct and, second, I am still exploring and I reserve the right to change my mind!

Setting the context

As I have already mentioned, there is much debate about the terminology of research and I have found that this does more to get in the way of good research than it does to encourage it. With that in mind the structure of this book is based on a framework of the research hierarchy I use with my students. The debate on whether a case study is a research method or a research strategy will no doubt continue for longer than I may be privileged to engage in that debate. The emphasis here is on the 'doing' rather than on the 'debating'. That said, it is impossible to ignore the philosophy and theory behind the research process but here that will only be introduced as context; any reader who is stimulated by this debate is strongly encouraged to follow the leads offered here and continue to read in more depth around the issues. One potential solution to stripping away some of the confusion is to develop a research hierarchy that provides a framework for designing and conducting research studies. There will no doubt be many who disagree with the structure offered here, even if that disagreement is related only to the use of terminology. I do not offer this as the *only* structure, it is offered as *a* structure that has worked for many neophyte and experienced researchers. The structure of the text follows the research hierarchy outlined below.

The research hierarchy

I would like to establish the way I use some standard research terms and the connections between those terms from the outset. Figure 0.1 describes the connections and relationships between various levels of the research hierarchy using work by Guba and Lincoln (1988) and building on that to include all major elements of a research study.

Figure 0.1 The research hierarchy (Pickard, 2002; Pickard and Dixon, 2004)

A research paradigm

Whether we are concerned with the philosophical forces driving the research or not, all research models begin at that philosophical level which defines the paradigm. Here I am using the interpretation of paradigm originally provided by Kuhn (1970) as a means of viewing the world, influencing but not controlling the assumptions and direction of research. This interpretation views paradigms as 'the entire constellation of beliefs, values, techniques, and so on shared by members of a given [scientific] community' (Kuhn, 1970, 146) and they 'provide the concrete puzzle solution or exemplar of how to solve a scientific problem' (Seale, 1998, 12). A paradigm then comes before the theoretical perspective of the research, it is the 'world view' that is accepted by members of a particular scientific discipline which guides the subject of the research, the activity of the research and the nature of the research outputs: 'Indeed, fundamental to the concept of the paradigm is its pre-theoretical and, in the final analysis, metaphysical character of a "guiding vision", "a view of the world", which shapes and organizes both theoretical reflection and empirical research and, as such, precedes both' (Corbetta, 2003, 11).

A research paradigm does imply a methodology, it is very often an individual's view of the world that dictates the nature of the research they engage with. Ideally it is the question that should dictate the nature of the 'asking', but very often this is not the case. Positivist thinking is associated with quantitative research, interpretivist thinking with qualitative research and postpositivist thinking with a dualism that attempts to include both methodologies.

Research methodology

This is the theoretical perspective of the research, that is the overall nature of the research activity, although the term is applied to many aspects of the research process in various disciplines. I believe there are only two fundamental methodologies: qualitative or quantitative. However, a methodology does not necessarily imply a particular research method; all too often assumptions are made concerning particular research methods that are essentially incorrect. A methodology is perspective, the angle the researcher wishes to take on the question being asked. An example of this would be examining use of a service by the users of that service; it may be that the angle is one of 'how many?', 'how often?' or 'when?'; this would be a quantitative angle on the question. On the other hand the angle could be 'why?', 'how?' or 'how do they feel about it?'; this then would be a qualitative angle. This is an over simplification of these definitions, which is intended to show the elementary difference between the two, not to provide any in-depth discussion. That will follow in Chapter 1. This perspective or angle does not necessarily imply a particular research method, although clearly there are times when it must.

Research method

This is the bounded system created by the researcher to engage in empirical investigation, the overall approach, often referred to as a 'strategy'. For us, for now the term 'method' is being applied in this way. Models of the research process rarely make any distinction between research methods and research techniques but take for granted some implicit understanding of the distinction. This is not the ideal approach to a rigorously constructed research design. A research method is not defined by the techniques employed within it to harvest data, but by the driving purpose of the investigation.

Research techniques

These are the individual data collection techniques applied within the method. The most obvious example of lack of distinction between method and techniques is the use of the terms 'survey' and 'questionnaire'; very often the two are used interchangeably within the research methods literature. This is misleading as a survey can include a variety of data collection techniques and is far more than a single questionnaire; it is in fact a research method. An individual method does not necessarily relate to a specific data collection technique, although we are often led to believe it does: 'Typically books about research treat techniques and method together, thereby implicitly limiting the use of a particular technique to a certain method' (Harvey, 2000, xv). There are many techniques which are strongly associated with particular research methods and this is perfectly legitimate, but it is wrong to assume that a method dictates a technique. Research design should be flexible enough to ensure that questions are addressed in the most appropriate manner without limiting potential discovery and innovation. A technique is the approach taken to data collection, the way in which empirical evidence will be harvested from the source.

Research instrument

This is the device that is designed or trained to collect the data necessary to provide insight or offer answers to the questions being asked. When engaging in experimental research the instrument used could well be a 'brass' instrument, a term that has emerged from laboratory experimentation when much of the equipment was made of brass. This term is applied now to refer to all experimental apparatus, although it may not of course all be 'brass'. The 'pencil and paper' instrument is the term used to describe a questionnaire as it has been written by the researcher and will be added to by the research participant. In interpretivist research the 'human' instrument is the researcher, someone who has been trained to look, feel, respond and collect data within a natural setting, sometimes using an additional instrument, sometimes not.

This handbook is designed to follow this research hierarchy, providing descriptions and examples of each stage of the research process and allowing you to make choices at each stage, in order to construct your own research model to satisfy your own goals and the goals of your intended investigation. It is important to remember that not every choice implies a subsequent choice, but some do.

Overview of contents
Part 1: Starting the research process

Part 1 focuses on the generic issues that are necessary for the majority of research investigations regardless of the methodology, method, technique or research instrument. This section opens with a brief discussion of the three major research paradigms in information science. I would like to emphasize the *brief* as it is impossible to provide the detail and depth of discussion necessary for a topic as huge as this.

The purpose of this first chapter is to provide an overview of current thinking within the field. Usually a discipline has a dominant paradigm, although this can and often does change over time. Because of the diverse nature of information science there is no truly dominant paradigm today, although it is fair to say that at the time of writing 'interpretivist' research is without doubt the newest paradigm and is only just beginning to emerge as a significant force in research in information and communication. Qualitative and quantitative methodologies are discussed and we look at the different approaches to demonstrating the rigour and trustworthiness of both methodologies. This debate is often neglected or, even worse, criteria used to demonstrate rigour in one methodology are applied directly to the other.

Literature reviewing, defining the research, sampling and preparing a research proposal are covered in this initial section. The ethics of research will be discussed here, including the still rather controversial ethics concerned with conducting research in 'virtual' environments. The practical exercises at the end of every chapter are designed to consolidate your learning from the chapter and to demonstrate just how 'doable' these activities really are. Research is very much a practical process - no real mystery just hard work.

Part 2: Research methods

Part 2 focuses on research methods, and the variety of potential approaches available to the researcher. Each chapter describes a research method, and gives examples of the type of question the method responds well to (this does not mean it cannot be tried on something new) and instructions on designing that method. You are again asked to engage in the exercises, which are provided to consolidate the knowledge you have gained from the description in the chapter. Each chapter ends with a selection of further readings, which deal very specifically with the research method discussed in the chapter. Once you have chosen your approach you can then go on to investigate the method further, if you choose to. I provide enough detail to apply the chosen method but you may well want other opinions, as I would in your position.

Part 3: Data collection techniques

Part 3 focuses on collecting data. The data collection techniques discussed in this book are essentially those relating to social or 'person-centred' research, but also include those used to examine and develop systems, although this is not an information systems text. 'Virtual' research techniques are included here as adaptations of the conventional techniques. Research in 'virtual' environments is still very new and I encourage you to experiment with your own adaptations as well as those discussed in these chapters. Once again there are opportunities for you to engage in practical exercises, which highlight the way in which the techniques work. Some of them are group activities.

Part 4: Data analysis and research presentation

Part 4 focuses on quantitative and qualitative analysis and presenting research. I have already recommended that you read widely on the method and techniques of your choice, and emphasize this even more in this section. It is outwith the scope of this text to provide the detail and depth necessary for you to master any of the methods of analysis covered here. There are entire texts dedicated to statistical and narrative analysis procedures. I do not repeat these procedures but rather discuss how to apply the procedures appropriately to the data gathered.

I strongly recommend that you gain wider experience of the various strategies introduced here before you go on to apply them within the research context. However, sufficient information and a number of challenging exercises should provide you with enough insight to make relevant choices. Included in this section is a chapter on presenting research, an activity that has turned out to be one of the most challenging aspects of research for a great many researchers. This is not surprising as so much relies on your ability to get your message across to your reader. All that hard work, effort, planning and investigation is only as good as the final product, the research output.

I hope you get as much pleasure reading and using this book as I have had in acquiring the knowledge and experience to write it. Don't ever get confused by the term 'expert' – it usually simply refers to an individual with a burning passion and someone who has been around long enough to learn from their many mistakes. This is my passion and I hope I can share some of that passion with you.

Part 5: Glossary and references

The final section in this book provides a glossary of research terms; generally the definitions provided are those commonly used in the disciplines from which they have emerged.

There is also a full list of titles referenced in the text. Further suggested reading is given at the end of each chapter.

PART 1

Starting the research process

PART 1

Starting the research process

In Part 1 I want to focus on the initial stages of any research investigation, the areas common to all research regardless of the character and purpose of that research. It is mostly very practical in nature, with the exception of the first chapter, which examines the philosophical underpinnings of research. Although this philosophical debate is not for the faint hearted, it is fundamental to understanding the entire activity we refer to as 'research'. I suggest you take the time to engage in this debate if for no other reason than to decide which side of the paradigmatic fence you sit on, to determine your view of the world and the manner in which you feel we can explore that world. I secretly hope that reading this first chapter will capture your imagination and encourage you to follow up the leads I offer; at the very least it should provide you with a broad overview of the fundamental differences between research paradigms and a framework for thinking about the research process.

Most of Part 1 examines the preliminary stages of research and provides practical guidelines and advice. It ends with a discussion of ethics in research. This is a very important and sometimes neglected area, and it is vital for anyone engaging in a research project of any size to take it into account.

Chapter 1

Major research paradigms

Introduction

This text is primarily concerned with the research process that is required in order to produce results. It has been said that too much time spent engaging in the 'higher' philosophical debate surrounding research limits the amount of actual research that gets done. All researchers have their work to do and ultimately it is the 'doing' that counts, but the debate is a fascinating one and it would be very remiss not to provide you with some level of introduction to it. If you find yourself reading this chapter and thinking 'so what?', take some time to examine the implications of a paradigm on the research process. What follows is a very brief discussion of the major research paradigms in the fields of information, communication and related disciplines.

We are going to take a tour of three research paradigms: positivism, postpositivism and interpretivism. For some this will be too much, for others too little. Those of you who want more can follow the leads at the end of the chapter; those of you who want less, please bear with me for the brief tour of the major research traditions of our discipline. Having at least a basic understanding of different research paradigms is important at any level, if for no other reason than making you aware of the potential implications of the choices you make: 'Being aware of paradigmatic blinders is a first step towards greater situational responsiveness and creativity in making methods decisions' (Patton, 1988, 118).

Guba and Lincoln go further and claim that 'paradigm issues are crucial; no inquirer ought to go about the business of inquiry without being clear about just what paradigm informs and guides his or her approach' (1998, 218). Of course it has also been said that attempting to write on this subject 'requires the skills of an individual who is at once presumptuous and masochistic' (Caldwell, 1994, 1). I hope I am neither, therefore I shall keep this discussion to a minimum and examine only that which I feel is important as background to the practical side of research.

According to Lincoln and Guba (1985), there are three major questions that help us to define a research paradigm: the ontological question, the epistemological question and the methodological question. 'Ontology' is the nature of reality; 'epistemology' is the philosophy of how we can know that reality; and 'methodology' is the practice of how we come to know that reality. The three questions are:

- What is the nature of reality? This is the ontological question concerning the nature and form of reality.
- What is the nature of the relationship between the knower and the known? This is the epistemological question.
- How we can come to know it? This is the methodological question.

It is in answering these three questions that paradigm boundaries are established. The three major research paradigms associated with our disciplines are positivism, postpositivism and interpretivism. By using the three basic questions above we can examine the beliefs of each of these paradigms and contrast the fundamental differences between them. A summary is provided in Table 1.1, which is adapted from Lincoln and Guba (1985, 109). You are strongly advised to read this essay for more detailed discussion.

This chapter provides a broad overview of the three research paradigms currently accepted within our disciplines. Of the three interpretivism is by far the most recent addition to our investigative toolkit; research is not a static subject, we are constantly learning and as a result practice is constantly evolving. Nothing is fixed in the research process and this provides great opportunities for innovation and adventure. I would like you to remember this as you explore the possibilities set out before you here.

Before we go on to discuss the three major paradigms let us remind ourselves of what we mean by a paradigm. In the Introduction I used Kuhn's definition of a paradigm as 'the entire constellation of beliefs, values, techniques, and so on shared by members of a given [scientific] community' (Kuhn, 1970, 146). That is to say it is 'a basic set of beliefs that guide action' (Guba, 1990, 17). Now we can go on and examine the positivist, postpositivist and interpretivist traditions in light of the three questions concerning the ontology, epistemology and methodology of each paradigm. I would also like to provide a very brief history of each paradigm for context. These are potted histories that do little more than provide you with an outline of the development. Table 1.1 provides an overview of the contrasting basic beliefs of each of the three paradigms.

Positivist research
Brief history
There are three generations of positivist thinkers who have influenced and shaped the paradigm as it is today: the original formulation of positivism attributed to Auguste Comte, the logical positivism associated with the Vienna Circle, and finally the standard positivism developed in the mid-20th century (Outhwaite, 1987). Standard positivism is the basis for today's postpositivist tradition so we shall leave that discussion for the next section.

In the early 19th century Auguste Comte devised social positivism as a means of examining social phenomena as an empirical science as opposed to the theological and metaphysical philosophies that dominated at the time. Positive knowledge was the discovery of causal laws of phenomena derived directly from observation. This was a rejection

Table 1.1 Characteristics of major research paradigms (adapted from Lincoln and Guba, 1985)

	Positivism	Postpositivism	Interpretivism
Ontological stance	'Realism'	'Critical realism'	'Relativist'
	Belief in a tangible, social reality. This reality exists independently of those 'creating' the reality. A social reality can exist just as a natural reality exists (water remains water whether someone is swimming in it or not).	Belief in a social reality but acceptance that knowing this reality will always be inhibited by imperfections in detecting its nature. The imperfections are the result of human fallibility.	Belief in multiple, constructed realities that cannot exist outside the social contexts that create them. Realities vary in nature and are time and context bound.
Epistemological stance	Objectivist/dualist	Modified dualist/objectivist	Transactional/subjectivist
	Investigator and investigated are independent of each other.	Acceptance that independence is not possible but objectivity is seen as the goal and demonstrated by external verification.	The results of the investigation are a product of interaction between the subject and the investigator. What can be known is a result of the interaction.
Methodological stance	Experimental/ manipulative	Modified experimental/ manipulative	Empathetic interaction
	Hypothesis testing, variables identified before the investigation. Empirical testing is conducted in order to establish the 'truth' of the proposition.	Hypothesis testing but more emphasis placed on context.	Investigator interacts with the object of the investigation. Each construction of reality is investigated in its own right and is interpreted by the investigator.
	Predominantly quantitative.	Quantitative and qualitative.	Qualitative, including hermeneutics and dialectic interchanges.
	Analysis by variables.	Analysis by variables.	Analysis by case.
Purpose	Prediction/control/ explanation	Prediction/control/ explanation	Understanding/ reconstruction
	Framing of general laws.	Generalizations.	Transfer of findings.

of the notion that society was beyond our physical perception and could not be examined in the same way as natural objects could be examined. Comte sought to take the rules and practice of the natural sciences of physics, astronomy and chemistry and apply the same investigative techniques to social theory and human behaviour. It has to be remembered that at this time natural science was still dominated by Newtonian mechanics. But Comte believed it was possible to 'reconstruct human knowledge in order to build a better society' (Smith, 1998, 78). Although Comte is seen as the 'father of positivism' much of his work was rhetorical, it was Emile Durkheim (1858–1917) who first pioneered empirical investigation of society, and he was labelled the first 'sociologist' (Corbetta, 2003). Durkheim began to examine social phenomena as a set of independent variables that could be empirically tested to determine any evidence of causal links.

Logical positivism emerged from a group of philosophers working in Vienna during the 1920s; they rejected Comte's positivism (they actually refused the title 'logical positivists' in favour of 'logical empiricists' in order to distance themselves still further from the tradition associated with Comte) (Outhwaite, 1987). Moritz Schlick began the movement in 1922 at the University of Vienna. Other notable members of this group, known as the Vienna Circle, were Rudolf Carnap, Philip Frank and Bertrand Russell. Russell developed the analytical tools of mathematics, which made the greatest distinction between Comte's positivism and the new empirical positivism. This was the first time statistical analysis was used to examine social behaviour. These philosophers believed that although Comte had attempted to adapt social theory to the model of the natural sciences, he had not gone far enough. They rejected totally the concept of the metaphysical and claimed that elements of this still existed within Comte's work. They 'asserted that only meaningful statements were to be permitted scientific consideration and accorded the status of knowledge claims' (Caldwell, 1994, 13). By 'meaningful' they referred to only those statements that could be verified or falsified by evidence.

Physical evidence is paramount to logical positivists: if there is no physical evidence then how can phenomena be verified or falsified? They believe that concepts such as motivation and affective influences on behaviour can only become metaphysical speculation as there is no visible means of verifying these 'unseen' behavioural influences. 'The stated aim of the logical positivist is to cleanse scientific knowledge of speculative thinking, for it is not tied in a direct and demonstrable way to experience' (Smith, 1998, 97). Examples of this way of approaching social investigation can be seen in the work of a group known as 'behaviourists' who based their work on the concept of classical and operant conditioning. This approach concentrates on the way individuals respond to various stimuli. From this behaviourist tradition emerged the 'classical conditioning' of Pavlov (1927), and Skinner's 'operant conditioning' (Skinner, 1987). This demonstrates that the basic premise of positivism, that of social engineering, still remained for the behaviourists although the approach had changed.

Ontology – realism

Positivism assumes the existence of an objective, independent and stable reality, which is available for discovery and analysis. Only observable phenomena are recognized; what is real is only that which can be observed. Metaphysics is strongly rejected, thereby denying the meaningfulness of human characteristics that cannot be demonstrated overtly. Social facts are seen to exist independently of human interaction just as natural laws exist. These social facts function according to their own laws, mechanistic and immutable. Newtonian mechanics were seen as transferable from the natural world to the social world of its inhabitants.

Epistemology – objectivist/dualist

The positivist view of the relationship between the knower and the known is one of 'objective observer'. The researcher can stand apart from that which is being observed and report on the reality that is discovered through this observation. This stance was seen as an obvious development from the natural sciences: if we can watch a flower grow and report on that growth, then watching a human interact with their environment in any way could also be observed and reported.

Dualism exists when two distinct entities are present with the research process, the researcher and the subject, existing independently of each other. Research is designed in such a way that objectivity can be demonstrated through replication; this will be discussed in more detail later in this chapter. This stance relies on the presumption that it is possible to observe without influencing that which is being observed.

Methodology – experimental/manipulative

Positivists believe that reality can be dissected into variables that represent the theoretical constructs that underlie observable phenomena. These variables can then be manipulated through experimentation and 'laws' can be determined from the results of those manipulations. Positivist research usually begins with a hypothesis, which is then tested empirically for verification through structured experimentation. This testing involves a complex statistical mechanism for determining relationships between the variables, and results in broad generalizations concerning the phenomena being studied. Quantitative methodology is used in positivist research.

Purpose – predication/control/explanation/verification

Positivist approaches are focused on explaining how things happen in order to predict what comes next and being in a position to control what happens. Social reconstruction was the driving force behind Comte's original ideas and this purpose remained constant throughout the various positivist traditions. Generalizations are derived from examination of the specific and applied to all occurrences of the incident, striving to demonstrate universal validity.

Postpositivism
Brief history

It is important to realize that the whole premise of positivism was an emulation of the natural sciences, particularly physics. Postpositivism was as much a reaction to the failings of positivism as it was to a shift in the emerging changes in the basic axioms of natural science. During the early 20th century natural science underwent an enormous shift; physics was the driving force behind this shift. There was a move from the rigid mechanistic Newtonian physics to the concept of 'uncertainty' and 'relativity'. Einstein and Heisenburg took physics from the language of deterministic laws to probability and uncertainty (Corbetta, 2003). The great shift here was not Einstein's theory of relativity, it was his statement about the tentative nature of discovery, that determinism inhibits the true goal of research which is discovery (Popper, 1963). If it was no longer possible to study the natural world from a mechanistic viewpoint then it was certainly no longer possible to study social facts in that way. This raised an enormous question for the study of human behaviour. There was a need for refinement and development in social research if it was to retain credibility as a true science. That development came in two major stages; standard positivism began in the 1930s and continued through to the 1960s, when it was replaced by the postpositivist paradigm as we know it today.

New theories of uncertainty and probability leading to the tentative nature of discovery were adopted in social research with the concept of 'falsification' introduced by Karl Popper between 1959 and 1963. It was no longer possible to 'prove' a hypothesis as it could never be certain that an alternative explanation did not exist for the relationship between the variables. Popper introduced the concept of 'critical realism'; the positivist view of the existence of objective social facts remained but this was now tempered with the notion that those facts were subject to interpretation (Tucker, 1998). This was translated into the practical claim that it was possible to prove the hypothesis was 'wrong' to falsify the claim, but not to verify that claim beyond doubt; uncertainty and probability would always prohibit this. Current postpositivism is rooted in the premise that any perception of reality cannot be an objective picture but is drawn from empirical observation and existing theory. There has been a shift within this paradigm but the basic concepts of quantification and generalization taken from original positivism remain predominant.

Ontology – critical realism

Objective social facts do exist independently of and external to human beings, but these facts are subject to uncertainty and probability. Cause and effect relationships do exist but it is not always possible to 'know' these relationships in their entirety. Human fallibility will always create imperfections but there remains the basic belief that a 'reality' is out there waiting to be discovered.

Epistemology – modified dualist/objectivist

The major difference between postpositivist epistemology and that of the original positivists was the ability of the 'knower' to be completely divorced from the known. Postpositivists accept that all discovery is subject to interpretation; it is the responsibility of the researcher to demonstrate objectivity during the discovery process. This objectivity is demonstrated by external validity, a notion that will be discussed later in this chapter.

Methodology – modified experimental/manipulative

The approach taken by postpositivists remains one of experimentation and hypothesis testing and although the procedure has been modified from that of the early positivists, they remain essentially the same. Variables are identified and manipulated, and the relationship between these variables is then measured using statistical techniques. The more 'qualitative' notion of 'interpretation' is often included in this approach allowing for the possibility of prior knowledge having an impact on the perceptions of results.

Purpose – prediction/control/explanation/falsification

The purpose of research within the postpositivist tradition remains very similar to that of positivism. The most significant difference is the notion of falsification; disproving the existence of a phenomenon had become a valid outcome of an investigation. Generalizations about the phenomena under investigation remain an output of the postpositivist approach to empirical investigation. Methodological dualism in the use of qualitative and quantitative is accepted practice in postpositivist research.

Interpretivist research
Brief history

'Interpretivism' is used as a covering term for a number of approaches to research. Essentially the areas we are concerned with can be sorted into two distinct groups: 'empirical interpretivism' and 'critical theory'. The former deals with investigation in natural settings of social phenomena; the latter engages in ideologically orientated investigation, examining current thought and social structures. Anthropology also falls into the interpretivist paradigm but it is beyond the remit of this book to cover that area in any detail other than to look at the generic issues that influenced the development of all interpretivism. In 1883 Wilhelm Dilthey published the first critique of positivism with his now famous distinction between the 'science of nature' and the 'science of spirit' (Corbetta, 2003). This was essentially a philosophical debate that commented on the difference between understanding human thought and explaining nature. Dilthey's critique was a direct response to positivism, a refutation that human beings could be investigated in 'cold' cause and effect terms.

The first proponent of empirical interpretivism was Max Weber at the beginning of the 20th century. Early interpretivists focused on ethnographic studies of colonial culture and immigrant culture in Europe and America, focusing on the work of Bronislaw Malinowski (Swingewood, 2000) and the Chicago School of sociology (Denzin and Lincoln, 1994). A new movement that attempted to formalize the procedures of empirical interpretivist research followed this early phase. One of the best examples of this approach can be found in the work of Barney Glaser and Anselm Strauss. They attempted to provide interpretivist researchers with a framework for analysis that had, up until this point, been missing from the paradigm (Glaser and Strauss, 1967). Following this, from 1970 to the mid-1980s there was an expansion of the paradigm into a myriad of approaches to interpretivism; these are listed in Table 1.2.

I am not suggesting that all approaches to research shown in Table 1.2 were developed during this short period; these approaches emerged throughout the 20th century

Table 1.2   Approaches to interpretivism

Human inquiry	Critical theory
Anthropology	Feminism
Constructivism	Marxism
Ethnomethodology	Post-modernity
Naturalist inquiry	Post-structuralism
Phenomenology	Structuralism
Semiotics	
Symbolic interactionism	

(see Swingewood, 2000, for in-depth discussion). The most recent development in inter-pretivism is the emergence of 'storytelling' or 'narrative' over 'theory building' (Denzin and Lincoln, 1994).

Ontology – relativism

Interpretivists belief that realities are multiple, constructed and holistic. There is no sin-gle, tangible reality, instead there are only the complex, multiple realities of the individual. Reality is seen as 'individual' and embedded in context, as opposed to 'universal' (Flick, 2002).

Epistemology – transactional/subjectivist

The known and the knower influence each other; all descriptions are time and context bound. It is impossible to separate cause from effect as all entities are in a state of simultaneous shaping (Lincoln and Guba, 1985). All knowledge we acquire is a prod-uct of the interaction between the known and the knower; the researcher and the subject are both 'changed' by the experience, and knowledge is a result of this interaction and is time and context bound.

Methodology – empathetic interaction

Interpretivists take the stance that any research activity will leave the subject of that research in an altered state. Heisenberg claims that 'what we observe is not nature itself, but nature exposed to our method of questioning' (1958, 288). The data that is gath-ered from that research might itself be, in part, a product of the research process. The time and context in which the data is gathered will also influence that data: 'Context is something you swim in like a fish. You are in it. It is you' (Dervin, 1997, 32). Inter-pretivism can offer understanding of the meanings behind the actions of individuals. 'From this perspective, meaning depends upon context, and the interpretation of action or opinion must take account of the setting in which it is produced' (Dey, 1993, 110). Interpretivism seeks to understand the entire context, both at the macro- and micro-environmental level. Qualitative methodology is applied including dialect interchange with participants and hermeneutics, depending on both the tacit and the explicit knowl-edge of the researcher.

Purpose – transfer of findings based on contextual applicability

Transferability depends on 'similarities between sending and receiving contexts, the researcher collects sufficiently detailed descriptions of data in context and reports them with sufficient detail and precision to allow judgments about transferability' (Erlandson et al., 1993, 33). The 'sending' context is the research location, the 'receiving' context is the context to which the research findings are applied. Interpretivist tradition is concerned with individual contexts, therefore 'research can only be particularized and generalization, in the traditional scientific sense, is impossible' (Dervin, 1997, 14).

As I said in the opening section of this chapter there are those who believe that discussions of paradigms have no place in the research process; you can make your own mind up about that. I believe that although the theoretical debate may not contribute greatly to 'getting the job done', it does provide an understanding of the intention behind the action. It would be very difficult to provide a simple definition of 'types' of researchers without over-simplifying the nature of these traditions. One useful if somewhat basic definition is supplied by Greene (1990), who suggests that positivists and postpositivists can be thought of as social engineers, interpretivists as storytellers and critical theorists as catalysts of social change.

Qualitative or quantitative methodology?

In the research hierarchy there is no doubt that a research paradigm implies a research methodology. Hopefully the explanation of the three paradigms given above should make this very clear. It is impossible to examine multiple, individual realities in any depth using a quantitative methodology, just as it is impossible to identify a single reality, measure it or quantify it in any other way than via a quantitative methodology.

Gorman and Clayton (2005) identify the fundamental argument between the two methodologies and present a summary of qualitative and quantitative approaches to an inquiry. Although they do not argue necessarily for paradigmatic purity, it appears implicit in the distinctions between the two. They begin by examining the basic assumptions of each mode of inquiry; quantitative methodology assumes the objective reality of social facts; qualitative methodology assumes social constructions of reality (Gorman and Clayton, 2005, 24-8). These assumptions are in fact two of the basic axioms of two separate belief systems, two conflicting paradigms. There is no consensus of opinion concerning the need for paradigmatic purity in research. Many social researchers see methodological dualism as the only pragmatic option. Feyerand argues that this eclectic approach to inquiry is not only possible but necessary if science is to advance, claiming that both 'methodologies have their limitations and the only "rule" that survives is "anything goes"' (Feyerand, 1975, 296). This is in fact the methodology associated with the postpositivist paradigm. The description of the two methodologies that follows may help you to answer this question for yourself.

Qualitative research design

The emergent design of qualitative research does not allow for a detailed plan before the research begins; 'the research design must therefore be "played by ear"; it must unfold, cascade, roll, emerge' (Lincoln and Guba, 1985, 203). However, it is possible to develop a design that allows for the iterative nature of the study. A design adapted from Lincoln and Guba's generic research model (1985, 188), their development of that model (Guba and Lincoln, 1998, 104) and Kumar (1999) is presented in Figure 1.1. This design illustrates the entire research process conducted within the boundaries of trustworthiness: transferability, credibility, dependability and confirmability. The human instrument applies appropriate data collection techniques, complemented by tacit knowledge, to the investigation. Purposive sampling is employed in order to achieve a sample of maximum variation, extreme case or typical case (Patton, 1987), to ensure that each new research participant contributes characteristics differing from preceding participants. This allows for multiple perspectives on the phenomena under study. Inductive data analysis is a vital part of both the selection of subsequent participants and the constant building of grounded theory (Glaser and Strauss, 1967). The emergent design (Lincoln and Guba, 1985) of individual data collection techniques is based on analysis of preceding data and the identification of concepts and ideas that require further and deeper investigation. This process produces individual studies, which are then reported back to research participants and discussed with the researcher. By analysing these individual studies, themes are identified which provide grounded theory to be transferred from the local to the global level (Deem, 1998).

The essential components of a qualitative research design are literature review, theoretical framework (to act as cognitive signposts not to restrict emerging concepts), fieldwork in a natural setting, using a human instrument, purposive sampling, appropriate data collection techniques, inductive analysis, emergent design, iteration of activities, grounded theory, negotiated outcomes, and forming a tentative working hypothesis, leading to transference of findings based on contextual applicability. Many of these stages are discussed in detail in subsequent chapters but there are a number of things we need to examine further before we go on.

Human research instrument

In order to study behaviour in context it is most appropriate to choose the human as instrument. Human lives and their interpersonal relationships create complexities that need to be understood and the researcher acting as the research instrument allows for understanding and depicting these complexities: 'These complexities . . . cannot be figured out, cannot be understood by one-dimensional, reductionist approaches; they demand the human-as-instrument' (Maykut and Morehouse, 1994, 27).

Qualitative research combines the individual research participant, the researcher as research instrument and appropriate data collection techniques in a collaborative process of producing meaning from data and using that meaning to develop theory: 'If a person is to be understood as a person and not as a thing, then the relationship between the researcher and the other person must be a dynamic and mutual relationship'

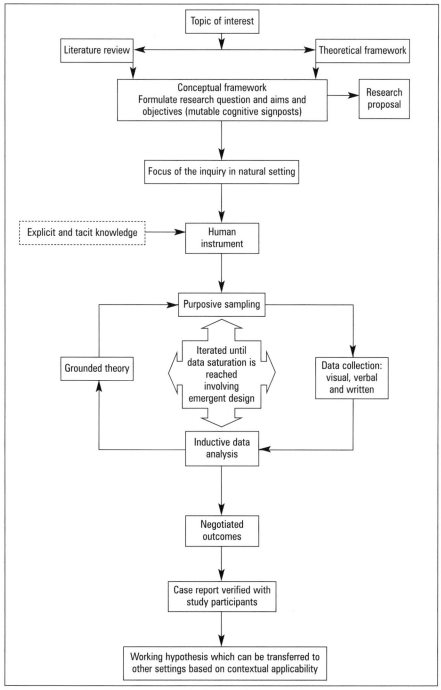

Figure 1.1   Qualitative research design (adapted from Kumar, 1999, and
Lincoln and Guba, 1985)

(Maykut and Morehouse, 1994, 37). When human experience and situations are the subject of the research, then the human as instrument is 'the only instrument which is flexible enough to capture the complexity, subtlety, and constantly changing situation which is the human experience' (Maykut and Morehouse, 1994, 26). The researcher as instrument is also in a position to apply appropriate tacit knowledge to each situation and event as it occurs. Tacit knowledge can contribute to interpretation of the observed evidence, although confirmation and justification of how this knowledge is applied must be possible. Tacit knowledge provides a springboard to generate theory but must be applied tentatively and these theories are only retained and developed when there is evidence to support them.

Emergent design

Emergent design is an integral part of all qualitative research yet it is rarely explicitly admitted outside the social sciences. The concept of an emergent design is based on the belief that the researcher 'does not know what he or she doesn't know' (Lincoln and Guba, 1985, 209) at the beginning of a study. Therefore it would be impossible to establish the means by which the unknown could manifest itself to the researcher during the course of the study. Because of this, qualitative research allows the design to emerge as the study progresses. A research model can and should be developed that allows for the iterative nature of the study. It takes the form of a plan that maintains the focus of the study without precluding the use of individual techniques, as they become apparent. This is one area in the investigation where the participants can be given a degree of control over the process, leading to a sense of ownership of the study: 'The [interpretivist] paradigm affirms the mutual influence that researcher and respondents have on each other . . . never can formal methods be allowed to separate the researcher from the human interaction that is the heart of the research' (Erlandson et al., 1993, 15).

An interesting example of this occurred during one of my own qualitative investigations involving teenagers. I had designed what I thought to be a very good search log (a diary of their information-seeking behaviour) for each participant in my study and asked them to use it. After 20 weeks of the field work, only two of the 16 teenagers had begun to use their logs to keep a record of their searches. They were happy with the organization and format of the log and thought that the information provided in it was clear and gave them a valuable framework for recording their work. The 14 teenagers who had made no entries gave a variety of reasons for not complying with my request: 'I haven't done any research projects', 'I forgot what to do', 'It interferes with my work', 'It takes up too much time', 'I can't be bothered' and 'I don't want to walk around with a great big yellow book, I feel stupid'.

A focus group meeting was held at each site to decide what could be done about this problem. I explained that I needed a detailed account of the searches the teenagers carried out when the researcher could not be present. It was to be a surrogate for the observations the teenagers were now accustomed to. Very productive discussions followed and the teenagers themselves identified ways in which they thought the search log could be a more effective tool. They suggested keeping a handwritten diary in their own words, storing data on a Microsoft Access database, and keeping a diary in a Microsoft Word file. One participant requested an audio tape so he could describe his actions verbally. Unfortunately the economic restrictions of the research would not permit this last suggestion although it would have been a very interesting data collection method. I agreed to logs being kept in one of four ways: on databases, on notebooks, as word-processed documents, and using the original log design. The search logs provided a rich source of data and were well maintained throughout the research. The level of involvement in the design of the log by the teenagers played an important role in the quality and quantity of information provided from this source. They had become stakeholders in the research and this appeared to encourage vigilance in maintaining the logs. After all, if their design was so much better than mine it had to work to prove them right! It certainly increased their diligence.

Negotiated outcomes

The dialectic nature of qualitative research is accommodated by interaction with participants where they are encouraged to compare and contrast the researcher's constructions of reality by debate: 'Because the realities that will be included are those that have individually and collectively been constructed by persons within the context of the study, it is imperative that both data and interpretations obtained be verified by those persons' (Erlandson et al., 1993, 31).

Stake claims that negotiated outcomes or 'member checking' is a vital component of a study, not just in terms of adding to the credibility of the study, but also in improving the quality of the final case report. He stresses that, 'all [his] reports have been improved by member checking' (Stake, 1995, 116). There is some debate on how far participants should be allowed to go in terms of altering what has been said or done but it is the responsibility of the researcher to control this procedure to allow for maximum information yield. Ultimately this is up to the researcher or the research team. I have always found it incredibly helpful to involve research participants in this process; there is rarely any real conflict concerning interpretations but there can be significant insight gained by this dialectic interchange.

The other aspects of qualitative research will be covered later in this book. The role of this introduction is to provide you with a broad picture of what qualitative methodology actually means and give you an outline of the research process.

Quantitative research design

The design of quantitative research is far more linear than that of the qualitative approach and I would suggest that this is probably the most attractive feature of this approach for new researchers. I have always found that students doing research for the first time prefer the appearance of this design as it provides a more concrete framework, but that does not mean to say I am recommending it over qualitative research, far from it. I am saying that we need to look beyond first impressions and make choices based on much more.

Quantitative research begins with a theoretical framework established from the literature review; from this framework a hypothesis will emerge and the variables within that hypothesis can be identified. The notion of a hypothesis can also be translated into research aims and objectives; it is only compulsory to have a hypothesis when true experimental research is chosen as the method. This will be discussed in detail in Chapter 3. From this it is possible to select the most appropriate research method, then calculate the sample and design the data collection instruments within that method. Once data collection is complete it is time to process and analyse the data. Once data analysis is complete the researcher has the 'evidence' either to falsify or to support the hypothesis. Please note the use of the word 'support', I am often frustrated by the use of the word 'prove'; it is rarely possible to prove anything that is related to human behaviour. There is also no need to make such an irrational claim, as support is a great achievement in any research. It is then time to make generalizations based on the findings or, in the case of experimental research, to formulate general laws (highly unlikely within our discipline). All of these elements of the research process are discussed in much more detail throughout this book. See Figure 1.2 for a summary of the quantitative research design process.

Criteria for judging research

Establishing the value of research findings has been and still is a hotbed of critical debate and conflict among researchers (Smith, 1990). Whichever paradigm you associate your research with, whichever methodological approach you take, demonstrating the value of your investigation is essential. This applies to practitioner research and student research: we all want our findings to be believed and are responsible for ensuring that they can be believed.

How do we do this? This question is particularly difficult to address when you consider the clear differences between the two methodologies we have looked at. It is clear that each takes a very different view of the nature of reality so it would follow that demonstrating the truth cannot follow the same pattern in both methodologies. I am constantly perplexed by attempts made to judge research conducted within one methodology by criteria established to judge the other. Wolcott's comments on the application of validity criteria devised for judging quantitative research being applied to qualitative research demonstrate the inappropriateness of applying criteria established for one research paradigm to another, conflicting paradigm. He claims that 'a discussion of validity signals a retreat to that pre-existing vocabulary originally designed to lend precision to one arena of dialogue and too casually assumed to be adequate for another' (Wolcott, 1990, 168). Understanding the methods of establishing the 'truth' of research is essential for researchers and they must understand that it is inappropriate to judge methodologies using criteria that are not only misleading, but fundamentally wrong. Table 1.3 shows the criteria applied to establishing the value of research findings from the qualitative, the quantitative and mixed methodological perspectives. The four concepts used by researchers to gauge the value of research have been 'truth value', 'applicability', consistency' and 'neutrality' (Lincoln and Guba, 1985).

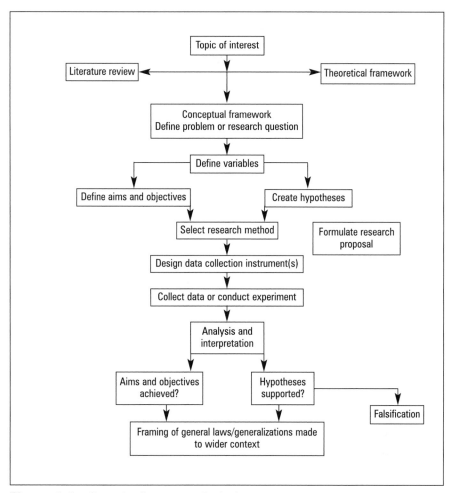

Figure 1.2 Quantitative research design

Table 1.3 Methods of judging value in research (adapted from Lincoln and Guba, 1985)

	Quantitative methodology (rigour)	Qualitative methodology (trustworthiness)	Mixed methodological approach
Truth value	Internal validity	Credibility	Validity/credibility
Applicability	External validity	Transferability	Generalizability
Consistency	Reliability	Dependability	Synchronic reliability
Neutrality	Objectivity	Confirmability	Objectivity

Establishing trustworthiness in qualitative research
Credibility
Credibility in qualitative research is demonstrated by prolonged engagement with the research participants, persistent observation of those participants, triangulation of the techniques used to study those participants and their contexts, peer debriefing, and member checks. Qualitative methodology often applies triangulation as a means of establishing credibility, including for example triangulation of investigators, theory, technique or sources (Denzin, 1978). As each source and type of data have both limitations and strengths (Patton, 2002), the use of multiple data collection techniques compensates for any limitations of individual techniques (Marshall and Rossman, 1989). There is also a need for what Mellon refers to as 'objective subjectivity' (Mellon, 1990, 42). Identifying that it is impossible to remove all subjectivity from a qualitative study allows the researcher to be constantly alert to this subjectivity and compensate whenever necessary.

Transferability
In terms of transferability Lincoln and Guba note that 'the trouble with generalisations is that they don't apply to particulars' (1985, 110). In qualitative research, the goal is to allow for transferability of the findings rather than wholesale generalization of those findings. Here the researcher provides 'rich pictures' on an individual level; the user of the research then gathers, or already has, empirical evidence concerning the cases to which they wish to apply the findings. If sufficient similarities between the two contexts are identified then it is reasonable to apply the research findings to the new context: 'Every context is by definition different, an intersection of a host of nameless factors. Because of this, research can only be particularized and generalization, in the traditional scientific sense, is impossible' (Dervin, 1997, 14). Erlandson et al. reinforce this: 'Because transferability in [an interpretivist] study depends on similarities between sending and receiving contexts, the researcher collects sufficiently detailed descriptions of data in context and reports them with sufficient detail and precision to allow judgements about transferability' (1993, 33).

Dependability
Dependability is established by an 'inquiry audit', where an external 'auditor' examines the research process. In order to allow for this an audit trail must be maintained by the researcher along with the research journal. The data produced can then be examined in terms of accuracy relating to transcripts and levels of saturation in document collection. Dependability is concerned with the manner in which the study is conducted; evidence needs to be provided that demonstrates that the methods and techniques used were applied appropriately and with relevance to the study. Lincoln and Guba (1985) recommend the use of the 'Halpern Audit Trail' as a means of ensuring that constructions can be seen to have emerged directly from the data, thereby confirming the research findings and grounding them in the evidence. Edward Halpern produced the audit trail as part of his doctoral dissertation in 1983.

Confirmability

Confirmability is vital to limit investigator bias. The notion of objectivity is still often used in postpositivist, qualitative research but it is becoming increasingly more difficult to defend even in the modified form in which it is now applied. 'How, when each researcher is embedded in prejudices, values and specific cognitive frameworks, can we move, however tentatively, towards something which might be called objectivity?' (Lazar, 1998, 17). The goal is to ensure that the results, accepted as the subjective knowledge of the researcher, can be traced back to the raw data of the research, that they are not merely a product of the 'observer's worldview, disciplinary assumptions, theoretical proclivities and research interests' (Charmaz, 1995, 32).

Establishing rigour in quantitative research

Quantitative research relies on what has been referred to as the 'trinity of validity, reliability and generalisability' (Janesick, 1994, 215). This is actually more true of the mixed methodological approach than it is of quantitative research, although the terms have been somewhat randomly applied. The way to establish the value of quantitative research is by testing it against the criteria of rigour noted in Table 1.3.

Internal validity

Internal validity relates to the way in which a causal relationship is demonstrated. Is it clear that the effect is indeed attributable to the cause? When examining causal relationships there are two sets of variables: dependent variables, the outcome, and independent variables, the variables that are manipulated in order to demonstrate a relationship. For example, if we are investigating the effect that playing music in a department store can have on shoppers' spending then music becomes the independent variable and spending the dependent variable. The presence and character of the music will be manipulated (no music, soft music, loud music and so on), and the resulting change, if any, in spending will be measured. Internal validity is concerned with the extent to which we can demonstrate any change in the dependent variable as a direct result of changes made to the independent variable, all other things being equal.

External validity

External validity is concerned with the extent to which findings from the investigation can be generalized to the wider context. This depends on the sample used in the investigation and to what extent it is 'representative' of the wider population. This is demonstrated by a statistical examination of probability; the significance of the sample is paramount and needs to be given considerable thought before the research is carried out.

Reliability

Reliability is concerned with stability of the research findings over time and across locations. Typically the test, retest method is used to demonstrate reliability. The research is conducted more than once and by other researchers. If the results are found to be significantly similar, then reliability is accepted. More recently statistical analysis software has provided a second solution to this, which allows for cross-sectional analysis of the data. This will be discussed in the final section of this book.

Objectivity

Objectivity is a very tricky topic to discuss; it is highly emotive and therefore you are likely to find much discussion and many opinions on the matter. I do not put forward an opinion here, simply an explanation of how it is used in quantitative research. Objectivity is measured by the extent to which the findings from an investigation would remain constant regardless of the character of the researcher. Findings are a result of the research investigation, not a result of the researcher's interpretation of those findings. The goal is to demonstrate that the investigation is value-free, free from any personal constructs of the researcher.

Summary

Some claim that striving and debating over paradigm and methodological issues does not help in achieving the aims and goals of the research. For example Miles and Huberman contend that 'researchers should pursue their work, be open to an ecumenical blend of epistemologies and procedures, and leave the grand debate to those who care about it' (1988, 223). Well I care about it and would encourage those of you who have been stirred by this debate go on and investigate it further.

 PRACTICAL EXERCISE

This is slightly different from the exercises you can expect in the rest of the chapters in this book. It focuses more on your own beliefs than strict procedures and hopefully it will help you to understand the relevance of paradigms and methodology in deciding on your own approach to an investigation. I am going to give you a research question; I want you to decide on the approach you would take in order to provide what you think would be a valid response to the question. At this stage I would not expect you to go into any real detail concerning the design of your investigation but I do expect you to say how you would approach the question. This is as much about understanding your own view of the world as it is about demonstrating that you understand the major traditions discussed so far.

Research question: 'What role do the media play in people's perception of internet technology and access to information?'

- What do you think you can reveal by investigating this question?
- What would be your personal preference in approach to this question?
- Can you say why?

Keep a note of your responses, it may be very interesting to look back at them after you have explored this topic in more depth.

Suggested further reading

Budd, J. M. (2001) *Knowledge and Knowing in Library and Information Science: a philosophical framework*, New York, Scarecrow Press.

Gorman, G. E. and Clayton, P. (2005) *Qualitative Research for the Information Professional: a practical handbook*, 2nd edn, London, Facet Publishing.

Guba, E. G. and Lincoln, Y. S. (1994) Competing Paradigms in Qualitative Research. In Denzin, N. K. and Lincoln, Y. S. (eds) *Handbook of Qualitative Research*, London, Sage, 105–17.

Swingewood, A. (2000) *A Short History of Social Thought*, 3rd edn, London, Macmillan.

Chapter 2
Reviewing literature

The design of all research requires conceptual bridges from what is already known, cognitive structures to guide data gathering, and outlines for presenting interpretations to others.
(Stake, 1995, 15)

Introduction

In order to establish the 'conceptual bridges' referred to by Stake it is necessary to determine the current state of knowledge within your topic area. If you think of your research as a grand adventure, then the literature review is the runway to that grand adventure; it is the thing that gets you off the ground and ready to fly. The literature review is an adventure in itself; discovering what is already known about a particular topic, sometimes from within a number of different disciplines, and bringing it together, often for the first time. This means exploring your topic both within your own academic discipline and across disciplines. For example if you were interested in how young people interact with information you may find yourselves exploring the literature in information science, communication, education, psychology and sociology. It is the topic that drives the investigation and that means sometimes having to look outside the obvious to determine the state of knowledge. A literature review is a 'runway' because it should:

- clarify your own research aims
- provide you with the depth and breadth of subject knowledge necessary
- form the theoretical framework for your own empirical investigation
- contribute to your research design.

The extent to which the literature is identified and reviewed depends very much on the nature of the research. In a piece of higher degree research it is expected that no significant work will have been omitted from the candidate's discussion of the literature and any such omission might seriously jeopardize a submission's chance of success. It is therefore imperative that a full and thoughtfully designed search for literature be carried out. Masters dissertations are usually expected to cover all of the major work in a particular field and undergraduate research would be expected to discuss all the most prominent research. Professional research may not always need to cover the literature to the same extent; it may be sufficient to provide context to the research by presenting the current situation. This will depend very much on the purpose and the audience of your research (Wilson, 1994).

A literature review is a critical discussion of all significant, publicly available literature that contributes to the understanding of a subject. In order to produce a literature review you must carry out a search of all the appropriate bibliographic sources in order to ensure that no significant documents have been missed. From the retrieved literature you must record each items existence uniquely, appraise each item in terms of its contribution to the body of knowledge on the subject of the search, and synthesize all of the literature located into an account of the research on which your project is built. This will convey a sense of the research data available, the validity of the methods you used to gather that data, the currency of your findings, the ideas and theories which have been formulated by previous researchers, any gaps in current knowledge and the predicted contribution of your own impending work.

The literature review process involves four distinct stages and requires four separate skills:

- **information seeking and retrieval**: the ability to search appropriate sources and scan the literature efficiently, using manual or online methods, to identify and obtain a set of useful articles, chapters and books
- **evaluation**: the ability to judge a source based on a number of criteria, including the source itself, the author and the subject
- **critical analysis**: the ability to examine and analyse the content of the literature systematically
- **research synthesis**: the ability to synthesize the various concepts and evidence you have found into a structured piece of discursive prose that provides context and background on your topic area.

Information searching and retrieval

When planning a search on any topic area it is important to be familiar with the *tertiary sources* (bibliographies of bibliographies), which will help you to identify the *secondary sources* (such as bibliographies, indexes and abstracts), which will then lead you to the *primary sources* for your review. The first thing you should do is formulate a strategy for your search. This presents us with something of a paradox: how can you start to search for literature until you have an idea of your theoretical framework? But how can you build such a framework without reviewing the literature? The answer is that you begin with a very loose framework, a research question maybe, and allow that question to guide your initial search. Over time as you build up knowledge of the area and identify relevant work, you will see a stronger framework begin to emerge. It is often very difficult to trust to the process, particularly if this is the first time you have ever carried out a literature review; you must try to allow the theory to emerge as the search and analysis progress. As you analyse the literature, new avenues will appear and your search will widen; it is an iterative process and you must allow ideas to move forward and not be afraid to adjust the research question. Remember that the literature review is there to allow you to formulate your research question more precisely; it is highly probable that as you become increasingly more knowledgeable the focus of the research may shift.

It is not the intention here to provide a detailed discussion of the principles and practice of information retrieval, there are a number of excellent guides and text books that already cover the topic in far more depth and detail than would be possible here (see suggested further reading at the end of the chapter). This is brief overview of the steps involved in the search for material for your literature review.

Define your search objectives

It is useful to begin by stating clearly the research question(s), determining why information is needed and how it will ultimately be used. This will help you to formulate boundaries to your search and may also suggest appropriate search systems. It is important to establish parameters for your search in order to avoid wasting time. You need to make some decisions early on in the process, and you may change your mind about these decisions as the search progresses. Examples of possible search limitations are country of publication, language of publication, and date or type of material (for example, only journal articles). By doing this you start by making sure you know exactly what you're not looking for! You then have to examine your subject and define a basic structure for your initial search. For example, research into how young people use the internet could potentially cover a number of areas, so the first step is to define your opening objective. One possible research question could be: What is the role of the internet as an information source in primary level education? That question would lead to a search covering topics such as 'information and learning', 'children's internet use', 'the national curriculum' and 'electronic information resources for education'. These topics are a starting point but the researcher's objectives may change as the search progresses. Once you have organized your subject into topic groups you can then go on to analyse the keywords within that group to make sure you are using the best possible search terms.

Identify keywords, phrases and subject categories to be used in the search

You must identify all the possible ways to describe the topic groups, noting synonyms, distinctive terms and alternative spellings, bearing in mind that there is often a significant difference between British and American spelling of the same word. Using a thesaurus always helps to ensure you are using the most appropriate keywords within your subject. The topic groups used in the example earlier could be analysed using the *British Education Thesaurus*. A comprehensive list of all search terms should be maintained, recording the success and value of each, in order to avoid unnecessary repetition. When the first useful items are identified, you should examine them for other keywords and concepts that were not predetermined and carry out a subsequent search to ensure that all items using these terms are located.

Identify and record the sources to be accessed in searching for information

The value of this step cannot be over stressed; only someone who has agonized over that vital lost record can understand the anguish caused by failing to note a source, only to realize that it was probably the most important reference available! It is also important that you maintain as full a record as possible of all potentially useful sources, and maintain an ongoing log of the search, recording the bibliographic sources and search terms you have used. It is useful to keep a log of your current search, which can also be stored and referred to in subsequent searches; re-inventing the wheel is never a good idea and we usually don't have the time, so keeping a log is always useful. Use dedicated software such as *Endnotes* or *Pro-Cite* but if you don't have access to such software then design a database yourself using fields such as author, date, title, publisher and location. Of course there is nothing to stop you using index cards to store the data manually. Whichever option you prefer make sure you record all the necessary information as you identify it.

Evaluation

Once you have carried out the search, it is important that you pause to examine the information you have retrieved. If you have restricted yourself to referred journals, books and so forth, there may not be a problem. However, with the increased availability of published information, particularly on the internet, you may need to examine the quality of the sources you have identified. There are a number of criteria you can use to evaluate the quality of the information you have retrieved.

Authority

You must consider the authority of the creator(s) of the document in order to appraise the reliability of the information provided. You should consider aspects such as the authors' previous research, their stature, their organizational affiliation, political stance, credibility and reputation among their peers. Much internet material does not even indicate authorship and documents that have no named author should always be treated with great caution. Where publishers are given consider whether they have a reputation for producing authoritative and high quality publications. Journal articles are often peer reviewed before publication but this is not always the case and you should check for information about the editorial policy of journals to determine the rigour of the review process. It is also worth investigating whether a source you have identified has been cited by other reputable authors. The *Social Sciences Citation Index*, available via the 'Web of Science' at http://wos.mimas.ac.uk/, allows you to do this with a large number of academic journals.

Scope

Consider what claims are made by the author(s) of the work. Most reliable pieces of research should set out clearly the scope, aims and objectives and the methods by which data were collected. Any works which fail to set out such information should again be regarded with caution.

Purpose

Think about why a work was produced as the reason may give an indication of its reliability. If a work was produced to convince buyers of the value of an information resource, it will scarcely constitute an objective and independent assessment of the value of that resource.

You will soon develop an understanding of your topic and become familiar with individual researchers or a core body of authors who publish extensively in your area. Until you develop that 'feel' it is useful to determine evaluation criteria from the outset to save you time and effort.

Critical analysis

There are a number of ways to approach critical analysis, but one thing they all have in common is 'reading with a purpose'. Every item you read will inform your argument and establish the background to, and justification for, your work. The technique used in this chapter demonstrates how to deconstruct an argument in order to establish the robustness of that argument. The same technique can be applied in reverse when you are constructing your own argument. Ensuring that the building blocks of your claim are supported by credible evidence and sound reason will strengthen your argument and make it difficult to refute. Two very effective approaches to critical analysis are those proposed by Toulmin (1958), who identifies the elements of an argument as *a claim, data, a warrant,* and *backing,* and Fisher (1993), who identifies *reasons, conclusions* and *evidence* as the elements by which an argument can be analysed. A more detailed description of both approaches can be found in Hart (1998), and further reading on this subject is strongly recommended. What is presented here is a technique that combines elements of Toulmin's and Fisher's approaches, but this is not the only potential combination, just one that happened to work for me and my students.

Essentially an academic argument should have a number of components. Any argument should consist of a *claim* (or conclusion), a *reason* (interpretation of data), *evidence* (data) to support that claim, and any *qualifications* of the claim. In order to analyse the argument of the author you need to read the piece and identify all of those components.

A claim

A claim is the essence of an argument; it is the conclusion the writer intends to demonstrate by applying all other components of an argument in support of that claim. A claim could be as simple as 'You must buy this CD!' or 'You must read this novel!' Academic conclusions emerging from research are essentially no different, although one would hope there is sufficient and detailed evidence to support them. Before believing any claim you would need to know a few things; you would need to know the reasons someone had for making such a bold claim, what evidence that person can provide to support the claim, and how far they take the claim - for example, whether there are any qualifiers. When reading a journal article, a conference paper, a section in a book or a report, you look for that highest level statement, the essence of the entire argument. Usually it is not difficult to spot a claim or conclusion; it is often there in a title or if not in quite so obvious a place then certainly in the opening paragraph as the writer defines the aim(s) of the work. Once you are aware of the writer's claim you then need to continue your analysis to establish how well that claim is supported.

A reason

The reasons a writer gives for making a claim are the first building blocks of any argument. Reasons comprise the second level of an argument, without which the first level, the claim, cannot stand. The argument would cease to be effective without a robust reason, which is usually the writer's interpretation of the evidence or data. There are three questions to ask when trying to establish the value of a reason:

- Is the reason relevant to the claim it supports?
- Is the reason effective?
- Is the value invoked by the reason likely to be universal or selective?

In order to be relevant to the claim there has to be a very clear link between that claim and the reason(s) for making the claim. That may sound like a very obvious statement but all too often conclusions or claims are made that appear to be a massive leap of faith from the reason(s) we have been presented with. The claim may be something the author believes in with great passion, but without providing relevant reasons the claim is little more than a personal position. Back to our example of the novel, then. If someone claims that we must read it, a relevant reason to support the claim would be that the quality of the writing is high, the story exciting or perhaps that previous works by the same author have been very well received.

If a reason is to be effective, it must relate to a value you can believe in and agree with. Value judgements are nearly always subjective; this means the value judgement of the writer has to agree with the value judgement of the reader. It is, therefore, always a good idea to restate the value being appealed to as clearly as possible in your own terms. If the reason our book critic gives for wanting us to read this novel is simply that their favourite author wrote it, we are unlikely to be convinced. This reason is too subjective. If, on the other hand, the reason is because it has won three book prizes and was written by one of the most highly acclaimed writers of our time, we may be convinced. On the other hand a subjective reason could be very effective if we shared the value judgement of the person giving it. For example, if the book were a science fiction novel and both the critic and the reader shared a love of that genre, then the subjective reason the critic gave would be effective for that particular reader. You, on the other hand, would be reading this as a reviewer, critically analysing each element and would not be convinced by such a value dependent reason.

Evidence

Most readers are unlikely to accept a claim based solely on the reason(s) given by the author; we would expect the author to support the reason(s). The more hostile or critical an audience, the stronger the evidence must be. It must be accurate, credible and given in sufficient quantity to convince the reader of the author's knowledge. Where is the evidence to support the book critic's assertion that this particular novel was written by one of the most highly acclaimed writers of our time? The evidence could be a list of all the writer's previous works and the awards that she has won.

When evidence comes in the form of empirical research data you need to ask yourself if the data is credible: were the statistics gathered from a reliable source and in a verifiable way? If you are given qualitative data in the form of opinions the same questions need to be asked. Where was the data collected? How was it collected? And how did the researcher interpret it?

Qualifiers

There are two types of claim, the unqualified claim and the qualified claim. By far the most common are qualified claims, whether made by our book critic, a research student or a practitioner sharing the results of their investigation, the majority of claims or conclusions are qualified in some way or another. This by no means lessens the value of the claim; if anything it makes it more reliable because the research has acknowledged the potential limitations of the work. An unqualified claim would be:

'Books by Isaac Asimov are enlightening.'

A qualified claim would be:

'Many books by Isaac Asimov are enlightening.'

When you are reading an article look for the qualifiers; they are words like *usually, many, most, often* and *a few.*

Drawing conclusions from critical analysis

Once you have analysed the text you must then draw your own conclusions from the work and begin to formulate your own argument; your review will ultimately provide a synthesis of the articles, research reports or other reviews that you have analysed. Your conclusions will provide the framework for that synthesis. This exercise is also very useful when writing up your own work. If your writing can stand up to the same level of critical analysis that you have subjected your chosen review items to, then you can feel fairly confident that you have presented a robust argument.

Marking up the text

When reading through an article it always helps to annotate the text as you go in order to establish which part of the article does what in terms of the overall argument, if you have a taken a photocopy that is! Fisher (1993) suggests one way of doing this:

- A claim is identified in the text by <u>underlining</u>.
- A reason is identified in the text by square brackets: [....].
- Evidence is identified in the text by placing an asterisk at either side of the evidence statement: *...*.
- Qualifiers are identified in the text by encircling them: ⬭ .

Using a template for analysis

After you have read through a text it is useful to take a separate note of what you marked up in it, and you should also keep a reference of the source. The template shown in Figure 2.1 provides a structure for making notes after reading an article or paper.

Full citation				
Scope				
Purpose				
Method				
Claim	Qualifiers	Evidence	Reason

Figure 2.1 Evaluation and critical analysis framework

This framework should be used for each separate item you are reviewing; the number of rows in the second half of this template are no indication of how many rows you will need, that all depends on the item.

Synthesizing the research: developing a theoretical framework

Once each item has been analysed, or as the analysis progresses, you are in a position to formulate a theoretical framework for your investigation. Of course this framework would have been growing as each additional item was analysed; the picture builds incrementally as each new item is added to the overall picture. Innovative frameworks usually draw on literature from more than the core discipline of study, and it is often necessary to extend the boundaries of your review in order to introduce new concepts. To begin with this can seems a very daunting task, as there is likely to be a lot to read, analyse and synthesize. Working your way through each item may appear to be laborious but there really is no 'quick fix' solution. While you analyse each item you will be in a position to 'place' the evidence you find in the item somewhere in your growing theoretical framework. One way to approach this is to draw a 'concept map': start to identify the various concepts within the literature and map out any connections between them. Seeing a 'picture' of your review and watching it take shape and grow in substance is a very good way of preventing information overload. An example from a study of how young people use electronic information as a learning resource (Pickard, 2002) demonstrates the growth of a theoretical framework that provides the conceptual bridges for further investigation. Figure 2.2 shows the various strands of the literature that provided the necessary background and identifies (in italics) the gaps in knowledge that existed.

All of the various concepts seen in Figure 2.2 come together to provide the theoretical framework for an investigation into the use of electronic information resources in the learning process. These various strands are linked together to provide a framework that covers all aspects seen as relevant to the initial question. The review is presented to the reader as part of the research study in order to provide him or her with the context and background for the 'new' theory that will hopefully

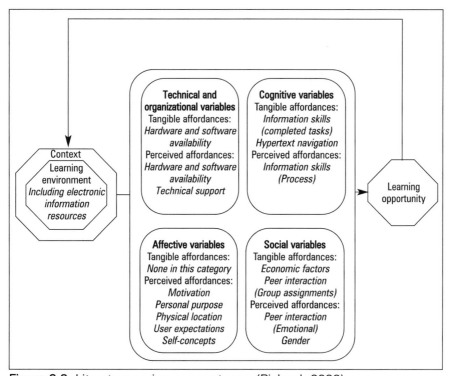

Figure 2.2 Literature review concept map (Pickard, 2002)

emerge at the end of your research. It also provides you, as the researcher, with the knowledge to move from the broad theory to a well-defined research question. This will help you begin to put into operation your own investigation, something we will examine in much more detail in the next chapter.

Using the literature review to inform your methodology

It is very natural to conduct a review of subject specific literature and apply this only to establish the theoretical framework for your research from the point of view of the subject. This is potentially a waste of valuable information. The literature review not only informs you of the 'state of knowledge' of the subject, it also provides you with insight concerning methodology. When any research is presented in published form, there will inevitably be a description of the research design applied to the study. Use this to assist you in designing your own investigation, extracting ideas of how not to do it, as well as ideas on how to do it. In a formal research report this will be written up as a separate section discussing only methodology, but your discoveries from the critical analysis can be applied again to discuss and justify your own research design. Although research methods texts are written as a guide to research activity you should also learn from the experience of other researchers and use their designs to inform yours.

Final synthesis: the review

Before you begin writing your review return to your purpose. You are writing a literature review to establish the context of your research, to demonstrate your knowledge of your chosen topic, and to identify any gaps that may exist in the published literature. Essentially this means you are justifying the need for, and contextualizing, your research. You are also developing your own conceptual bridges, the starting point of the empirical investigation you are undertaking.

Writing a literature review is very like writing any academic report; you are writing a formal piece with a recognized structure and format. A critical review is a robust and well supported discussion in the form of discursive prose. First time reviewers often think it should be an annotated bibliography, providing a list of entries consisting of a reference followed by a brief discussion of that reference. This is a very common mistake and should be avoided at all cost. Nor is a literature review a list of every single item you have read, however much you want to impress your reader with the extent of your reading; it is a critical discussion of relevant work. It is not your purpose to present everything, only that which creates a picture of the current state of knowledge and issues being investigated; it may be painful to discard some of that hard won literature but you must make informed and appropriate decisions.

Blaxter, Dodd and Tight (1996) provide a list of what references should and should not be used. References should 'justify and support your argument; allow you to make comparisons with other research; demonstrate your familiarity with your field of research'. However references should not be used to 'impress your readers with the scope of your reading; litter your writing with names and quotations; replace the need for you to express your own thoughts; misrepresent the authors' (115).

Your review will consist of the following sections.

Introduction

The introduction should include a clear statement of your purpose, outlining the scope and coverage of your review so your reader knows what to expect and understands the reason for any apparent omissions. Go back to the early section where we discussed how to establish the scope of your literature search. Provide your readers with the reasons for the choices you made at this point. This opening section will say what you have reviewed and why.

Methodology

You may want to let your reader know how you engaged in the review process. This is not always included in a review, it depends on the nature of the report you are presenting.

Discussion

This is the main body of the review, where you discuss the collection of items reviewed and put forward your own 'argument'. It is highly likely that you will want to arrange this discussion under headings that reflect the individual concepts you have used to synthesize your findings. In order to check that you have written an evaluative and critical review that is robust why not apply the critical analysis technique to your own work at this point?

Conclusion

This is your closing statement; there should be nothing new here as you have already provided your argument. This is a clear and concise statement of that argument based on the evidence you provided in the discussion. The conclusion should end with a statement of the problem or research question that still remains, after all you already know has been investigated.

References

The referencing for a literature review should be of a very high standard; the list of references is as a much a part of the review as the discussion and should be treated as such. A very useful online resource is 'Cite Them Right', which can be found at www.unn.ac.uk/central/isd/cite/.

Summary

The four major skills of the reviewer – information searching and retrieval, evaluation, critical analysis and synthesis – are, like all skills, developed and honed through practical application. The paradox of the literature review is that you need a review to allow you to frame a relevant and worthwhile research question, but you need to have a question before you can investigate the literature. The truth is the literature review process is a continuous one throughout the lifespan of the research project; there will be a point at which your individual critical analysis of items will be synthesized but you will not stop there. You will add to the review each time you locate a relevant piece of work that has a place in your theoretical framework. What you begin with is an idea for your research, a particular curiosity that needs to be formalized and placed within current knowledge surrounding that idea. From your review you can then move on to the next stage in the research process: framing your research question, aims and objectives or hypothesis based on what you have discovered from within the published literature.

 PRACTICAL EXERCISE

1   Look at this excerpt from an article. See if you can identify all of the components of an argument in the article using the text markings suggested in this chapter.

Any approach to managing electronic resources should take into account the value and impact of these resources on the users and how the nature of provision can influence and impact on this relationship (Dixon, Pickard and Robson, 2002). The value of electronic information resources is not only concerned with the resource itself but also intrinsically linked to the environment in which use occurs. The construction of an environment that ensures that these are affordances and not barriers is the responsibility of all those who design and control that environment. This includes schools, public libraries, home and in fact any location that provides access to information. Developing a framework that can be applied to monitor and measure the value of this constructed environment is dependent upon the involvement of all stakeholders. This includes those delivering the service, those using the service and those relying on the service to contribute to the wider needs of the individual and the community. This framework needs to be flexible enough to accommodate all local conditions whilst providing sufficient rigidity to allow for suitable measurements of value across environments. Value as social construct varies according to context, it is therefore necessary to provide a framework that can be used to measure value in such a way that individual contexts are not marginalized. Electronic information resources have become swathed in symbolism and surrounded by their own mythology. Myths have been created and compounded by marketing strategies, imaginative exaggeration and distorted perceptions of reality (Klienmann, 2000). Training and education in the use and application of these resources are necessary to develop a clear understanding of the value of these resources to the user.

References

Dixon, P., Pickard, A. and Robson, H. (2002) Developing a Criteria-based Quality Framework for Measuring Value, *Performance Measures and Metrics*, 3 (1), 5–9.

Klienmann, G. (2000). Myths and Realities About Technology in K-12, Education Development Centre Inc, www.edc.org/LNT/news/issues14/feature1.htm.

Source: Pickard, A (2004)

2 Now apply this technique to an entire published article; it may be a good idea to do this with an article you have already read. See if applying a structure such as this to your reading opens up the contents of the article any more than your initial reading did.

Suggested further reading

Cooper, H. (1998) *Synthesizing Research: a guide for literature reviews*, 3rd edn, London, Sage.

Fink, A (1998) *Conducting Research Literature Reviews: from paper to the internet*, London, Sage.

Hart, C. (1998) *Doing a Literature Review: releasing the social science research imagination*, London, Sage.

Hart, C. (2001) *Doing a Literature Search: a comprehensive guide for the social sciences*, London, Sage.

Chapter 3

Defining the research

The formulation of a problem is often more essential than its solution, which may be merely a matter of mathematical or experimental skill. (Einstein and Infeld, 1938)

Introduction

Now you have developed a theoretical framework for the research from the literature review; the next step is to use that theoretical framework to construct a conceptual framework. Both qualitative and quantitative research demand the development of a theoretical and conceptual framework; after the conceptual stage the two approaches begin to move forward in their own discrete fashion. Table 3.1 outlines the divergence that takes place at this stage in the research, if it has not already done so at least in the mind of the researcher.

Table 3.1 Pre-operational structure of quantitative and qualitative research

Quantitative research	Qualitative research
Topic of interest	Topic of interest
Literature review	Literature review
Theoretical framework	Theoretical framework
Conceptual framework	Conceptual framework
Define variables	Identify a tentative research question
Define hypothesis *or* aim and objectives	Define aims and objectives (mutable subject to investigation)

The theoretical framework covers the theories, concepts and issues which surround your chosen topic. It needs to be narrowed down, as not every one of those theories, issues or concepts will relate directly to your investigation. When you move from theory to concept you begin to identify the true focus of your research, to define the boundaries of your own work as it relates to the wider theory that already exists. This is essentially your research question. It is at this stage that we make final decisions on that approach, although it is very probable that you already had a very firm idea of how you wanted to proceed before getting this far. The literature may have suggested an approach that appealed to you or you may have external pressures that require you to take a particular approach. Whatever the situation, it is now time to engage in one of the most creative aspects of research: to begin to design your own study.

Designing a conceptual framework

There will be a number of factors influencing you at this stage: your own agenda, external requirements, resources available to you, and not least your own experience of research. Essentially the research question should itself determine the design of your study but it is usually the case that naturally qualitative researchers ask questions such as: Why? How? What?, and naturally quantitative researchers ask such questions as How many? How often? Where? This is of course far too simple a distinction but lets you see the potential for creating an appropriate research question. It is at the stage of the conceptual framework that you make these methodological choices. If we return to the example of a theoretical framework used in the previous chapter, it is evident that it would be possible to approach that question in a number of ways. It would be possible from that theoretical framework to focus on one or more aspects of the theory and identify those concepts which provoked the most interest. The approach taken to the research would be influenced by the concepts, the preferred approach of the researcher and the intended research output.

In this chapter I will present a number of possible approaches to the research questions, which can be developed from the theoretical framework in the previous chapter. I should point out at this stage that the research undertaken based on that framework was actually a highly interpretivist research study involving 16 collective case studies (Pickard, 2002). I made the decision to take this approach for a number of reasons: my own particular preference for interpretivist research at that time, because I wanted to investigate individuals in great depth over a long period of time, and because I wanted to explore the issues in a way that had not been done before in our disciplines. That aside, it would have been possible to explore the same concepts in a number of ways; the approach would have altered the research but that is why we make decisions like this at this stage.

So let us look at the ways in which we could explore the issues surrounding the use of electronic information resources in the provision of learning opportunities for young people. Our research question for this stage in the process will be: 'Does access to electronic information resources have a role in breaking down barriers to learning opportunities encountered by young people?' (Pickard, 2002, 5). We shall explore the possible approaches available to us when defining a research design to address this question. Looking back at Chapter 1 we know that the research question can be approached in a number of ways depending on our ontological and epistemological stance. It is at this stage that we must make a decision about how we are going to construct our research; this choice will be guided by our own views, the purpose of the research and very often the research traditions within our professional field. How we proceed from this point on will determine the choices we have to make relating to our research method: sampling, data collection, data analysis and presentation of our findings. Based on what we have learned from our theoretical framework and other influencing factors we make the first decision: whether this is to be a quantitative study, a qualitative study or a postpositivist combination of the two. Let us explore the possibilities in relation to the original research question.

The research hypothesis

Hypothesis testing is only carried out in quantitative or positivist research; very often qualitative or interpretivist research will culminate in the generation of a working hypothesis but it is not the driving force behind the research design. Although devising and testing hypotheses is useful in most quantitative research, it is an essential part of statistical inference. Hypothesis testing is an attempt to investigate the relationship between two or more variables. The hypothesis is a 'scientific guess' (Busha and Harper, 1980, 10) at the nature of that relationship, established before the empirical investigation takes place and developed from the theoretical framework.

According to Popper (1963), there is no logical way of evaluating how researchers draw up a hypothesis; it is a result of their own interests, knowledge of the theory and a way of constructing a framework to engage in empirical activity. Popper claimed that 'proving' a hypothesis in social research was almost impossible, therefore it is of more value to falsify that hypothesis. Falsification is definite; we may not be able to 'prove' a hypothesis, only offer support that the hypothesis may be true or prove that it is not.

In quantitative social research it is very dangerous to make claims about proving the link or relationship between variables. Experimental research is as close as we can get to this but even then it is difficult to abstract one element, or just a few elements, of the subject under study while holding every other element constant (Lincoln and Guba, 1985). Schwartz and Ogilvy demonstrated that it was 'in principle impossible to separate a thing from its interactive environment' (10). The Heisenberg Indeterminacy Principle (Heisenberg, 1958) had already shown that in physics it is impossible to predict the future state of a particle as the act of experimentation to determine that state would itself create the observed state (Capra, 2000). Any act of experimentation or observation will inevitably alter the state of the subject being studied; any research activity will leave the subject of that research in an altered state. Heisenberg states that 'what we observe is not nature itself, but nature exposed to our method of questioning' (288).

The data gathered from any empirical investigation may itself be, in part, a product of the research process. We will look at this again in Part 2 when discussing experimentation. For now it is enough to say that formulating a hypothesis has great advantages in quantitative research, but claims made concerning the outcome of the research in relation to the hypothesis needs to be realistic. In the majority of research studies involving human subjects in real-world conditions, it is impossible to conduct completely 'clean' hypothesis testing. This can only be done in experimental conditions where the researcher has control of all variables; even then there is an argument that it is impossible to control everything.

Burns identifies three essential steps in using a hypothesis to engage in scientific discovery:

1. The proposal of a hypothesis to account for a phenomenon.
2. The deduction from the hypothesis that a certain phenomenon should be observed in given circumstances.
3. The checking of this deduction by observation (2000, 106).

The hypothesis must be capable of being tested; from a theoretical proposition we must create an 'operational' (Burns, 2000, 108) hypothesis. A hypothesis must be:

- a proposition that implies a relationship between two or more concepts,
- which is located on a lower level of abstraction and generality than the theory,
- and which enables the theory to be transformed into terms that can be tested
  empirically.   (Corbetta, 2003, 61)

Defining variables

From our theoretical framework we now need to identify the concepts we wish to investigate in terms of connections and relationships. These concepts will provide us with the variables we need to construct the research hypothesis, and then the operational hypothesis we will use to engage in the empirical investigation. 'A variable is an *operationalized* concept' (Corbetta, 2003, 68).

There are three types of variable: nominal, ordinal and interval variables. The classification is related to the functions that can be performed on the particular variable. A *nominal* variable is one that can be classified by categories which cannot be ordered, such as gender and colour. The variable value will have names. An *ordinal* variable is one in which the order of data points can be determined but not the distance between data points, for example letter grades such as 'A' and 'B'. The variable value will be numbers but only ordinal numbers. An *interval* variable is one in which both order of data points and distance between data points can be determined, as in percentage scores and distances. There are two forms of interval variable: *discrete variables*, which have a definite value and can be counted, and *continuous variables*, which can occur on an infinite number of points on a continuum such as a tape measure. The variable value will be numbers with cardinal properties.

It is obvious that the variables you select to create your hypothesis will determine the nature of your data collection and analysis later in the process. It is important to think about this from the outset; too many research projects have been thwarted as a result of identifying variables that ultimately did not lend themselves to practical data collection and/or analysis. We will look at this again in more detail in Part 3. You need to be aware that your choice of variables has implications for your empirical research design.

Looking back at the theoretical framework in Chapter 2 there are a number of potential variables we could focus on to form the basis of our hypothesis. I would like to point out that using them all would be a great mistake unless you had unlimited resources. Your choice of variables is concerned with the research question. Our question for this example is 'Does access to electronic information resources have a role in breaking down barriers to learning opportunities encountered by young people?' (Pickard, 2002, 5). The following variables could be identified from the map in Figure 2.2 (page 33):

- access to electronic resources – interval variable, which is either continuous or discrete depending on how we want to measure or count it, for example, the number of times a PC is accessed or length of time of access
- social background – nominal variable if we are using recognized named social groupings; ordinal if we are using a predefined classification scale such as the Standard Occupational Classification
- academic attainment – ordinal variable
- IT literacy – ordinal variable
- gender – nominal variable.

Once we have decided on our variables it is then time to construct a hypothesis that would allow any relationship between the variables to be tested.

Constructing your hypothesis

We now have a research question and a list of potential variables to help us respond to that question. It is now time to examine those variables and decide what relationship, if any, may exist and how we can test for its existence. As pointed out earlier, the resources available to you as well as the research question may influence this decision; there is a limit to what can be done in a single investigation so it is important to think very practically at this stage. The literature review may have already identified potential relationships between these variables, for example, there may be evidence to suggest that young people who spend more time than others accessing electronic resources are those with higher levels of IT skills. You may want to test this for yourself with your own sample group or you may want to introduce a third variable to find out if that has any influence on the relationship.

Hypothesis testing is deductive: the problem is stated then data is collected in direct response to the stated problem. You can see that there is a rigid structure to this approach that dictates the empirical data collection. An experimental hypothesis will have three types of variable: an independent variable, a dependent variable and intervening variables. The *independent variable* is the condition that is manipulated by the researcher; the *dependent variable* is the effect of this manipulation; intervening variables are all of those things the research has no control over. It is important to acknowledge the potential impact of *intervening variables* on any research findings. In the majority of research within a natural setting there is no manipulation of a variable; the independent variable becomes an existing condition. In our example below of whether access to electronic resources has a role in breaking down barriers to learning opportunities encountered by young people, the independent variable could be IT literacy and the dependent variable academic attainment. We would be looking to see if levels of IT literacy had a relationship with level of academic attainment among our sample group. From the variables we have identified there are a number of possible hypotheses we could decide on, for example those shown in Example 3.1.

Example 3.1 Possible approaches to research questions
There are a number of possible approaches to any research question; here are three possible approaches to the same question.

Research question: 'Does access to electronic information resources have a role in breaking down barriers to learning opportunities encountered by young people?'

Hypothesis 1: 'Higher levels of IT literacy in young people will lead to higher levels of academic attainment in assignments where electronic information resources are used.'

Hypothesis 2: 'Young people from the top two groups of the Standard Occupational Classification will perform better in assignments where access to electronic information resources is needed.'

Hypothesis 3: 'Young males are more confident in navigating electronic information resources and this confidence leads to more successful use of these resources.'

If this approach is appropriate to your investigation then you have chosen a quantitative research design; this would then imply that your research design may include probability sampling. Your research method is likely to be experimental, quasi-experimental or a large scale survey.

Research aims and objectives

Hypothesis formulation is all very well when you know exactly which variables are involved in your intended investigation and you have decided how those variables will be counted or measured. What happens when you want to engage in an investigation that is not concerned with measuring or counting anything? When your purpose is to investigate a particular phenomenon in rich detail, then it may well be impossible to define variables before you begin the investigation. Even if you were aware of likely variables, the purpose of the research is very different; exploration becomes the focus of the investigation, not testing or measuring.

Chapter 1 explains the major differences in approaches to research. A very basic but important distinction between the approaches is that it is rare, if not impossible, to test a hypothesis in qualitative research. In qualitative research the purpose is to explore a research question in depth, not to focus on specific variables and test relationships between those variables. In this case we need to establish the aim(s) of the research and a set of objectives. In recent years many qualitative researchers have adopted the approach of finding a focus (Lincoln and Guba, 1985) – providing a focus of inquiry that guides the investigation but does not restrict discovery. Aims and objectives focus the research without eliminating a major characteristic of all qualitative research, that it must 'be "played by ear"; it must unfold, cascade, roll, emerge' (Lincoln and Guba, 1985, 203).

The conceptual framework you construct will provide a starting point to finding this focus; the 'conceptual bridges' discussed in Chapter 2 form the building blocks of your research aims and objectives. We have a research question, a question that emerged from our investigation of the current state of knowledge within our particular area of interest. We know what is known; we have decided on which element of what remains unknown we wish to explore. Now we have to frame a focus that will guide our investigation. In order to do this there are a number of questions that we have to ask about our research question:

- Why am I doing this research?
- What is the purpose of this research?
- What do I hope to learn from this investigation?
- What do I need to know in order to provide an answer to my research question?
- Who can provide access to that knowledge?
- What will be the likely output from this investigation?

The answers to these questions allow us to frame our aim(s) and from that to construct the objectives of the investigation. It is at this point that many new researchers become confused, asking 'What is the difference between a research aim and an objective?' It would be very easy to over complicate the response to that question but in reality it is simple (see Example 1.2).

An *aim* is concerned with the conceptual level of the research, the overall purpose, which is not necessarily time and context bound. It is related to the wider research question and any intended research outputs. It would be the answer to the question 'What is the purpose of this research?' If we look at Example 1.2, one aim is quite simply to answer the research question that has been identified and, having found an answer, to provide more specific detail to that answer. The overall purpose is to provide others with evidence-based guidelines for their own practice. A research aim is concerned with the *why* and the *what,* why we are doing it and what we hope to produce by doing it.

A research *objective* is concerned with the *'how'* of the research activity; defining objectives comes from answering the question: 'How will I achieve my stated aim(s)?' This is very much an operational list of activities that will guide the practical side of the research. You could almost call it a task list so it is not surprising that most objectives begin with a verb. Simple as this sounds it does help when constructing objectives to consider the type of words you should be using, words such as 'examine', 'identify' and 'establish' are usually the first words of a research objective. The operational list of activities will ultimately lead to you achieving your aim(s); they are the pieces of the puzzle that need to be understood and put in place before the whole picture can be revealed.

Example 3.2 Aims and objectives

Research question: **'Does access to electronic information resources have a role in breaking down barriers to learning opportunities encountered by young people?'**

Aims:
- To answer the question 'Does access to electronic and digital information resources have a role in breaking down barriers to learning encountered by young people?'
- If so, how and why does it have this role and what are the circumstances that influence this role? To provide a clear understanding of the use of these resources.
- To suggest a guide to good practice in managing electronic information resources (EIRs) and develop a criterion-based framework of potential learning opportunities in the electronic information environment.

A set of seven specific objectives has been established arising from these aims:

1 Identify and evaluate contemporary use of electronic and digital information by young people.
2 Establish the current context set by central government, local education authority and individual school policies.
3 Establish what young people assume they are doing in relation to the process witnessed by the researcher.
4 Consider motivation to use electronic information and the effect this has on participants' learning.
5 Establish the level and quality of information skills training available to young people, and examine its application during the information-seeking process.
6 Examine the conditions that influence use.
7 Establish the conditions under which access to electronic and digital information does impact positively on learning.

(Pickard, 2002, 5)

Summary

At this stage in the research design major decisions are made about the approach, nature and purpose of the investigation. We have taken the same research question and looked at how we can respond to that question from each of the major research traditions discussed in Chapter 1. Decisions are based on the purpose of the research as well as the researcher's experience, preference and understanding. It is vital that once those decisions are made the purpose of the research is expressed in an appropriate and practical manner. If you are to achieve your research goals then you must create a design that will lead to a logical and defendable outcome. Your research design must ensure **rigour** or **trustworthiness**, depending on your chosen approach.

 PRACTICAL EXERCISE

1 Identify the dependent and independent variables in the three hypotheses given below.
2 Discuss in seminar or write a brief discussion on the major problems with testing these hypotheses in a natural setting.

   Hypothesis 1: 'Higher levels of IT literacy in young people will lead to higher levels of academic attainment in assignments where electronic information resources are used.'
   Hypothesis 2: 'Young people from the top two groups of the Standard Occupational Classification will perform better in assignments where access to electronic information resources is needed.'
   Hypothesis 3: 'Young males are more confident in navigating electronic information resources and this confidence leads to more successful use of these resources.'

3 You are working in an academic library and have been asked to investigate students' perception of the importance of information literacy to their academic study in a particular university. Construct an aim that adequately reflects the purpose of this investigation. Once you have established an aim, list a set of no more than five objectives that arise from this aim.

Suggested further reading

Burns, R. B. (2000) *Introduction to Research Methods*, 4th edn, London, Sage, Chapter 7.
Corbetta, P. (2003) *Social Research: theory, method and techniques*, London, Sage, Chapter 3.
Silverman, D. (2000) *Doing Qualitative Research: a practical handbook*, London, Sage.

Chapter 4

The research proposal

Why write a proposal?

There are a number of reasons for preparing a research proposal. In the case of funded research it is quite simply that there will be no funding without one. All funding bodies have their own framework for a submission of a research proposal; in many cases these frameworks are now in electronic form and very structured, sometimes restricting the writer to a specific number of characters in each section. These proposal frameworks are created to ensure that all the necessary requirements of the funding body are covered in the proposal and to provide uniformity when examining their merits. This is usually a highly competitive arena and proposals will be seen by a number of referees who will rate each one according to a predefined, criterion-based evaluation. Proposals that achieve the highest grades will usually be funded according to the budget available. This approach to bidding for research funding is clearly defined and the purpose of submitting the proposal is very clear. However, the role of a research proposal is far more extensive than this; it has a very important function in the research process whether or not funding is an issue. It may be that even though actual funding is not available, you will need to convince your line manager or tutor that this is a viable and worthwhile research project, one that is worthy of your time and effort. Small scale, work-based projects are still costly. Even without direct funding, there is your time to consider, resources that may be needed and possibly the time of potential participants if they are in the same organization.

Academic research such as a dissertation will always require some form of proposal. Sometimes this is assessed as part of your taught course of study, other times it is an intrinsic part of your dissertation module. This chapter will not discuss specific proposal frameworks such as those provided by research funding bodies, here we will look at the various elements of a research proposal: what needs to be said, why it needs to be said and how best to say it. It is up to you to take these elements and translate them into the framework you are required to follow, be that a formal funding application, a written response to questions from a line manager relating to your proposed research or an academic proposal with defined marking criteria. Whatever the external requirements, a research proposal should cover what Kumar describes as the *what*, *how* and *why* of the research:

- *what* you are proposing to do;
- *how* you are proposing to do it; and
- *why* you have selected the proposed strategy (1999, 170).

But remember there are two major purposes to a research proposal: to provide others with the information they need, and to provide yourself, the researcher, with a plan that will guide you during your investigation. A well-constructed research proposal will provide you with a very useful tool throughout the research investigation. We will discuss this function of a research proposal later in the chapter.

Structure of a research proposal

Usually the idea of producing a formal document is rather intimidating, but it should not be. A formal document means that there is a formula which, if followed carefully, ensures that you have covered all of the areas you need to cover in order to present your proposed research. Although requirements for a research proposal can often differ slightly according to funding body, academic or professional body regulations, there is an almost universally accepted 'list of contents' that is expected. It is important to pay very close attention to any specific instructions you have for presenting a proposal and use this as a guide to individual sections within that proposal. As already discussed, many funding bodies have their own proposal framework ready to receive your input, regulations differ from university to university and often within individual departments - be aware of exactly what is required. The aim here is to provide as comprehensive a list as possible of the detail that should be included in a proposal. It is your responsibility to make sure you conform to the requirements of the target audience, whether reviewers, academic research supervisors or your line manager.

In order to convey this information here is one suggested structure. Under each heading we will look at how it is possible to present the information when the intention is to engage in a qualitative study that is likely to be of an iterative nature. Remember that research proposals are almost always subject to very stringent word counts; in the case of forms that are completed online you may be limited to a certain number of characters per section. It is up to you to say all you have to say within the required word limit. Bear this in mind when you examine this proposed structure, which includes:

- a clearly defined title and introduction
- a statement of aims and objectives, or a hypothesis
- a review of the literature
- a research design
- an intended sample
- a list of procedures for data processing and analysis
- a definition of anticipated research outputs
- a statement of anticipated constraints

- a note of any ethical considerations
- a project timetable.

Clearly defined title and introduction

Make sure you get your title right. This may sound painfully obvious but it is amazing how little attention is often given to composing a clear, accurate and literate research proposal title. It will be the first thing that any reviewer or tutor reads so it is vital that it is an accurate reflection of what you are proposing to do and that it is clear and concise. Remember that it may well be a working title – things can and often do change as the research progresses – but that is no excuse for not getting it right at this stage. Titles that swell to two or more sentences generally only do so because the author has not taken the time and care to provide a more concise reflection of the intended research or because he or she is trying very hard to cover as many aspects of the problem as possible. This can be done without presenting a rambling title that means very little.

The introduction to the proposal should include a brief rationale explaining where the idea for the research began and some evidence from the literature that there is a need for this particular investigation. This is a brief preamble that sets the scene for the rest of the proposal and gets the message across that this would be a useful and productive research activity. It is not necessary here to provide a lot of detail – that will follow in the other sections. The introduction highlights the contribution this proposed research will make to the body of knowledge that already exists. This sounds like rather a taunting claim but remember that there are rarely large leaps in knowledge; knowledge grows incrementally with each new contribution, however small or localized that contribution might be.

Statement of aims and objectives, or a hypothesis

It is vital that you present clear and concise research aims and objectives or state the hypothesis or hypotheses you intend to test. At this stage any statement you make must clearly reflect your understanding of the problem or question and your understanding of the capacity of research to respond to it. The detail of methods and techniques will follow later in the proposal but do not make the mistake of making over ambitious claims at this stage.

Review of the literature

This is your initial review. At this stage in the process nobody would expect you to know all there is to know and be aware of everything that has been published in relation to your intended research. At this stage your review of available literature has two main functions: to acquaint you with current thinking in your subject area, and to find out about methods and research processes used by other researchers investigating this topic. The contents of this review will depend very much on the topic of your research. There may already be an extensive body of literature specifically focusing on your topic; in this case you will be expected to have identified the major theories in your area and be aware of the most prominent researchers in the field. You are providing a broad overview of the topic area, identifying what is already known and what is not known or remains largely neglected in terms of empirical research. The 'newness' of your proposed research will depend very much on the level and nature of the project. An undergraduate research project is unlikely to be attempting anything completely new, whereas an element of 'newness' and contribution to knowledge is a requirement of doctoral research. These are the two extremes and there are many variations in between. A small-scale, localized study may be seeking to investigate a particular phenomenon only as it relates to the local setting. Here novelty and 'newness' are not the issue, what matters is that the researcher has knowledge of current thinking on that particular phenomenon and how theories have been developed.

This section will follow the same conventions as a more extensive and detailed review outlined in Chapter 2. You will begin with a broad overview of the topic and any related topics. From there you will take the reader to the central focus of your investigation; depending on your topic the main themes you should aim to cover in this review, if they exist in your subject area, are:

- major theories in the field, providing an overview of current thinking
- the historical development of theory and major practical advances
- major published research findings
- the main problems or issues that remain.

The initial review for a research proposal needs to be clear, concise and sufficiently detailed to demonstrate your understanding of the field.

Research design
In this section you will be expected to present your plan of action for the research investigation, setting out the major processes and procedures you intend to follow. This applies to both quantitative and qualitative research designs, although it is understood that many qualitative research projects will be iterative and very open to change. This does not mean it is impossible to present a plan that provides a framework while still allowing for the emergent nature of the research. It is possible to begin with a broad research design and still remain responsive to discoveries made in the field. It is important to remember that it is not sufficient to say what you intend to do; you must defend and justify your choices from the appropriate research methods literature. This section should be referenced, too; not as heavily referenced as your literature review, but it is necessary to demonstrate your understanding of the methodology and that you have read around the subject. Every choice, every decision relating to research design, should be supported and justified from the published material you have read. As you work through this book you will see that it follows the same structure recommended here.

The structure of this section should follow the research hierarchy as outlined in

Figure 0.1 in the Introduction to this book: state your methodology, and explain your data-collection techniques and research instruments.

Methodology

Begin by stating your methodological position; the questions you should be answering are:

- Is this study qualitative, quantitative or mixed methodology?
- Why have you made this decision?
- Why is this the most appropriate decision?
- What are your research methods?

Once you have discussed your methodological choices you can then go on to state which research method(s) you will be applying to this investigation. The questions you should be answering are:

- What research method(s) are you applying to the study?
- Why have you made this choice?
- How do you intend to structure the method(s) for your investigation?

Data collection techniques

Defining your method(s) may well imply you will use a particular data collection technique but whether this is the case or not, it is necessary to explain how you intend to collect the data you need for your investigation. The questions you should be answering here are:

- What data collection techniques will you be using?
- Why have you decided to use these techniques?

Research instruments

Many data collection techniques imply a particular research instrument has been used, so this section may actually be included as part of the discussion of those techniques, but this is not always the case. The previous section has explained what techniques you will be using and why; this section needs to explain how you will be applying those techniques. If you are using questionnaires, will they be pencil and paper questionnaires or online questionnaires? If you are using interviews to collect data will there be a formal interview schedule or will you be using open ended interviewing techniques where the researcher becomes the primary research instrument?

You need to present a clear, concise and well supported research design; your choices should be directly related to your research question. You may decide to follow recognized tradition in the field or you may decide to take a very different approach to what has been done before. Whatever choice you make you will need to demonstrate that you understand the nature of the choices you have made.

Intended sample

Your choice of sampling technique will depend very much on your research design. In the following chapter we examine sampling in detail; it is vital to make the correct choice of technique in order to fulfil the goals of the research. It is important in a research proposal to identify how a sample will be achieved, and the technique and procedures that will be used. It is also important to identify the research population, the size of the sample that will be used, if this can be determined at this stage, and how the sample will be contacted.

Also give a brief description of the research setting, whether an organization, a community or group, or a very specific geographical area. It is important that you provide detail on salient issues relating to your research topic, explaining what it is about this particular setting that makes it an ideal choice.

Procedures for data processing and analysis

At this stage it is not normally necessary to demonstrate any of the techniques that will be used for processing and analysing the data but it is important to explain *how* this will be done. The sort of detail that is usually expected is a description of the procedures you will use, which must relate directly back to the type of data that is to be collected. In quantitative research this could mean being very specific about statistical tests to be performed and how this will be done. It may be pertinent to highlight the major variables in the study and how these variables will be tested. A typical error when proposing a qualitative study is to neglect to mention any specifics concerning analysis, usually because the assumption is made that analysing descriptive data is straightforward. The complexity of analysing this type of data should not be under-estimated and there are recognized and very formal procedures available; demonstrating an understanding of data processing is vital in a proposal.

If you are planning to use computer software for your analysis then discuss it here and explain why it is appropriate.

Anticipated research outputs

All research must have clearly defined outputs regardless of the level and nature of that research. Students frequently fail to see beyond the academic exercise of the research, focusing only on the work as another part of their programme of study. This is all very well and of course that is a very important aspect of the research but there is wider potential. All good research has a contribution to make, however small that contribution may be, and it is important to state that potential contribution clearly in a proposal. That is not to say that you should make over-ambitious claims, but you should realistically and honestly highlight what you, the researcher, hope to achieve. Research outputs should relate directly back to the stated aim(s) of your research, to clarify the intended output return to the original purpose of your investigation. This section should be very concise, stating exactly what you hope to achieve, who will benefit from the research and how.

Anticipated constraints

All research is restricted to some degree by constraints, and these constraints fall into two major categories: *limitations* of the study based on design, and *potential problems* relating to logistics. It is important to state any potential constraints in the proposal; it is highly likely that other things may occur during the course of your investigation but at this stage it is still possible to highlight constraints that you know will in some way impact on the overall output of the investigation.

Limitations based on design

Limitations are inevitable in many research studies. It is far more usual to make compromises in research design than it is to do everything we would like to do, exactly as we would like to do it. What matters is that these limitations are identified and explained from the outset. It may be that your sample is smaller than would be ideal; why is this? What impact will it have on the data you collect? The research method you decide on may not be the ideal method but it may be the very best you can do under the circumstances. Be sure to share this information at this stage in the process, to clarify your awareness of the research process and ensure that you will respond to any impact on the data when you engage in that process.

Problems relating to logistics

Problems with the research design are related to the actual logistics of the research. It may not be possible to foresee every problem at this stage but you need to highlight the obvious ones and suggest possible ways of minimizing the impact they will have. Usually problems relate to difficulties contacting research participants, gaining access to data and the quantity of data that is collected.

Ethical considerations

All research concerned with human participants needs to consider ethical issues. Universities and many other organizations have their own policy on ethics relating to research. Depending on what you are intending to do, where you are intending to do it and who will be involved in your study, there will be different regulations and standards concerning the ethics of your research. In your research proposal you must show that you understand the regulations you are bound by and that you have designed your study to conform to those regulations. Ethics in research will be discussed in detail in Chapter 6.

A project timetable

All research proposals need to include a realistic and well organized timetable. You must avoid the temptation to present a list of activities, this is not a research timetable. You need to present a schedule of work that includes all elements of the research, both desk-based and empirical work. This should be structured in such a way that critical incidents are highlighted, periods of intense activity can be easily identified and each activity has been realistically scheduled.

The proposal as a research framework

Once a proposal has been successful it still has a crucial role to play in your research study. It becomes the anchor that will remind you of your focus as the research progresses and grows. Remember the hapless Alice as she chased after the white rabbit? You will encounter many white rabbits in your research and you will be very tempted to follow them down some dark, forbidding tunnel. Sometimes this may be the right thing to do but more often than not it will lead you away from your focus and be very costly in terms of satisfying your original goals. In large scale research studies it is often possible to follow many new avenues, but this is not an action that is recommended in small scale studies that are restricted by time and resources. Even when engaging in highly iterative qualitative research, there is a need to hold on to your focus; only in the most open ended ethnographic investigations is it possible to follow every new avenue and see where it takes you.

Not only is your research proposal your anchor, it also forms the foundation of your research report. Your initial literature review does not become useless, it is the foundation of the more extensive review that will emerge from your research project. Your research design may alter slightly during the process but it will be the foundation for discussing your methodology when you come to present your work.

All good research is made better by personal reflections from the researcher, a sharing of the process 'warts and all'; this reflection is made easier by having your proposal as the basis for the reflection: What worked? What did not? Why?

So, beware white rabbits; once you begin following them down that tunnel they have a nasty habit of changing character. The soft, fluffy, innocent and very interesting fellow you met at the tunnel opening becomes a different creature half way down. Remember the scary white rabbit with the big white teeth who fooled the Monty Python team? He can fool you too. Your research proposal, with clearly stated aims and objectives or clearly defined hypothesis, is your anchor. It will keep you focused and allow you to make sensible choices about following new issues. This is not to say that you will just ignore or forget these new and interesting issues; what you should do is make a note of them. You can always recommend that someone else asks these questions or you may decide that your next research study will investigate these issues further. It is rare that a single study can answer all of the questions surrounding a research problem; it is equally rare to engage in any research and not identify new questions. You are opening a can of worms as soon as you begin to ask questions; do not expect to find all of the answers. More importantly, do not neglect to mention the new questions you have discovered. Your research proposal will remind you of why you are here, why you are asking these questions and what you wanted to achieve. Do not waste this vital research resource.

Summary

In this chapter we have looked at the research proposal, the reasons for preparing a proposal, the structure of that proposal and its content. Although there is an accepted formula to presenting a research proposal, the content depends on your own situation, the nature and level of the research and local requirements. It is important that you are very familiar with what is expected of you before you prepare your proposal. It will not matter how 'worthwhile' the proposed research may be if you fail to acknowledge requirements and meet expectations. Be sure to follow any guidelines provided and fit your detail into those guidelines, not the other way around. Your proposal may well be dismissed for not meeting basic requirements. Once you are familiar with these requirements be sure to provide as much detail as you can under each of the sections. Be realistic, this is not a theoretical exercise. You are preparing the rationale and presenting the plan for an actual research study. Time, effort and logical planning at this stage will serve you very well indeed when it comes to engaging in the research activity. Define your aim(s), objectives and/or hypothesis clearly and concisely; become immersed in the theoretical background to your topic; become familiar with research traditions in your field, you may wish to follow established tradition or you may wish to take an independent route; be prepared to argue your case either way. Provide a realistic research design in as much detail as possible; think about practicalities: entering the subject area, the resources available to you, and ethical issues you may have to face. Ultimately this means you will understand your own capabilities as much as you understand the research process. Also remember that the audience for your proposal will undoubtedly have extensive knowledge of the research process, so do not attempt to avoid or dismiss potential problems. Your audience will see through this and it will serve you no useful purpose when it comes to actually beginning your research.

 PRACTICAL EXERCISE

1 Prepare a brief overview of a research study you would like to engage in. At this stage it is not necessary to concern yourself with technical terms relating to methodology; that will follow later. For now write an overview of a study that appeals to you. Organize your overview under the following headings:

- The research problem
- One major research question to be asked
- Data to be collected
- The potential research population
- The importance of the problem.

This overview should take up no more than two sides of A4.

2 If you are in a position to share your overview with colleagues in a
seminar setting or electronic discussion forum then pass on copies of it
and ask for either written feedback or open discussion about it.

Suggested further reading

Bell, J. (1999) *Doing Your Research Project*, 3rd edn, Maidenhead, Open University Press,
    Chapter 2.
Kumar, R. (1999) *Research Methodology: a step-by-step guide for beginners*, London, Sage,
    Chapter 13.

Chapter 5

Sampling

Why sample?

Sampling is used when it is not possible or practical to include the entire research population in your study, which is usually the case. Sampling is the process of selecting a few from the many in order to carry out empirical research. It needs to be accepted from the outset that a sample represents a form of trade off between the desirable and the attainable, but this is more often the case in statistical sampling than it is in descriptive sampling. In qualitative descriptive sampling the case is selected based on what we can learn from the case and the goal is rarely to make inferences about the wider population based on this discovery. There is discussion concerning the use of generalization in qualitative research but I would always tend to discourage this; transfer of findings is very different from generalization and if generalization is the purpose of the research then the applicability of qualitative research should be questioned. In most quantitative research the point is to take a sample and make inferences about the rest of the population based on that sample. With both approaches it may well be much more informative to study the entire population but this would almost always be impossible based on cost and time. For this reason we sample.

The method of sampling used plays a major role in any research investigation. Very often it is the characteristics, composition and scale of the sample that give weight to any findings that emerge from the investigation. You must take care when selecting a sampling technique; there are a number of different approaches to sampling and choice of approach should be influenced largely by the purpose of the investigation. You will need to demonstrate the appropriateness of the chosen sample to the nature and output of the research. It is totally inappropriate to engage in a small scale, localized qualitative study then attempt to generalize from the findings. Likewise, it is inappropriate to engage in a large scale, broad study and attempt to provide any real detail concerning individuals (unless it is a large scale investigation involving many researchers investigating many people in a great deal of depth!).

A rather simplistic rule of thumb is to assume that quantitative research will tend to use probability sampling techniques and qualitative research will tend to use purposive sampling. Remember that here when we are talking about qualitative research we are talking about in-depth rich pictures, not short anecdotal snippets of detail collected from many in order to add detail to the quantifiable evidence gathered. Qualitative research may produce theoretical generalization, which means it is possible to generalize from, for example, a case study to a wider theory based on the findings of the case study. Replication of the events in the case study would then go on to add confirmation to the theory. There remains some conflict in the published literature on research methods concerning this particular aspect of the process. Payne states that positivist and interpretivist researchers 'may have very different ideological roots but there is a common concern in ensuring that respondents are *representative*' (1990, 23). The word representative needs to be used carefully. Interpretivists would argue that a sample need only be representative when commonalities are being sought; there are many occasions when participants are selected because they are different or extreme and represent nothing other than themselves (Morse, 1994a).

Your sample selection much be directly related to the type of study you intend to conduct, the research question you are asking, and the type of evidence you need to present in order to respond to that question. For example, would you take a random sample of 13- to16-year-old teenagers from a particular region if you wanted to investigate their use of the internet? What if, when your random sample was decided, none had ever touched a computer? Think carefully about the research question you are asking and the nature of the response you want: do you want to be in a position to make general statements or do you want to provide detailed insight? Your answer will often determine the research method(s) and sampling techniques that are appropriate to accomplish this.

Population and sample

So how do we go about selecting a sample and what do we select the sample from? Your research population is the entire set of individuals about which inference will be made. For example, before a political election opinion polls are used to gauge the general trends that are emerging within the population; these opinion polls are drawn from a small section of the entire population in order to make inferences concerning the likely outcome of the election, when every member of the population should cast their own vote. So, the expressed opinion of a small number of the population is used to infer political preferences within the entire population. This example should also indicate that inferences could sometimes be wrong! Be wary of making over-exaggerated claims or extended generalizations based on relatively small samples. Remember you are making a trade off but that does not mean your discovery has no significance, you just need to be honest with your reader when you put forward your inferences, make them aware of the sample and also make them aware that it is impossible to account for all individual traits. This is a discovery based on a 'best possible estimation'.

Probability sampling

In order to provide a statistical basis for generalizing from a research study to a wider population, probability sampling must be applied. There are a number of techniques available that allow for statistical generalization but remember that the logic of statistical generalization demands that certain conditions are met. These conditions are that the:

- sample is *representative* of a wider *population*;
- wider population is properly defined;
- sample was drawn from a population using *probability sampling* methods.

Even where a sample is obtained using probability sampling methods, the ability of such sampling to produce a representative sample will depend on:

- the adequacy of the *sampling frame* from which the sample was drawn;
- any *bias* in response and non-response from the selected *sample units*

(De Vaus, 2002a, 149).

These conditions apply regardless of the sampling procedure you choose and you must always be aware of the limitations of your final sample when you discuss the nature and consequences of your research findings. It is always preferable to calculate the sampling error present in your research as this provides your reader with a more realistic understanding of the significance of your findings. 'Error' in this case does not mean a 'mistake', it is the term used to demonstrate the likely variance between results obtained from the sample and characteristics of the population as a whole. A general rule is that the larger the sample size the smaller the sampling error.

For the purposes of the examples in this section let us assume that our research population is *the entire membership of a professional association.*

Simple random sampling

Random sampling is a procedure of creating a sample where each member of the defined population has an equal chance of being selected for inclusion and the selection of one participant depends on the selection of any other from that population. A simple random sample can be drawn in several ways.

- We could write the name of every member of the professional association on a separate slip of paper; all of the names could then be placed in a large container. We then draw out random slips of paper until we have the number required for our sample. Remember that each slip would need to be replaced after the name was noted in order to ensure the number of slips in the container remained constant. If this number decreases (if we did not replace the slips) then the probability of selection would improve for each new participant.

This method is the most basic way of selecting a simple random sample, but it can also be the most unwieldy; if the research population is very large this could prove a very arduous task.

- An alternative is to use a random number table, a table of numbers where the numbers are listed in no particular order and no number occurs any more frequently than any other. Using our example and assuming the association had a membership of 3000 we would give each association member a number from 1 to 3000 on a separate population list. Using the random number table and entering the table at any point we would work horizontally or vertically through the table until we had drawn the required sample, ticking off the membership number on our population list as they were selected. This process can be performed using a computer program that numbers each member of the population, generates a list of random numbers and then produces a sample list based on those numbers.

Stratified random sampling

Very often a research population will have recognized groups or strata within that population. There are two ways of dealing with this if you wish to include the distinct groups as an element of the sample design: stratified random sampling or cluster sampling. Stratified random sampling allows for random selection within each group or strata. This is a two staged process. First the groups are identified and the research population is listed within their groups. Once this list has been prepared a random sample is taken from the group in the same way as a simple random sample would be drawn from the entire research population. It is important here to remember that each group should be represented in the sample in equal proportion to the size of that group in relation to the entire research population. Using our example of association membership, one possible choice of grouping or strata could be 'duration of membership'; members would be listed according to the length of time they had been members (see Table 5.1).

Table 5.1 Sample composition using stratified random sampling

Length of membership	No. in research population	No. in final sample
6–10 yrs	450	45
11–15 yrs	670	67
16–20 yrs	590	59
21–25 yrs	420	42
26–30 yrs	350	35
31–35 yrs	270	27
36–40 yrs	120	12
41–45 yrs	90	9
46–50 yrs	40	4
Total	3000	300

Each group within the research population should be taken as a separate population, then simple random sampling can be carried out to draw the correct number from the group using one of the techniques discussed in the previous section.

Cluster sampling

Very often a research question is concerned with group activity rather than that of individuals, or at least it is concerned with the way a group functions or performs. It may well be that data is still gathered from individuals but it is the group activity as a whole that is central to the research question. When the research population is very large and often spread over a wide geographical area, or groups demonstrate a common characteristic that has a direct relationship with a main variable in the research question (similar to stratified sampling), clusters may be selected by the researcher.

Clusters can be identified based on geographic location. In the case of our professional association this could be done based on regional groups if it were a national association. If we were identifying clusters based on the nature of professional activity clusters could be identified as sub-groups within the association. This type of sampling is most common in educational research (Burns, 2000) where it would be impossible to take a sample based on, for example, the entire population of children in compulsory education. Based on the assumption that all state run schools will be following a similar curriculum it is possible to select individual schools based on geographic location.

Quota sampling

Quota sampling is sometimes referred to as convenience sampling as it is based on the researcher's ease of access to the sample. With quota sampling a required percentage of the total research population is identified (the quota). There may be some visible characteristics that are used to guide the sample, for example the researcher wishes to draw a sample that is 50% female, 50% male. The researcher then takes up position in a convenient location and asks all possible participants who pass to be involved in the research. This is often the technique used by market researchers when identifying random members of the public in shopping centres or other such public places. Remember that it is not as simple as standing on a street corner stopping members of the public.

There are a number of concerns when using this particular technique. I would rarely recommend this approach other than when it is being used in a specific location, a place where permission can be obtained and the researcher is safe from potential harm. Using our example of the professional association, the researcher would set a quota, that is determine the size of sample required for the research. The researcher would then seek permission to take up position in one of the central common rooms in the association headquarters. The researcher would approach every member who enters the common room until the quota for the sample has been achieved.

Purposive sampling

> The logic of purposeful sampling lies in selecting *information-rich cases* for study in depth. Information-rich cases are those from which one can learn a great deal about issues of central importance to the purpose of the research.   (Patton, 2002, 169)

There are two possible approaches to purposive sampling: a priori sampling, which establishes a sample framework before sampling begins; and snowball sampling, which takes an inductive approach to 'growing' the sample as the research progresses. It is the second of these that is the more truly qualitative as it maintains the emergent nature of the research. It is also a very 'loose' approach that often makes neophyte researchers very nervous. To walk out into the field not having an a priori sample map, not knowing who you need to include in your investigation, can be a very nerve-wrenching experience, even for the more experienced researcher. It can also be very difficult if you are restricted by time; many academic research studies have to be undertaken in a relatively short time frame.

If this is your first attempt at qualitative research, or if you are very restricted by time, you may want to create some boundaries to your sample by applying a more rigid structure. A priori sampling would provide you with that structure. It is not, strictly speaking, consistent with the concept of emerging theory but from a practical sense it offers some security while still allowing for theoretical sampling within the structure. As with all sampling, it is the purpose of the research that should drive the choice of sampling technique; a priori criteria sampling is more useful for 'analysing, differentiating and perhaps testing assumptions about common features and differences between groups' (Flick, 2002, 63). Snowball and theoretical sampling are processes that allow for 'on-going joint collection and analysis of data associated with the generation of theory' (Glaser and Strauss, 1967, 48).

A priori criteria sampling

A priori criteria sampling may represent a trade off between a totally emergent research design and a more structured a priori design but it also allows for an element of inductive design within the framework that is created. In a similar way to probability sampling criteria are identified from the conceptual framework of the research study, those cognitive signposts developed from the literature review. These signposts form the basis of a sampling framework, a broad outline of the nature of participants needed to provide insight on the main issues of the research. Criteria are identified and used to create a grid. Once this is done each cell within that grid needs to be represented in the final sample. This is as far as the a priori determination of the sample goes; within each cell sampling can be done in an inductive way. The researcher can now engage in snowball sampling to populate each cell.

Let us return to our example of the professional association; we have investigated the literature on the issue and have discovered that the significant criteria that appear to influence a professional's attitude towards their association are gender, type of membership and location. Using this information we construct a sample grid for our investigation (see Table 5.2). We know we have to identify members who fit these cells and attempt to fill each cell as evenly as possible to build our sample. Once the overall structure has been determined we can identify individuals in an inductive manner more appropriate to qualitative research until the cells are evenly populated.

Table 5.2 Sample grid

	Associate		Affiliated		Fellow	
	Male	Female	Male	Female	Male	Female
NE						
NW						
Mid						
SE						
SW						

Snowball sampling

Snowball sampling, or interactive sampling, as it was originally referred to by Denzin (1978, 89), is the technique that is most commonly used to identify a theoretical sample and it can be accomplished in two ways. The first and original method of this type of sampling is to make initial contact with key informants who, in turn, point to information-rich cases. The second is to begin with an initial participant who, through the process of interview and observation, will point out characteristics and issues that need further inquiry. These characteristics form the criteria used to identify subsequent cases in order to provide a suitable sample (Lincoln and Guba, 1985; Patton, 2002). 'Purposive and directed sampling through human instrumentation increases the range of data exposed and maximises the researcher's ability to identify emerging themes' (Erlandson et al., 1993, 82). 'The sample was not chosen on the basis of some "a priori" criteria but inductively in line with the developing conceptual requirements of the stud[y]' (Ellis, 1993, 473).

This type of sampling demands a viable exit strategy. As there are no a priori numerical restrictions placed on the sample, the danger of over-saturation could become highly significant. The sample itself is likely to converge as the number of differing characteristics falls. The purpose of this sample was to maximize information yield. It would then follow that termination of the sample could only occur once no new information was being added to the inquiry via new samples. This redundancy is the only criteria for termination. Therefore the size of the sample could not be predetermined: 'the criterion invoked to determine when to stop sampling is informational redundancy, not a statistical confidence level' (Lincoln and Guba 1985, 203). However, Lincoln and Guba do suggest that 'a dozen or so interviews, if properly selected, will exhaust most available information; to include as many as twenty will surely reach well beyond the point of redundancy' (235). As they relate this suggestion only to the interview situation, it could not be as readily applied to long term observation and multiple interviews, which may be a part of an in-depth study of each case. The researcher makes the decision to terminate sampling, based on information redundancy and other restrictions on the study, such as time and resources. Like any form of sampling, snowball sampling may also be subject to compromise.

Snowball sampling can be applied to building various types of sample. Patton (2002) provides definitions of six types of sample that can be built applying snowball sampling techniques: extreme or deviant cases, typical cases, maximum variation cases, critical cases, politically relevant cases, or convenience samples. The type of case (sample unit) that is identified depends on the purpose of the research.

Identification of the initial participant in snowball sampling can often be a matter of convenience and therefore 'limited (and presumably, thoroughly biased)' (Ford, 1975, 302). The subsequent gathering of new participants will reduce this bias. The fact that the initial participant serves a very clear purpose and should never be claimed to be representative of anything other than the individual in question limits the restrictions of this bias. In order to reduce this bias still further, very often initial participants used are taken as a 'dry run', and although they are used to identify subsequent participants, they would not be included as case studies in the final analysis.

Theoretical sampling follows a very similar process to snowball sampling; the difference is in the purpose of sample selection. With theoretical sampling emerging theory drives the selection of subsequent participants. This technique is particular to grounded theory, where the purpose of the research is to generate theory, not to produce generalizations about a wider population outside the study sample: 'Theoretical sampling is the process of data collection for generating theory whereby the analyst jointly collects, codes and analyses his data and decides what data to collect next and where to find them, in order to develop his theory as it emerges. This process of data collection is controlled by the emerging theory' (Glaser and Strauss, 1967, 45).

Summary

Sampling is a vital stage in the research process; the outcomes, rigour and trustworthiness of your research all rely on the robustness of the sample and how that sample was identified. The sampling technique you apply must be appropriate to your research goals and conform to the research tradition you have chosen for your investigation. Any claims you make concerning generalization, applicability, transferability and significance will all be judged in view of your empirical evidence and the source of that evidence. But we are all aware that reality and theory are rarely a perfect match; compromise is inevitable in research and all sampling has limitations. What is important is that you choose a technique that matches your research design, you are open and honest about your sample composition and you provide your reader with sufficient detail to understand the significance of your findings and any bias that may exist as a result of your sampling: 'These techniques are, of course, the ideal. Few researchers, apart from government bodies, have the resources and time to obtain truly representative samples. For most research, investigators often have to make do with whatever subjects they can gain access to. Generalisations from such samples are not valid and the results only relate to the subjects from whom they are derived' (Burns, 2000, 85).

In qualitative research this is exactly as it should be, generalization, in this sense, is not a goal of qualitative research but it often is in quantitative research. Whichever tradition you are following be very careful about claims you make based on the sample you have studied. Do not make the mistake of assuming all dogs are vicious because you were once bitten and do not attempt to convince your readers of findings that go beyond the evidence you have presented.

 PRACTICAL EXERCISE

The following exercise can be done either as a self-test activity or as a shared task in a seminar or electronic forum. If you are doing this as a self-test activity discuss your responses with your supervisor, mentor or a colleague if you have the opportunity.

A researcher is attempting to gather data on students' reactions to an electronic information gateway that has been recently designed and implemented by a particular university. The entire population in this example is every student registered to study with the university.

Below are six scenarios of how the sample for study was identified by the researcher. You have two tasks:

1 Identify the sampling procedure being applied in each of the scenarios.
2 Provide a brief discussion of the major disadvantages of each of these
   procedures in terms of research output.

Scenario 1
The researcher draws up a sampling frame of all student registration numbers and arranges them in no particular order other than the way they were taken from the university registration database. A sample size of 10% has been determined. The researcher takes each 10th student registration number from the database and adds that student to the sample for the research.

Scenario 2
The researcher draws up a list of all student groups based on the subject they are studying and the level of study at this point in time. From this list the researcher selects the following groups:

- undergraduate year 3 – history
- undergraduate year 3 – mathematics
- undergraduate year 3 – applied science
- undergraduate year 3 – English literature
- postgraduate – history
- postgraduate – mathematics
- postgraduate – applied science
- postgraduate – English literature.

Every student in each of the groups is added to the sample for the research.

Scenario 3

The researcher draws up a list of characteristics based on a theoretical framework identifying the characteristics that most influence use and perception of electronic information resources. The characteristics are:

- level of study (postgraduate or undergraduate)
- gender
- mode of study (campus or distance learning)
- subject (science or humanities-based discipline).

This provided a structure of 16 fields; sampling continued until all 16 fields were filled as evenly as possible.

Scenario 4

The researcher decides on a sample size of 1% based on the purpose of the research, the budget for the project and the time available for the investigation. The entire student population of the university is 28,650. The researcher decides that the central library building would give access to the largest volume of students that would be likely to be in a position to comment on the new electronic information gateway. After gaining permission from the relevant parties involved, the researcher takes up a position in the foyer of the library and approaches every student that enters the library. This goes on until 286 students have taken part in the investigation.

Scenario 5

The researcher obtains access to the central database of student registration numbers; these numbers are then listed according to mode and level of study. The researcher then has four separate lists of student registration numbers:

- undergraduate, campus
- undergraduate, distance learning

- postgraduate, campus
- postgraduate, distance learning.

A sample size of 10% has been determined. The researcher selects every 10th student registration number from each of the four lists, providing 10% of students from each of those lists.

Scenario 6
The researcher identifies an initial research participant willing to commit a series of data collection activities. This student is a first year undergraduate history student with very little IT experience but advanced research skills. Once this student has been 'signed up' to the research project the researcher then goes on to identify another first year undergraduate student in computing science, who has very advanced IT skills but is not very familiar with research techniques. This process is repeated until the researcher has exhausted all possible combinations of characteristics identified from the initial research participant.

Suggested further reading
Probability sampling
Burns, R. B. (2000) *Introduction to Research Methods*, 4th edn, London, Sage, Chapter 6.

Henry, G. (1990) *Practical Sampling*, London, Sage.

Kumar, R. (1999) *Research Methodology: a step-by-step guide for beginners*, London, Sage, Chapter 12.

Payne, P. (1990) Sampling and Recruiting Respondents. In Slater, M. (ed.), *Research Methods in Library and Information Studies,* London, Library Association, 22–43.

Non-probability sampling
Erlandson, D. A., Harris, E. L., Skipper, B. L. and Allen, S. D. (1993) *Doing Naturalistic Inquiry: a guide to methods*, London, Sage.

Maykut, P. and Morehouse, R. (1994) *Beginning Qualitative Research: a philosophic and practical guide*, London, Farmer Press, Chapter 6.

Miles, M. B. and Huberman, A. M. (1994) *Qualitative Data Analysis: a sourcebook of new methods*, 2nd edn, London, Sage, Chapter 2.

Chapter 6

Ethics in research

Research ethics is a field which is constantly changing, and its boundaries are at times quite fuzzy. What might be acceptable research behaviour one year, may be unacceptable the next.

(Bow, 1999, 254)

Introduction

Research ethics is discussed in all research methods texts - or if it is not, then it should be. Although many of these texts will tell you the same, or similar, things, there is some conflict of opinion. A very public and often cited example of this conflict can be seen in the reaction to the research of Laud Humphreys (cited in Punch, 1994). Humphreys investigated the behaviour of homosexuals in semi-public places. His research was primarily concerned with the social background of the men who met for casual encounters in public toilets. From a vantage point in a city park he observed the behaviour of the men and secretly recorded their car number plates. Using this information he located the individuals, then visited them at their homes; this time he was in the guise of a medical survey researcher. In this way Humphreys acquired a considerable quantity of personal information about these men, which he later published. The reaction to his work demonstrates the conflict of opinion regarding research ethics. Humphreys was awarded one of the highest accolades available by an American research association for his work, but at the same time there was a campaign going on to have his PhD revoked for misconduct; he even received a thump in the jaw from another researcher (Punch, 1994).

Although this rather extreme example is in no way typical of the majority of social science research today, it raises a number of issues that, to a greater or lesser extent, face all researchers when engaging with other human beings in the research process. I would like to point out that although there is a school of thought that advocates that covert research is acceptable, the stance taken here is that research should be overt, meaning that all research participants have the right to know they are being studied and why they are being studied (Bell, 1999). Their knowledge of the research activity may well have an impact on their behaviour but that will be discussed in Part 2 as we look at individual research methods. There is an argument that observing people in public places needs no permission or consent as their behaviour, by definition, is public and therefore available for all to see, study and analyse (Marvasti, 2004). This argument works in so far as we agree on a definition of 'public place'; a street, a park or a shopping centre may well be public but is a person's place of work 'public' just because the public are allowed access to it? There need to be careful and agreed definitions of an individual's right to privacy and how far your intended research goes towards invading that privacy.

Since the mid-1970s professional bodies and universities have established their own codes of practice which set out guidelines for all research carried out within the profession or university. Although these codes are very useful and should be followed, there will always be times when decisions must be made and there is no obvious right or wrong. For this reason I would recommend that knowing and understanding the codes of practice of your own institution is essential. It is also essential to develop your own ethical code. It is impossible to predict every possible event that may occur in the field but it is possible to identify the major ethical concerns of a study at the planning stage. Ethical strategies should be included in all research proposals and procedures set in place to ensure that the research is conducted in an appropriate and ethical manner. It is vital to be aware of any formal ethical consent procedures from the earliest point in the planning. If your research proposal has to go before an ethics committee it may take some time so build this in to your schedule. Information and communication studies cover a wide range of sub-disciplines and therefore are subject to a variety of codes of practice. The health information sector has extremely rigorous codes and it is usual for any research proposal to go before a committee before the research can begin. You will save time and effort if you are aware of ethical expectations before submitting the proposal. It is essential to know your own field and prepare your research in accordance with accepted research behaviour in that field.

It is important that, as a researcher, you take responsibility for decisions you may have to make quickly and without the guidance of a supervisor or a specific instruction in a code of practice. This chapter is primarily concerned with helping you to understand the possible consequences of research decisions and the implications these decision have for you as the researcher, your research participants, the value and quality of your research findings and the funding body or institution that is associated with your research.

Gaining access to the field

The keys to access are almost always in the hands of multiple gatekeepers, both formal and informal. In most cases those gatekeepers, before giving assent, will want to be informed about the inquiry in ways that will permit them to assess the costs and the risks that it will pose, both for themselves and for the groups to which they control access.

(Lincoln and Guba, 1985, 253)

Gaining access to a research site requires careful planning and should come very early in the research process, usually as soon as a proposal has been approved but often even earlier. It is prudent to approach a number of potential research locations to identify the most appropriate location and to 'get a feel' for the environment. It may be relatively simple to identify the formal 'gatekeeper' within an organization, the head of a library service, the head of a school or principal of a college, or the director of a company. You should write a formal letter of request to the formal gatekeeper asking permission to carry out your research, detailing the nature of the study and exactly what you will be doing while you are on site. It is recommended that you provide as much detail as possible at this stage; asking for more time than you ultimately take is far better than asking for a little then outstaying your welcome. It may be that the formal gatekeeper is very interested in your research and is more than willing to allow you access; he or she may also offer additional help in organizing your data collection. If so then it is very likely that this person will also want something from you in return. Usually this is no more than being given a copy of your research report, but be sure to establish this relationship from the outset.

Many of you will be thinking about engaging in research within your own organization. This does not mean that because you are already a member of this community you do not need permission to engage in the research – you do. Be sure to identify the most appropriate gatekeeper and prepare a formal letter of request detailing your intended research activity. You may be fortunate enough to have the research activity included in your workload; even then resist the temptation to feel that you do not need to ask permission because you are there anyway.

Gaining access to a research site comes in two stages: being granted permission to be 'on site' by the individual or group responsible for the site, then gaining the trust and cooperation of the individuals who populate that site. An interesting dilemma here is one of non-participant observation. If you were given permission to spend a number of days observing activity in an academic library, who has the right to give you that permission? You would have prepared a letter requesting permission from the head of the library service to engage in the observation. If you receive written consent to enter the library and carry out your observation from the head of the library service, is that enough? It may be that in your view it is, and it may certainly bring you in line with any code of practice you are following, but does it satisfy you as a researcher? After all, it is not the head of the library service you are observing. What about the individuals whose place of work you are invading? Gaining access and informed consent are very similar once we get down to personal space. It may be sufficient to have written permission to be there but a researcher depends very much on the cooperation of research participants and often 'sufficient' is not enough when it comes to winning the trust of individuals. It is my opinion that every participant in a research study, however small a part they play, has the right to be asked if they are willing to take part.

Informed consent

When research participants give informed consent it means that they understand what they are agreeing to, accept what is being asked of them and are comfortable with the purpose of the research and the intended use of the data they are providing. The most transparent way of achieving this is to prepare a formal informed consent form that is read, understood and signed by all research participants or their parents or guardians. Informed consent forms create a mutual understanding that remains constant throughout the research and provides a reference point for both the researcher and the participants. Schinke and Gilchrist claim that 'all informed-consent procedures must meet three criteria: participants must be competent to give consent; sufficient information must be provided to allow for a reasoned decision; and consent must be voluntary and uncoerced' (1993, 83).

It is of course your decision as to how far you go to achieve informed consent; depending on the purpose of your research, the research activity, any code you are bound by, and advice from your supervisor or line manager. Although I would always advocate that you should obtain informed consent from your research participant, there are cases when exceptions might be made. If you think it appropriate to ask for informed consent, get the agreement of your supervisor or line manager; never make this decision on your own. There are occasions when it is impossible to engage in research without understanding, agreeing to and signing a formal consent form. Individuals who are below the legal age of consent, or those not classed as competent, should *never* be questioned, observed or investigated in any way without the formal written consent of their parents or guardians. The majority of research with children in information and communication studies takes place within some 'bounded system', such as a school with formal gatekeepers who are in a position to request and receive consent on your behalf. If the formal gatekeepers do this to a standard that is accepted by you and the other stakeholders in your research then it is sufficient, but make sure you know what has been said, as ultimately you are responsible.

Providing sufficient information about your research can often be problematic, particularly in qualitative studies where the design of the research is likely to emerge and your needs could well change. Be sure that you are very clear about the fact that the research design could change slightly. In this case remember to be specific about the *most* you will be asking. It is inappropriate to request a minimum then hope that people will be willing to give you more as the need arises. Include details of the purpose of the research, who will see and read your findings and what rights the participant has in terms of reading and commenting on your analysis before you share it with anyone else. This usually means providing a written statement, giving your potential participant time to read and take in the information, then sign only when they are satisfied with the procedures. It always helps to leave a signed copy of the informed consent form with your research participants so they have this for reference.

The question of coercion is sometimes rather a 'fuzzy' one; take for example the researcher carrying out an investigation into the use of a school learning resource centre. The researcher has permission to question all of the children in the school. A questionnaire has been developed and teachers have been asked to give out the questionnaires to all pupils during their tutorial class. The questionnaires are given out in class and pupils are asked to complete and return the questionnaires during the tutorial period. There are two possible levels of coercion here: did all of the teachers actually want to take up the tutorial period with the questionnaire or did they do it because the head asked them to and they felt obliged? The next question concerns the children. They were given a questionnaire during a class period and asked by their class teacher to complete the questionnaire and hand it back. This could almost be an assignment. Are the children taking part voluntarily or are they doing it because they feel they have to as their teacher told them to? How would you resolve this dilemma? Would it be sufficient to ask the head to give the teachers a choice and ask the teachers to give the children a choice?

In this situation it is the environment that is likely to control the responses of the teachers and the children. They may be given a choice but feel that they do not actually have a choice as refusal could put them in a bad light with those in authority over them. Voluntary participation is not always easy to secure and may be out of the researcher's control. In this example the researcher could choose to request to give out the questionnaire in person, perhaps in a lunch period, and make sure the children understand that they do not have to complete the questionnaire. This may reduce the return rate for the questionnaire, and be more time consuming for the researcher, but it would go much further to assuring voluntary participation.

These are choices which have to be made and ultimately it is the researcher who has to make any decisions that are not specifically covered in a code of practice. In my opinion it should be standard procedure in all research for those involved to complete an informed consent form (see Example 6.1). But this is not always practical and may not be necessary, particularly with one-off data collection techniques such as a single questionnaire. In this case one could argue that by completing the questionnaire and returning it the research participant has consented to take part in the research and have their information used in the analysis. Again, this is about choice and adhering to local codes and regulations.

Example 6.1 Informed consent form

Title of the research project: Access to electronic information resources: their role in the provision of learning opportunities to young people. A constructivist inquiry.

Purpose of the research: The purpose of this research is to find out if electronic information resources (such as the internet) have a role to play in the provision of learning opportunities for young people. The aim is to discover if these resources have the potential to provide

Continued on next page

learning opportunities, how this can be encouraged, what works well and what does not. This will create a better understanding of these resources and how they are used naturally, in order to produce guidelines for managing these resources within schools and colleges.

Data collection and handling: This study is designed to take an in-depth approach to finding out how these resources are used; because of this the data collection will continue for a period of approximately 18 months. During that time you will be interviewed, observed in a number of locations, asked to keep a diary, write a short autobiography and take part in focus groups. At this stage it is impossible to say exactly how long each of these activities will take and how many you will be asked to participate in. Initially all data collection will take place in school during school time and at no point in the research will you be asked to do anything during school holiday periods. All of these activities will be arranged at a time that suits you.

Confidentiality and anonymity: You are guaranteed total confidentiality with regard to anything you say, do or write in relation to this research within the normal boundaries of the law. You will not be asked to reveal anything that could harm or distress you in any way. All data will be identified by a fictional name that is only known to the researcher. Total anonymity cannot be guaranteed as contact with you has been made through your school and you will meet the researcher face-to-face, but no data will be directly associated with you by your real name and in the event of publication no identifying personal data will be revealed. All data will be sorted at the home of Alison Pickard and destroyed at the end of the formal period of retention. The only people with access to this data are the researcher's supervisors and examiners who may request to see it but in no way will they attempt to identify you through this data.

Voluntary involvement: You are free to end your participation in this research at any time, you may refuse to answer any questions or take part in any activity you do not wish to engage in. You are encouraged to ask as many questions as you wish. A process known as 'member checking' will be used to allow you to see how the data you have provided is being used.

Please sign and date this form (as you are under 16 years of age both you and your parent/guardian must sign this form)

                    (Pickard, 1998, Informed consent form, unpublished]

Anonymity or confidentiality?

In the example of an informed consent form you will see that there is a distinction made between anonymity and confidentiality. Very often these two concepts are discussed as if they were the same thing. They are not and I would recommend that you be very clear about what you can promise and what you cannot promise when asking for participation. *Anonymity* implies that the research participant remains totally anonymous during and after the research activity; this can never be the case if the researcher is to meet that person at all during the research process. It is even less likely if the researcher has made contact with the participant through a third person, which is the case in most research studies. You can promise and provide *confidentiality*, which means that the identity of the participant will not be revealed when using any data provided by that participant. Anonymity means nobody knows who the participant is; confidentiality means nobody will be told the identity of the participant. These are very different things. Once you have made promises to participants make sure you honour these promises, be careful about labelling audiotapes or attaching names to computer files. It is usually better to remove all identifying data at the earliest stage to avoid overlooking anything later.

A common tactic used to provide confidentiality is to refer to participants by a pseudonym or code depending on the research method being used. I prefer pseudonyms in case study research as they retain the personal element of the individual, but codes can be used if you prefer. The point is to ensure that no real names or identifying information is given when you report the research. This is actually a lot more difficult than it seems; there are occasions when it is almost impossible to hide the identity of an individual or an organization. Many individuals are easily identifiable by their role in an organization, for example there is only one head of a library service. How could you offer anonymity to someone in that role when it would be very obvious to everyone both within the organization and externally who that person was? The same applies to a lot of roles within library and information services, small organizations, schools and colleges. Simply changing someone's name is not always sufficient to disguise their identity. When this is the case you need to be sure that from the outset you do not promise more than you can deliver, that the individual concerned understands the transparent nature of their identity when associated with their role, and that you think very carefully about what data you will use and how you will use it.

Protecting participants

In information and communication studies it is often quite easy to dismiss the idea that any research in this field could cause 'harm' to research participants, but this depends on what you mean by 'harm'. It is highly unlikely that any research in our field would include anything that would cause participants physical harm, but it may be that questions we ask could cause some level of distress. Asking people about their behaviour, their opinion of their role in a community, their skills and competencies – or anything else that encourages a degree of introspection or analysis

– could cause a negative reaction. It is vital that the researcher handles any such questions with sensitivity and is prepared to stop the questioning or observation at the first sign of a negative reaction.

Harm could also be caused by our interpretation and presentation of research findings. Be open and honest about the purpose of the research from the outset and remember that however anonymous you have attempted to make your participants, they will know who they are. In Chapter 1 a process called 'member checking' was discussed. This is a usual step in case study research and will be considered in more detail later in the context of case study work. Here it provides a very useful means of clarifying how you have interpreted, analysed and intend to present the participants' data. Allowing them to see what you will be writing about them should strengthen their trust in you. Stake states that 'all (my) reports have been improved by member checking' (1995, 116). Member checking may appear to the participants as a courtesy; it will also benefit your research.

Ethics online

> Because online research practice is still in its infancy, the critical researcher will be confronted by quandaries at almost every point in the research process. Email interviews, real-time focus groups or online 'observation' all present dilemmas with which the online researcher must grapple, yet there are few research practice conventions available.
>
> (Mann and Stewart, 2000, 47)

As online research activity continues to increase it is clear not only that this type of research is subject to all of the ethical considerations already discussed but also that new questions are being raised and new issues identified. The 'virtual' nature of online activity brings with it new challenges of *overt observation, informed consent, protection of participants* and *handling of information*. Here we will look at the more general issues in relation to online ethics; issues specific to individual data collection techniques will be discussed in the relevant chapters.

Overt research in virtual communities poses a number of practical and ethical problems for the research as a result of the very nature of these communities. Requesting general permission to observe and analyse activity within a virtual community is difficult when the population of that community is likely to change, with new members appearing and disappearing sometimes daily. The role and responsibility of the researcher in online environments may not always be clear; there are a number of conflicting views when it comes to the nature of personal information and interaction online. Rafaeli argues that: 'We view public discourse on CMC [computer mediated communication] as just that: public. Analysis of such content, where individuals', institutions' and lists' identities are shielded, is not subject to 'Human Subject' restraints. Such study is more akin to the study of tombstone epitaphs, graffiti, or letters to the editor. Personal? – yes. Private? – no' (1995, 116).

This may well be the case but King argues that 'when the messages posted to

Internet communities are subject to analysis, there is a possibility of causing psychological harm to the author of the note' (1996, 120). This said, King also accepts that announcing the presence of a researcher in the community could cause a real problem. 'Requesting permission from the group to conduct a study based on the messages that the group generates is often a gross disruption of the very process of interest' (1996, 120). Online communities, groups, lists and chat rooms are populated by human beings; there are individuals at the end of each and every emotion or thought that is expressed in those arenas. Researchers need to remember that disembodied communication does not mean the people they communicate with have disembodied sentiments. Using the techniques already discussed in this chapter it is possible to achieve a balance between ethical integrity and contextual purity. Some online techniques will be considered in Part 3 when we look at specific data collection techniques. Until such time as more rigorous guidelines are established it is left to the individual or individual groups to establish the rules of ethical behaviour in online research.

Summary

This chapter is designed to identify and discuss potential ethical issues that can impact on research in information and communication studies. This is a guide but ultimately the responsibility for decisions made during the research process is yours. Be sure to remain open and honest about your research. If you are engaged in an academic research project discuss issues with your supervisor. If your project is work-based use your line manager as your mentor whenever possible. What you must never do is attempt to ignore or dismiss possible problems; they will not go away and you are ultimately responsible for everything that happens during your research investigation. This may sound too simplistic but I find that a very good question to ask yourself when it comes to any action you take in research is, 'How would I feel if that was done to me?' Remember, your research participants are real people and by agreeing to take part in your research they have done you a considerable favour. Respect them, their rights and the details of the lives they share with you, at all times. 'Do not deceive, coerce, breach privacy and confidentiality for your own ambition, prestige or ego' (Burns, 2000, 23).

 PRACTICAL EXERCISE

1 Looking back at Example 3.2 in Chapter 3 (see page 46), list the major ethical concerns associated with investigating the stated aim in this Example.
2 What procedures could be put in place to ensure that ethical concerns were addressed in this particular research activity?

Suggested further reading

These are general guides; always read and become familiar with the codes of practice within your own organization.

British Sociological Association (BSA) (2002) *Statement of Ethical Practice,*
    www.britsoc.org.uk/about/ethic.htm.
Buchanan, E. (ed.) (2003) *Readings in Virtual Research Ethics: issues and controversies,* New
    York, Ideal Group.
Council for American Survey Research Organisations (CASRO) (2002) *Code of Standards and
    Ethics for Survey Research,* www.casro.org/codofstandards.cfm.
Hine, C. (2000) *Virtual Ethnography,* London, Sage.
Mann, C. and Stewart, F. (2000) *Internet Communication and Qualitative Research: a handbook
    for researching online,* London, Sage, Chapter 3.

PART 2

Research methods

PART 2

Research methods

Part 2 focuses on research methods, which we have already defined as the bounded system created by the researcher to engage in empirical investigation, the overall approach to the investigation. Often the choice of method is dictated by a number of factors, not least of which is the individual researcher's own paradigm preference. That said, very often external forces can drive our choices – the purpose of the research, the audience, resource constraints and so on. This second part describes and illustrates eight research methods. I am not claiming these are the only methods available but they are by far the most commonly used; some are more common than others within information and communication related fields. I accept that what follows will have other labels within the research methods literature; they may be referred to as research strategies, research approaches or methodologies. I have already explained why I have chosen this particular terminology and can only say that, particularly for neophyte researchers, this has proved to be a logical approach to organizing an empirical investigation.

Part 2 will focus on defining, designing and conducting eight research methods. In any single research study it is possible to use one or more of these methods. A single study is not restricted to a single method; depending on the purpose of the research and the resources available more than one method may be applied to the research design: 'Methods are selected because they will provide the data you require to produce a complete piece of research. Decisions have to be made about which methods are best for particular purposes and then data-collecting instruments must be designed to do the job' (Bell, 1999, 101).

During the planning stages for this book I had intended to discuss online research in every chapter, looking at a 'virtual' case study as if it were inherently different from any other case study. The truth is, it is not. A research method follows the process and structure of that method regardless of the environment in which the method is applied. A research method remains that method regardless of location. A case study and ethnography continue to be just that; what changes is the nature of data collection within the method. The true implications of computer mediated communication (CMC) are manifest in data collection, not in research method. A case study conducted in the disembodied world of virtual communities will still be organized and structured as any case study; only when we apply data collection techniques must we recognize the very different worlds in which fieldwork is conducted. Recently many of my postgraduate students have decided to engage in online research: 'virtual ethnographies', 'online case studies' and 'online surveys'. On every occasion the basic axioms of the method hold true. For this reason, this part of the book deals with the structure and process of methods; in Part 3, when we look at individual data collection techniques, we will consider the often very considerable differences we have to accommodate when entering a virtual world, which may well strip away many clues and signposts a researcher would traditionally rely on to contribute to their data collection.

Chapter 7

Case studies

Qualitative cases study is characterized by researchers spending extended time, on site, personally in contact with activities and operations of the case, reflecting, and revising meanings of what is going on.

(Stake, 2003, 203)

Introduction

Case studies are not as simple to define as many other research methods, because of the nature and form of the method. A case study can be both the process engaged in to investigate a phenomenon and the written output of that investigation. The study is both the fieldwork and the report of that fieldwork. Leaving aside the written output for now, we shall focus on the method of investigation. The most commonly applied definition of case study research is provided by Yin who defines it as: 'an empirical inquiry that investigates a contemporary phenomenon within its real-life context; when the boundaries between phenomenon and context are not clearly evident; and in which multiple sources of evidence are used' (Yin, 2002, 23).

Although you will find this definition is the one most often used by authors discussing case studies, you must remember that many case study researchers claim Yin takes a rather positivist approach to the case study method, and that a case study can be either qualitative or quantitative depending on what it is you are investigating and how you can acquire knowledge of the case.

Case study research is a method designed to study the particular within context and has a very specific purpose. The term has been used very broadly to cover a far wider remit than is appropriate: 'The case study has unfortunately been used as a "catch-all" category for anything that does not fit into experimental, survey or historical methods. The term has also been used loosely as a synonym for ethnography, participant observation, naturalist inquiry and fieldwork' (Burns, 2000, 458).

It is not surprising then that definitions of 'case study' have become rather blurred. A case study should be a study of 'a functioning specific' (Stake, 1994, 236). That is to say a system that operates within well defined boundaries; the size and nature of that system are not the issue, what dictates the case is the purpose of the investigation. For example a student or a learning resource centre may be a case, both are specific, but the student's *learning* could not be the case; this does not provide sufficient boundaries. The purpose of a case study is to provide a holistic account of the case and in-depth knowledge of the specific through rich descriptions situated in context. This may lead to an understanding of a particular phenomenon but it is understanding the case that should be paramount.

Types of case study

Stake identifies three types of case study:

- The intrinsic case study
- The instrumental case study
- The collective case study (Stake, 1994, 237).

The *intrinsic* case study is one that is carried out for no other purpose than to give us a better understanding of the case; the case is studied as much for its ordinariness as for any peculiarities. For example you may wish to examine your own service or department in considerable depth; with an intrinsic case study you would be doing that for no other purpose than to acquire a deeper understanding of the service. If your service happened to be a learning resource centre in a school, your research would focus on the centre and all the associated complexities associated with it. You would not be conducting this study to gain knowledge of a particular phenomenon within the case, for example how the students search for information. This may be something that emerges from the study but it is not the purpose of the study.

If we wish to examine a particular phenomenon then we would conduct an *instrumental* case study. In this case the purpose is to investigate a particular phenomenon or theory and the case itself becomes less important other than as a vehicle for our investigation. The term *collective* case study is used to describe a research study that uses more than one case to investigate particular phenomena; usually the study is a collection of *instrumental* cases as it is rare for a study to focus on multiple cases for their own sake, although it is possible.

Triangulation

Triangulation within a case study can be achieved by using multiple data collection techniques or multiple sources of evidence, or very commonly both. Triangulation can be used for two purposes within a case study, depending on the overall approach of the research. Yin claims that the purpose of triangulation is 'to collect information from multiple sources but aimed at corroborating the same facts or phenomenon' (2002, 92). This is a very legitimate reason for triangulation but it also serves another purpose which is 'to pick triangulation sources that have different biases, different strengths, so they can "complement" each other' (Miles and Huberman, 1994, 267). Very often data sources will be selected in order to achieve both of these purposes within a single case.

Qualitative case study research as an interative process

The design of qualitative case study research is very much an iterative process; once in the field the researcher will allow the design of the study to develop as he or she gains an insight into the salient issues. What follows is a basic outline of the stages in case study research but they should not prevent the researcher from shifting that design in order to respond to issues as they emerge. When engaging in a qualitative case study it is important to create a post-fieldwork plan that has considerable flexibility and allows for discovery and exploration. The emergent design of interpretivist research does not allow for a detailed plan before the research begins: 'the research design must therefore be "played by ear"; it must unfold, cascade, roll, emerge' (Lincoln and Guba, 1985, 203).

When discussing *naturalistic* inquiry Lincoln and Guba identify three major phases in the research process; although they do not relate this specifically to case study research it provides a useful framework for organizing the case study process. Those phases are:

- phase 1 of the investigation, which should be the 'orientation and overview' phase
- phase 2, 'focused exploration'
- phase 3, 'member checking' (1985, 235-6).

These phases are used here to organize the stages in a case study, because although many of these stages are iterative and will not occur in a linear fashion, they will occur within a single phase of the process.

Phases in case study research (see Example 7.1, page 93)
Phase 1 'Orientation and overview'
Begin with the research question

The first step in this type of case study research is to establish a research focus to which you can refer over the course of study. Remember the rule: you will achieve more by attempting less. The research focus in an instrumental case study is usually a programme, a person or a group of people; an intrinsic case study would look at all of these aspects. This will be done by establishing a broad aim and identifying a number of objectives at the outset. These objectives are usually specific enough to be operational in achieving the aim(s) but also flexible enough to allow for emerging issues to be followed. Stake (1995) suggests using 'issue subquestions', which will 'draw us towards observing, even teasing out the problems of the case, the conflictual outpourings, the complex backgrounds of human concern' (17). It is very important at this point to decide on the boundaries of the case, as the research project will probably have strict time and resource constraints. Qualitative case study research can grow beyond the original aim(s) of the research once issues are identified and discoveries begin to surface. The researcher needs to remain focused on the purpose of the research and not be distracted by issues that are not necessarily related.

Single or multiple case designs

During this phase of case study research, the researcher determines what approaches to use in selecting single or multiple real-life cases to examine in depth. When using multiple cases, which would make the study a 'collective' case study, each case is treated as a single case. The conclusions from each case can then be used as data contributing to the whole study, but each case remains a single case. This creates an additional layer of analysis, as the individual cases must be analysed before any themes can be examined across and between the cases.

Selecting the site(s)

The purpose of a case study should drive the selection of an appropriate site. Very often the site is already known in advance, particularly when researchers choose to study their own environment. It is important from the outset to select a site that will provide rich and detailed insights. This means ensuring that multiple data collection techniques will be possible, and there will be access to artefacts and people holding relevant information about the case. Gaining entry does not only include the formal aspects of signing off and gaining permission, it also includes establishing trust and building up a rapport with all of the stakeholders: participants, informants and gatekeepers. The researcher must explore what the salient issues are within the context and begin to determine who can provide insight into these issues.

Decide on the unit of analysis

Within a case study the unit of analysis can be a single person, a group of people, a programme or a system. It is up to the researcher to determine the appropriate unit of analysis to provide insight.

Purposive sampling

Qualitative case study research always uses purposive sampling to identify information-rich sources within the case. It should be noted that the case or cases will also be selected using purposive sampling, although often this will mean a sample of only one site. In any 'bounded system' there are 'key informants' who will have a great deal of knowledge about the case as a whole and what goes on at a variety of levels within the case. These key informants may include the gatekeepers who were responsible for allowing you access to the site but they will not be the only key informants within the case. Lincoln and Guba (1985) encourage the use of informants, as 'by virtue of their position within the context, such informants can provide the inquiry team with an "inside" view of the norms, attitudes, constructions, processes, and culture that characterize the local setting' (258). They can also assist in identifying and recruiting the remaining members of the case study sample. Depending on the type of purposive sampling being applied there are a number of steps which can help to define profiles of potential research participants; read Chapter 5 on sampling for more detail. One way of identifying who should be included in the sample is to draw up broad profiles of potentially information-rich sources, but it is important to remember that things could change as the study progresses and discoveries are made.

Setting up a case database

During a case study you will collect and store multiple sources of evidence. This needs to be done comprehensively and systematically, in formats that can be referenced and sorted so that converging lines of inquiry and patterns can be uncovered. There will be vast amounts of data to handle; it is important that this is structured from the beginning. There are a number of choices available but the earlier in the process the data is structured the better, as this type of case study produces not only vast amounts of data but data from many sources and in many forms. You may want to set up a database that stores data by personal source: who said, wrote and did what? Or you may decide to structure the database by data collection technique, interview transcripts, observation notes, focus group records or artefacts. It is up to you to decide how to do this, but early structuring is essential to retain control of the emergent design of data collection.

Determining data collection techniques

Qualitative case study design does not allow for a priori selection and design of individual data collection techniques and instruments. The emergent nature of the investigation means that very often it is impossible to say exactly what data collection techniques will be applied until you have a feel for the site and begin to establish what is needed from whom. The purpose of the study is defined within the context of the 'social actors' inhabiting the study; it is they who are at the heart of the investigation with their own experiences and the meanings they attach to those experiences (Hamel, Dufour and Fortin, 1993). There are obvious data collection techniques available to capture these experiences and meanings, so it is possible at this stage to indicate likely techniques, such as interviews and observations. It is essential that the capacity of a case study to accommodate emergent design is not inhibited at this early stage so identify your key informants and gatekeepers. Data collection usually begins with very open interviews or discussions with these individuals. This will give you an overview of the issues within the case study site and alert you to salient topics and possibly other key individuals; your sampling will begin using information collected from these key informants. Observations will also take place in this initial phase, although they are unlikely to be particularly well focused at this stage.

Once you have identified the issues and your initial sample it is possible to decide on your approach to the more focused data collection. At this stage you will be in a position to identify who needs to be interviewed next, if further observation is necessary and what other techniques would be appropriate. Try to resist the urge to become too prescriptive; remember to allow your design to emerge and respond.

Phase 2: 'Focused exploration'
Data collection

This is the stage at which you will engage with your sample and begin gathering data on the case study. It is not necessary to have all members of the sample identified; an interview with one respondent could lead directly to another member of the case study. There can be no rigid structure imposed here, to do so would be to lose one of the greatest benefits of a case study, the ability to respond as your knowledge of the case increases.

A number of data collection techniques are available to the case study researcher: interviews, observations, document analysis (including research journals) and focus groups. Sometimes questionnaires may be appropriate. Part 3 discusses data collection techniques in detail, so use that section to determine the appropriateness and design of your data collection.

When deciding on which techniques to apply it is vital to do so in terms of the appropriateness of the technique to the research question and the feasibility of the technique in the context. You must consider practical issues such as the time you have to conduct the fieldwork, availability of the people you have sampled, the nature of the environment and the feelings of those you have sampled. Always be aware that you must retain a rapport with the community; you are not making a one-off visit then leaving with your rapidly harvested data. You will be spending some time in this environment so it is essential that you remain sensitive to the demands you are placing on your sample group.

Iterative analysis

> The word derives from the prefix 'ana' meaning 'above', and the Greek root 'lysis' meaning 'to break up or dissolve'.   (Bohm, 1983, 156)

A major strength of case study research is that it allows for confirmation or refutation of emerging themes as the researcher is aware of them before vacating the site and can adapt the data collection to respond to these emerging themes. As Dey points out, 'there is a difference between an open mind and an empty head. To analyse data, we need to use accumulated knowledge, not dispense with it' (Dey, 1993, 65). To carry out data analysis it is necessary to be open to all eventualities and not allow prior theory to drive the analysis. The emphasis must always remain on theory emerging from the data.

Immediately after each data collection exercise has taken place the researcher usually transcribes interviews and observation notes. Carrying out the transcription personally can help you to begin to analyse them while you can recall the event. Then you can interrogate the transcriptions manually and identify initial categories; each category should emerge directly from the raw data. You should purposely ignore any assumptions or interpretations at this point, although you can take and retain notes, and include them in subsequent stages of the analysis. In this way you will ensure that the data will jump and is not pushed, that categories are not forced, they emerge (Melia, 1997).

The creation of initial categories or themes will not only inform the analysis, it also allows you to identify salient issues which may need to be revisited during subsequent phases of the fieldwork: 'Important leads are identified in the early phases of data analysis and pursued by asking new questions, observing new situations or previous situations with a slightly different lens, or examining previously unimportant documents' (Maykut and Morehouse, 1994, 44).

Phase 3: 'Member checking'

> Because the realities that will be included are those that have individually and collectively been constructed by persons within the context of the study, it is imperative that both data and interpretations obtained be verified by those persons.
>
> (Erlandson et al., 1993, 31)

The dialectic aspect of case study research can be accommodated in a number of ways: by workshops where participants are encouraged to compare and contrast the individual constructions of reality by debate, by individuals reading their own individual accounts or through full case study reports. This gives the participants the opportunity to confirm the credibility of their stories and examine the cross-case themes as interpreted by the researcher. Those involved are given the opportunity to read their case reports and encouraged to comment on the contents, adding their own interpretations.

Stake claims that member checking is a vital component of a study, not just in terms of adding to the credibility of the study, but also in improving the quality of the final case report: 'I think I can say that all my reports have been improved by member checking' (Stake, 1995, 116). There is some debate on how far participants should be encouraged to go in terms of altering what has been said or done but it is the responsibility of the researcher to control this procedure to allow for maximum information yield. It is also necessary to complete the dialectic aspect of the study: 'We have found that members' feed-back is very valuable and sometimes helps us see or emphasize something we missed' (Maykut and Morehouse, 1994, 147).

Exiting the field

An exit strategy can be designed early in the research process. Information redundancy is usually the predominant criterion for leaving the field; when all data collection tools cease to reveal any new information then it is time to close the fieldwork (Maykut and Morehouse, 1994). This may also be tempered by time restrictions on the study. Exiting the field is not always the clinical process described in the literature.

The participants in a study can become involved in the research process to an extent that may be beyond the past experience of the researcher. The rapport necessary to carry out in-depth case studies places a great deal of responsibility on the researcher to develop a strong rapport with participants while remaining removed from the situation. This can be more difficult than originally assumed. It helps if the researcher begins to refer to the end of the fieldwork during Phase 2, to make it clear to participants that the work with them will come to an end at some point. At the beginning of the fieldwork it helps if each participant is given a study outline; dates should be included even if they are broad estimates, in order to give the participants a definite picture of the structure of the study. Once it becomes apparent that the fieldwork is not yielding new information the researcher should tell participants that the study will end soon and refer them to the original study outline.

Cross-case analysis for multiple case designs

In multiple case designs the cross-case analysis can only take place when all individual cases have been completed. The final phase of member checking with each case needs to be completed, then the findings from each case can be used as the raw data for the cross-case analysis. That said the themes for this analysis would emerge as each case is being analysed; the nature of the process makes it impossible to separate the points at which themes grow and develop. This approach to case study research aims to present rich, descriptive narratives at a micro level, to provide detailed descriptions, which will allow the reader to make sufficient contextual judgements to transfer the holistic case studies to alternative settings. It will also draw out the concepts and tenets of a theory using cross-case themes as they emerge from the analysis.

Writing up the case study

In Part 4 we will discuss specific techniques for presenting research findings. Case study research can be presented in a number of ways; the most commonly used method is to use a convincing story (Yin, 2002), which relies on rich pictures created by descriptive narrative. This is not the only option available to the case study researcher. Depending on your audience you may wish to provide visual descriptions of the case; if so you will construct 'rich pictures' using diagrams and evidence. The options will be discussed later in more detail but an important thing to remember is that constructing narratives is also a form of analysis. Writing theory as it emerges from the field is always recommended; it is not necessary to leave this until the end. You will certainly have to present your research participants with some form of written description if you are to allow them to contribute to an informed member check. Trustworthiness in case study research is demonstrated using the criteria discussed in Part 1 to establish *credibility, transferability, confirmability* and *dependability*.

Example 7.1 Sample case study fieldwork schedule

Phase 1: Maintain researcher's diary throughout all phases:
- Make initial contact.
- Obtain consent via sign-off forms.
- Interview to identify salient issues.
- Observe the participant using electronic information sources.
- Begin iterative analysis.
- Identify subsequent participants using snowball sampling.
Time: 3 months

Phase 2: Focused exploration, using:
- interviews
- observation
- non human sources; content analysis of documentation
- interviews with experts, who are likely to be learning resource managers, librarians and/or teachers and librarians
- iterative analysis throughout.
Time: 8 months

Phase 3: Compile preliminary case studies:
- Check members: case study is subject to scrutiny by participants individually and during workshops.
Time: 2–3 months

Write up final case studies.

(Pickard, 1998)

Summary

Using case studies is the most appropriate research method when the purpose of the research requires holistic, in-depth investigation of a phenomenon or a situation from the perspective of all stakeholders involved. When context is vital to a research question then the investigation must allow for context, space and time to become part of the analysis of the situation. Although emergent design is a significant advantage of case study research, it is still possible to formulate a broad research design from the outset allowing the researcher a degree of control over the process. The role of the researcher is very much that of being a 'research instrument', interacting with the research community and allowing that community some degree of 'ownership' of the research. Analysis is ongoing; although there will be a lot of work remaining after the fieldwork is over, it is impossible to conduct a viable case study without engaging in that analysis from the initial data collection. Case studies are not intended to produce generalizations, they are intended to allow for transferability of findings based on contextual applicability.

PRACTICAL EXERCISE

Using a 'bounded system' you are very familiar with, design an intrinsic case study. The 'bounded system' you choose could be an event you were involved in, your place of work or a community you belong to. There is no particular issue to identify at this stage, you are investigating the 'whole'.

Design the case study following these steps:

1 Define the case boundaries.
2 Describe the nature and function of the case.
3 Identify the key informants in the case.
4 Decide on a number of appropriate ways to collect data from the case study site and/or members of that community.
5 List your major concerns in terms of what could go wrong with your case study.

Suggested further reading

Hamel, J., Dufour, S. and Fortin, D. (1993). *Case Study Methods*, Newbury Park, CA, Sage.

Stake, R. E. (2003) Case Studies. In Denzin, N. K. and Lincoln, Y. S. (eds), *Strategies of Qualitative Inquiry*, 2nd edn, London, Sage, 134-64.

Tellis, W. (1997) Introduction to Case Study, *The Qualitative Report*, **3** (2), www.nova.edu/ssss/QR/QR3-2/tellis1.html.

Yin, R. K. (2002) *Case Study Research: design and methods*, 3rd edn, London, Sage.

Chapter 8

Surveys

The aim of a survey is to obtain information which can be analysed and patterns
extracted and comparisons made.   (Bell, 1999, 13)

Introduction

The purpose of survey research is to gather and analyse information by questioning
individuals who are either representative of the research population or are the entire
research population. The term 'survey' usually refers to a study that has used a
representative sample; if the entire population is involved in the study it is a 'census'.
Questions must be asked using a standardized questioning procedure applied
equally and consistently to all research participants.

The aim of survey research is to study relationships between specific variables,
which are identified at the outset of the research and stated as either a hypothesis or
a research question, or to describe certain characteristics of the population. The
findings from the survey can then be generalized to the wider population. Survey
research can include qualitative and quantitative research, but is usually quantitative
with a limited qualitative element, which is more likely to be anecdotal than truly
qualitative.

The term 'survey' is often used interchangeably with 'questionnaire'; the two are
not the same thing and it can lead to confusion if the distinction between the two is
not made very obvious. A survey is a research method, the purpose and aims of
which have already been stated; although data collection must be standardized,
there are options for data collection within a survey. A questionnaire is a very specific
data collection technique, which can be used within a variety of research methods. A
survey, then, is the research method used to structure the collection and analysis of
standardized information from a defined population using a representative sample
of that population. Probability sampling is vital in order to make valid generalizations about the wider population. When non-probability sampling is used you
must take care with any statements you make that attempt to generalize to the wider
population.

There are two types of survey: *descriptive* surveys or *explanatory* surveys. It is possible to apply both methods in the same study, as will become apparent when examining the nature of the two approaches.

Descriptive surveys

> The *descriptive* survey aims to estimate as precisely as possible the nature of existing conditions, or attributes of a population; for example, its demographic composition, its attitude to abortion, its religious beliefs, voting intentions, its child-rearing practices.
>
> (Burns, 2000, 566)

The purpose of a descriptive survey (see Example 8.1) is to describe a situation and/or look for trends and patterns within the sample group that can be generalized to the defined population of the study. The data gathered in this type of survey is usually a combination of measurements, counts and brief narratives, which are then analysed using descriptive statistics such as measures of central tendency and standard deviation. Because of the approach to sampling (usually random sampling) and the nature of the data gathered, this method does not lend itself to more sophisticated statistical analysis, indeed this is not its purpose. It is usual for researchers to put some interpretation on the results based on a combination of the current facts gathered and previous research.

Example 8.1 A descriptive survey

Pay and status: latest *survey* results
Presents the findings of the 2004 CILIP survey of UK library and information professionals conducted to gather information on salary levels relative to qualifications, responsibilities, employment sectors and solo working. Other information collected includes job titles and membership of professional organizations. Among the findings are that more than half of the 3,039 respondents earned less than £25,000 per year and that the median amount was £22,400. Also reports respondents comments and suggestions for action by CILIP to campaign for improved salaries, promote the appreciation of the profession by employers and merge or work more closely with other LIS professional bodies.

Creaser, C. and White, S. (2005) Pay and Status: latest survey results, *Library and Information Update*, **4** (6), (June), 40–3.

This descriptive survey was conducted in order to describe the current situation within the library and information profession in the UK. Data was gathered on a variety of variables including salaries, qualifications and sector information. This survey presents a picture of the profession using descriptive statistics which provide an overview of current working standards and trends.

Explanatory surveys

The *explanatory* survey seeks to establish cause and effect relationships but without experimental manipulation; for example, the effects on teachers' motivation of merit schemes, the effects of social climate on adolescent values.   (Burns, 2000, 566)

The definition offered here by Burns talks about 'cause and effect' when in reality any attempt to demonstrate causation within the natural human condition is fundamentally flawed. The closest we can hope to come to examining relationships between variables in a natural setting is not actually causation, it is covariance or correlation. Surveys always take place in a natural setting and under these conditions it is impossible to establish definitive cause and effect relationships, at best we can demonstrate a probable link between variables in a study. Later, in the chapter on experimental research (Chapter 9), we will go further into this discussion of the nature of causality; here it is sufficient to say that it would be totally inappropriate to claim that a survey could result in demonstrating definitive causality.

Many surveys begin with a hypothesis and attempt to support or refute that hypothesis; this can be appropriate but never be tempted to claim that the purpose of the survey is to *prove* the hypothesis; this claim will never withstand serious critical review. Explanatory surveys (see Example 8.2 overleaf) apply inferential statistical techniques to numerical data to establish relationship between variables. This does not mean that all the data gathered must be in numerical form; it means that all data must be coded in order to allow for statistical manipulation. The purpose of this type of survey is to identify and offer explanations for relationships between variables. Sampling is vitally important in this type of survey as it has major implications for the generalizability of the findings.

The survey process
Although there are differing types of survey, the process follows a very similar pattern whichever approach is being taken. Survey research usually follows a linear and structured process; steps in the process are clearly defined and rarely overlap, and the survey process consists of the follows stages.

Identify a general topic area
This will very much depend on your situation. It may be that you have been given a specific topic to investigate within your workplace, in which case the topic is already decided for you. If this is a research project being done as part of an academic qualification then identifying the topic is up to you with guidance from your course tutors. At this stage it is important to remember that you will have to remain motivated throughout the research so make sure the topic is one that will hold your interest and enthuse you. (See Chapter 3.)

Example 8.2 An explanatory survey

How experts and novices search the web

This study was undertaken to advance the understanding of expertise in seeking information on the Web by identifying strategies and attributes that will increase the chance of a successful search on the Web. The strategies were as follows: evaluation, navigation, affect, metacognition, cognition, and prior knowledge, and attributes included age, sex, years of experience, computer knowledge, and info-seeking knowledge. Success was defined as finding a target topic within 30 minutes. Participants were from three groups. Novices were 10 undergraduate pre-service teachers, intermediates were 9 final-year master of library and information studies students, and experts were 10 highly experienced professional librarians working in a variety of settings. Participants' verbal protocols were transcribed verbatim into a text file and coded. These codes, along with Internet temporary files, a background questionnaire, and a post-task interview were the sources of the data. Since the variable of interest was the time to finding the topic, in addition to ANOVA and Pearson correlation, survival analysis was used to explore the data.

Tabatabai, D. and Shore, B. M. (2005) How Experts and Novices Search the Web, *Library and Information Science Research*, **27** (2), 222–48.

In this study data was gathered in numerical and narrative form. All the data was coded in such a way that the researchers were able to test the results using standard inferential statistical techniques to establish correlation between the variables.

Investigate the literature

All research begins with an exploration of what is already known. Regardless of whether you have selected your own topic or been given a topic to investigate then you must familiarize yourself with the context and background to it. Reading reports of past research will also provide you with valuable insight of appropriate design features for your own survey, such as appropriate sampling, specific areas to be covered in the questioning and also hints on what not to do. (See Chapter 2.)

Establish an hypothesis or aims and objectives; identify variables

Remember that in all research you usually achieve more by attempting less; keep the hypothesis as simple and as clear as you can. You may be attempting to *support* a hypothesis but a survey will never *prove* it; it may however *refute* the hypothesis and this is usually as informative as *supporting* it. There is not always a clear distinction here but as a general rule descriptive surveys will have aims and objectives, explanatory surveys will state a hypothesis; this is not always the case but more often than not this distinction applies. (See Chapter 3.)

Identify a suitable population

This is the entire population, the group that you will be making generalizations about once you have reached your conclusions. It is important that you define the population from the outset in order to give credibility to your findings. You are not attempting to say something about everybody or everything, only the population you have identified. In the first example of a survey used here the entire population is all UK information and library professionals. Data was gathered from a sample of that population then findings generalized to the entire population. (See Chapter 5.)

Apply an appropriate sampling technique to draw your sample from that population

There are a number of practical constraints to consider at this point, whichever sampling technique you apply. Be practical and only attempt what you can legitimately estimate will be achievable. It is always tempting to try and cover everything but this could do more harm than good in the long run. Thorough and rigorous analysis of a smaller sample is always more worthwhile than sloppy analysis of an enormous sample. Remember to take account of the time available to you, who you can reach in the location you have access to, geographic limitations and financial constraints. You will need to demonstrate that all attempts were made to make the sample as good as it could get under the circumstances. Examine ways of making the most of what you have, not attempting to exceed your limitations. (See Chapter 5.)

Select and design data collection instrument(s)

At this stage you will know how you intend to collect your data, and will have planned questionnaire, interviews, structured observation and so on. As this is survey research you will need to design the data collection instrument(s) in such a way that it will produce standardized responses. So many times we read reflections on research with such comments as 'Responses to this question were difficult to analyse as there was clearly some misinterpretation of meaning by the respondent.' This is usually because there was an error in the construction of the question; pay close attention to how questions are worded and make sure responses can be coded. (See Part 3.)

Pilot a data collection instrument

Always pilot your data collection instrument, amend and try again. This is almost certainly the single most important step in the chain. You may think your questions are crystal clear with no hint of ambiguity. You will be amazed at how many meanings can be given to an apparently straightforward question or instruction.

Collect data

At last, the fieldwork itself. Now you can actually do your observing, interviewing, and administer your questionnaires. The mechanics of doing the administrative aspects of these activities should not be underestimated. (See chapters on individual data collection instruments for discussions of application.)

Analyse data

In survey research analysis does not usually begin until all data has been gathered, unless it is a staged survey with a number of rounds. Even in this case analysis of each round will only take place after the data has been collected. This is another significant difference between surveys and case studies. That said, it does not mean you cannot prepare for the analysis long before this point. If questions have been well constructed and responses been pre-coded then this stage will run a lot more smoothly. Be prepared for this before your data collection is complete. This is likely to be the single most challenging aspect of the research and the point at which you may well feel the most isolated. Make this stage as comfortable as you can by being prepared for it and knowing exactly what you are looking for and how you will find it. (See Part 4.)

Present findings and conclusions

I think it is fair to say that this is the stage where motivation becomes key: the data is gathered and analysed, the literature review written, it almost begins to feel as if the work is done and often the presentation stage is the most demanding in terms of actually sitting down and writing it all up. Presenting the findings in graphs, tables and charts may seem a clear cut, even simple, process but this is often not the case. It is very common for a researcher to examine their discovery and begin to think 'So what? Is this such a great discovery after all?' Remember that by this stage you will have become so steeped in the topic that what appears obvious to you will not be so obvious to others.

Take care when selecting ways of presenting your data, after all this is what all of that hard work has been about. Make sure that you link your conclusions directly back to the original purpose of the investigation; close the loop if you like. More importantly, make sure you select the most appropriate form of presentation for the data you have analysed and that your findings lead naturally on to your conclusions. You should almost be able to hear your reader saying 'Ah yes, I see' or 'Yes, obviously, that's what the data was implying'. Conclusions should never come as a surprise, you are highlighting your discoveries not introducing them for the first time; this should have been done as you were presenting your findings. (See Chapter 24.)

It is the linear nature of survey research that usually attracts the neophyte researcher; there is an order and structure that in itself provides a broad framework and stable procedure. This is a perfectly understandable reaction as the research process can be a rather daunting one the first time you embark on a project, particularly when you are doing it on your own either as an academic exercise or individually within your organization. This does not mean that conducting a survey is easy: you are engaging in a rigorous research activity that must demonstrate validity. The linear process may give you a feeling of security but those stages can be complex and demanding.

Summary

Surveys are used when the purpose of the research is to describe a population or characteristics of that population (descriptive survey), or determine the relationship between specific variables within a population (explanatory survey). It is important to distinguish between a survey as a *research method* and a questionnaire as a data collection technique. Although the terms are often used interchangeably within the literature, they are not synonymous. Surveys rely on representativeness and standardization in order to generalize findings from a sample to a wider population. Data collection techniques appropriate to survey research are questionnaires, structured interviews and direct, structured observation.

The important thing to remember with a survey is that questioning must be *consistent*, that is, you must ask the entire sample the same questions in the same way and usually restrict their potential responses within precoded parameters. This is probably the greatest difference between a survey and a case study, there are many other ways in which these two methods differ but the most obvious difference is in structure: surveys are designed to produce a generalization within the population, case studies are concerned with individual perceptions, beliefs and emotions. If interviews are used in a survey then those interviews need to be structured in order to allow for grouping of responses; the same applies to observation.

 PRACTICAL EXERCISE

Designing a survey

You are involved in a new local initiative to promote fiction reading among adults. At the outset of the campaign you are set the task of identifying current reading trends within your region in order to establish the most appropriate way of targeting the campaign. There may be a number of critical demographic variables you want to investigate such as gender, age, employment and education in relation to reading habits. You have been charged with designing a survey to provide an overview of the current situation.

To begin with you will have to address the following issues:

1 Construct a research question or a hypothesis; what is it you really want to know?
2 Will this be a descriptive survey or an explanatory survey?
3 What is the total population of the survey?
4 What type of sampling techniques will you apply and how will you construct your sampling frame?
5 How can you estimate an appropriate sample size?
6 What data collection techniques might you apply to gather the necessary data?

At this stage there is no need to design a data collection instrument, we will be doing that later.

Suggested further reading

De Vaus, D. (2002) *Survey Research*, London, Sage.

Punch, K. (2003) *Survey Research: the basics*, London, Sage.

Sapsford, R. J. (1999) *Survey research*, London, Sage.

Chapter 9

Experimental research

It is almost impossible to establish an experimental situation involving human subjects where a benchmark accurately measures every possible relevant variable present in the pre-test situation.   (Bertrand and Hughes, 2005, 46)

In social research there is a familiar slogan that states, 'covariance is not causation'. The two concepts are very different in terms of their context: the concept of causation is theoretical, whereas covariance is empirical.   (Corbetta, 2003, 91)

Introduction

Experimental research epitomizes the positivist paradigm discussed in Chapter 1. The opening quote in this chapter may appear to be very negative; the reason it is here is to highlight that experimental research has its place in library and information science but I would rarely advocate the application of this method in a study that involved human subjects. This is not to say it has not been done, it has, but I would argue that there are too many unstable elements involved ever to be in a position to construct a true experiment involving human beings and all the complex internal and external variables they are subject to. Experiments are possible on systems with stable functions, variables that can be systematically controlled; the human condition does not fall into this category. 'Effects studies' have been carried out in many branches of social science, but inference made from these studies is usually tenuous at best.

Before you decide to embark on experimental research you need to be very sure about what you are doing and the level of control you have over the situation. An experiment is a controlled research situation, which means '(a) that unwanted variables and external influences can be kept out of the experimental environment, and (b) that the researcher can establish the experimental conditions down to the smallest details' (Corbetta, 2003, 94). When these conditions are not entirely met then the researcher has a responsibility to identify the extent of the error. 'Experimental error occurs when a change in the DV (dependent variable) is produced by any variable other than the IV (independent variable)' (Burns, 2000, 134). As we can have no way of controlling all variables acting on a human subject at any one time, not only can we never avoid experimental error but the majority of the time we cannot locate the variable responsible for the error, therefore we are unable to measure the extent of error. A true experiment eliminates the effects of all intervening, spurious and antecedent variables. Tests and trails are not experiments and should not be labelled as such in a research context. If you intend to carry out an experiment, then you must understand the nature of experimentation and experimental error to enable you to establish the level of significance of any inferences drawn from your research.

In experimental research we are dealing with a number of different variables:

- *the independent variable (IV)*: the phenomenon or situation that is manipulated by the researcher
- *the dependent variable (DV)*: the behaviour or effect that is measured by the research as a result of the manipulation
- *the moderator variable (MV)*: the factor which is 'measured, manipulated or selected' by the researcher to determine whether or not it changes the relationship between the IV and DV
- *the control variable (CV)*: a potential IV that is artificially held constant by the researcher throughout the experiment (Burns, 2000).

Many studies claim to be experimental when at best they could be termed 'quasi-experimental'. It is not an experiment when 100 random users are asked to test a system just because they are given exactly the same search terms or search strategies, then provided with the same system to engage with. Take for example the testing of a new information skills training programme. It could be claimed that as long as the following procedure was employed then the design was a true experiment:

- Random selection was used to identify a study group then random assignment was used to divide these subjects into the test group and the control group.
- All subjects were given a test to rate their information skills.
- One group was given the new training (IV) and one group was not.
- Both groups were then re-tested and their scores compared (DV).

If the test results demonstrated that those who had undertaken the training programme showed significant improvement in the test and those not given the programme had not, then is it possible to say that the improvement was a direct result of the training? Well maybe, if no other factors had influenced the outcome.

The nature of causality

Experimental research is an attempt to establish causality, to *prove* that the dependent variable (DV, the variable being measured by the research) is a direct result of the independent variable (IV, the variable being manipulated by the researcher to determine the extent to which manipulation effects the dependent variable). In order to demonstrate causation it is necessary to show that the effect (Y or DV, dependent variable) is not only preceded by the cause (X or IV, independent variable) but that X produced Y and will do so repeatedly, temporal precedence being essential (Pearl, 2002). Causality is essentially a theoretical concept, a hypothesis that is impossible to verify empirically. 'Perhaps the best we can do is to note covariations together with temporal sequences. But the mere fact that X and Y vary together in a predictable way, and that a change in X always precedes the change in Y, can never assure us that X had produced a change in Y' (Blalock, 1961, cited in Corbetta, 2003, 89). Covariance is the empirical equivalent of causation, the closest we can get to demonstrating a relationship between phenomena.

The true experiment

An experiment is an attempt to empirically verify or corroborate the hypothesis of a causal relationship between variables. Experiments cannot demonstrate causation, only covariance; they are designed to measure the degree to which a relationship exists between the identified variables (Field and Hole, 2002). Covariance assumes temporal precedence of the independent variable and the elimination of all other variables from the research context. For this reason only the laboratory setting can offer a suitable environment for the true experiment. Here test variables can be controlled and unwanted variables removed; this allows inference that Y (effect or DV) is a direct result of X (cause or IV).

The basic model of a true experiment (see Example 9.1 overleaf) includes the subject of the experiment, the independent variable, and the measured dependent variable. A true experiment is used not only to demonstrate:

If X then Y

But also to demonstrate:

If no X then no Y

If the researcher succeeds in providing evidence to support both of these statements then X has been isolated from all other potential causes of Y, that is to say the treatment or cause can be seen to be the only phenomenon acting to create the identified effect. This means that there has to be at least two 'clean' tests carried out on two random groups at the same time in order to measure Y as a direct result of X. One test involves the subject being exposed to X then measuring the outcome, Y; the second test (the control test) involves the subject *not* being exposed to X and identifying and measuring the outcome. It also means all intervening variables are controlled, if not eradicated, then measured to determine level of error indicated by these variables. Figure 9.1 shows the basic design of a simple experiment.

Example 9.1 The true experiment
White, K. J. and Sutcliffe, R. F. E. (2006) Applying Incremental Tree Induction to Retrieval from Manuals and Medical Texts, *Journal of the American Society for Information Science and Technology*, **57** (5), 588–600.

This research investigated the 'applicability of ML (machine learning) algorithms based on decision trees to the IR (information retrieval) process'. A number of experiments were conducted on records generated from a collection. Based on a random selection of records, decision trees were created for each record. The decision tree could then categorize the record as relevant or irrelevant based on the query used to retrieve the document. In order to evaluate the decision tree each record was presented to the tree, which then produced an 'irrelevant or relevant' response to the original query. This was then compared with the performance of an inverted indexing system to evaluate levels of performance.

From this series of experiments a number of conclusions could be drawn about the use of decision tree forests in comparison with inverted indexing systems.

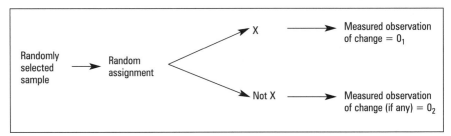

Figure 9.1 A basic randomized two-group experiment

There are a number of variations on the basic model shown here which include two or more experimental groups and the control group or alternative treatment groups. True experimental research can claim high *internal validity* because of the control imposed on all intervening variables; this could be interpreted as high integrity of findings if there is sufficient evidence that intervening variables have in fact been controlled. This research design is the most suitable for testing hypotheses which involve causal relationships, but be sure you have read and understood the section on causality before you attempt to demonstrate it using this approach. Experiments are a very expensive form of research in terms of facilities needed. A laboratory is a major resource as is the time of the research participants, and they are dependent on strict control features, which are not always possible.

The problem with true experiments comes in the form of *external validity*, or the extent to which findings can be generalized to a wider population. Because of the 'clean' nature of experiments, the forced laboratory conditions which enhance internal validity, the likelihood of applicability in a natural setting is reduced. In addition to this there are the problems which reduce *internal validity* such as *maturation;* changes in the subject which have nothing to do with the manipulated variable, for example fatigue brought on by engaging in the experiment. Learning from the pre-test is always a problem; many subjects may adjust responses as a direct result of thinking about the pre-test and not as a result of enforced changes in X.

Quasi-experimental design: the 'effects study'

The word 'quasi' means 'as if' or 'almost', so does that mean that a quasi-experiment (see Example 9.2) is almost a true experiment? In a sense, yes it does, but not in the sense that this suggests a lesser form of research, it simply means it has some of the components of experimental research, but not all. It is rarely possible 'to replicate social, organizational or behavioural conditions in a laboratory setting. Therefore

Example 9.2 The quasi-experiment
Ritchie, A. and Genoni, P. (2002) Group Mentoring and Professionalism: a programme evaluation, *Library Management*, **23** (1/2), 68–78.

This research investigated the value of a group mentoring programme, 'to provide evidence of the value of this particular type of mentoring in supporting an individual's emerging professional identity'.

Research design: there was no random selection used in this study as all those in the experimental group volunteered, thereby being self-selecting. The study was a three-group design:

- Experimental Group = 23 subjects
- Control Group 1 = 18 subjects (no current mentor)
- Control Group 2 = 22 subjects (had a mentor during the period of the investigation).

Study variables were: demographic information, professionalism, career and psychosocial development, sources of stress, and experiences of mentoring functions.

Data collection was done using pre- and post-test questionnaires. 'These questionnaires included the various scales which were used to measure the main outcome variables – professionalism, career and psychosocial development. Because the outcome measures were calculated by subtracting the pre-test scores from the post-test scores they were designated: professional identity index (difference), career index (difference) and psychosocial index (difference).'

Continued on next page

This research discovered that: 'the previously established dichotomy of mentoring outcomes into career and psychosocial functions does not adequately describe the full range of benefits derived by participants'. The research also provides evidence to support the differentiation between 'professional function' and 'career and psychosocial outcomes'. Another outcome of this research was the clear need to develop a more standardized instrument to test for outcomes in professionalism and to investigate the roles of mentoring in relation to professionalism.

observation in a field setting, say, might be preferable to experimental because the advantage of realism outweighs the loss of control' (Gray, 2004, 77).

Quasi-experiments differ from true experiments in purpose and process; where true experiments aim towards covariance, quasi-experiments aim to establish levels of correlation between observable variables. Correlation is used to identify both the degree and direction of a relationship, a scaled version of covariance which makes no temporal assumptions. True experiments involve deliberate manipulation of the independent variable whereas quasi-experiments or correlation observations do not intervene and aim to identify correlation between variables as they exist, with no temporal restrictions (Field and Hole, 2002). For this reason quasi-experiments can be conducted in a natural setting still making it clear that intervening variables may be acting on any results. The mistake that is often made is the claim that Y (effect or DV) is a direct result of X (cause or IV); this can never be the case in a natural setting. Where true experiments use random selection to identify research subjects, quasi-experimental research tends to study 'the effects of the treatment on intact groups rather than being able to randomly assign participants to the experimental or control group' (Mertens, 2005, 135).

There are two types of quasi-experimental research design: the *non-equivalent group design* and the *time series design*. The non-equivalent group design is very similar to the basic true experiment design, the only differences being the selection of study participants (non-random selection) and the location of the study (field setting not laboratory). The time series design follows the basic design of the non-equivalent group; the difference here is that observations are made at a number of time intervals pre-test and a number of time intervals post-test. Longitudinal observations provide substantially more observational data and more detail on progressive change or continuity.

Internal validity is always seen as the greatest threat to quasi-experimental research design; lack of control over intervening variables means it is almost impossible to eliminate rival explanations of any relationship between variables. External validity is however a great deal stronger in the sense that 'real world' conditions are present in the experiment.

Summary

True experiments are used to trace cause-and-effect relationships between pre-defined variables; as such they rely completely on controlled variables. This requires conditions where the researcher is in complete control of all independent variables, being in a position to add, remove or manipulate in some way every independent variable in order to trace effect. Many systems provide a sufficiently stable environment to perform experimental research. Retrieval systems are a prime example, although once we move beyond the controlled context of automatic performance and include human reaction, we tread into the much less stable environment of human behaviour.

Causal inference poses significant problems when we are dealing with the human condition; many variables will always remain outside the control of any research as cognitive, affective and social variables relating to the individual are almost impossible to predict and certainly impossible to control in most cases. Any research of this nature that involves humans in social settings will be quasi-experimental at best; only those entities that remain under the complete control of the researcher can be used as a basis for true experimentation. Your goal with this type of research is to demonstrate correlation not causation.

 PRACTICAL EXERCISE

1 Identify the IVs (independent variables) and DVs (dependent variables) in the following hypotheses:

a) Adults find it easier to recall a sequence of words than a sequence of numbers.
b) Performance is improved by practice.
c) Girls search more efficiently than boys when they are searching for information on a topic of personal interest.
d) Children with IT literate parents are more confident in using computers.

2 Select one hypothesis from this list and discuss whether or not the researcher could manipulate the IV.
3 Identify possible moderator variables for each hypothesis.
4 Identify likely control variables for each hypothesis.

Suggested further reading

Burns, R. B. (2000) *Introduction to Research Methods*, 4th edn, London, Sage, Chapter 10.
Corbetta, P. (2003). *Social Research: theory, method and techniques*, London, Sage, Chapter 4.
Field, A. and Hole, G. (2002) *How to Design and Report Experiments*, London, Sage.

Chapter 10

Ethnography

Introduction

> The goal of ethnography is to combine the view of an insider with that of an outsider to describe a social setting. The resulting description is expected to be deeper and fuller than that of the ordinary outsider, and broader and less culture-bound than that of the ordinary insider.
>
> (Wilcox, 1982, 462)

As with 'case study' the term ethnography refers to the research method and the research output; ethnography is the process of engagement and the written account of that engagement (Agar, 1996). The most common use of ethnographic research is in anthropology, although social science research has increasingly adopted this method, which focuses on interpretations of behaviour or specific events in the everyday lives of individuals.

The primary data collection technique is participant observation although other methods of collecting information concerning the context are often used. An ethnographic study begins with no a priori assumptions; the researcher seeks to explore and although the research will have a focus, the theoretical framework acts as cognitive signposts rather than controlling the direction of the investigation. Ethnography uses descriptive narrative to analyse and present the findings from the investigation; the purpose is to build theory by describing situations as they are and presenting patterns within a context.

Many of my students have asked me what the difference is between a case study and an ethnography, an understandable question as these methods are similar. Conducting an ethnographic study may, on the surface, appear to be very similar to case study research but it is the extent to which the researcher is immersed in the context that is the real and most obvious difference. The focus of ethnography is to describe and interpret a cultural and social group, whereas the focus of case study is to develop an in-depth analysis of a single case. A case study site is usually visited at regular intervals to engage in data collection that can be largely predefined, whereas ethnography demands prolonged engagement within the context (Creswell, 1998).

Case studies are essentially etic – outsider research – although the researcher attempts to gain as much 'local' knowledge as possible.

From a practical viewpoint, it would be very difficult to engage in ethnography while engaged in any other full-time occupation. I have supervised postgraduate dissertations that have taken an ethnographic approach but these have been rare and usually only when the researcher has chosen to study their own daily context. True, ethnography usually demands at least a year in the field; that in itself means it is not at all practical for many researchers. This method is more likely to be applied in a doctoral study where the researcher has funding to engage in prolonged fieldwork with no other full time commitment; that is not intended to discourage the use of this method, just to remind you that, as tempting as it may be, it is difficult to engage in this type of research anywhere other than your own social context. That said there are a number of examples of research studies which have taken an 'ethnographic approach' and applied the principles of the method to specific events and even systems as a means of evaluation. Othman (2004) applied the ethnographic process to the evaluation of the retrieval features of 12 databases. This may be an unorthodox application of the method but the study was a success and provided insights that may not have been possible applying any other method. Bouthillier (2000) carried out an ethnographic study of the nature and role of the public library in Quebec. Atton proposes the use of ethnography in collection development; the librarian already being an 'insider' can interpret and reflect on interaction with resources. 'One way to make sense of these resources is to attempt to understand how they are being used, and by what kinds of people, to undertake an ethnographic study of the resources as a prologue to acquiring them' (1998, 154).

There has been a considerable shift from the original positivist ethnographic studies of Malinowski (1922) and Mead (1960), with researchers claiming total objectivity and the ability to observe and record the 'reality' of a new context in an almost automatic fashion. It has been accepted for some time that all researchers enter an ethnographic study steeped in their own social and cultural biases but these are now explained and presented rather than being ignored and assumed to be irrelevant. Ethnography is both 'emic', or insider research, and 'etic', or outsider research; although the researcher is an outsider, the emphasis is on the 'going in' and not standing apart from the context. In some cases the researcher is already part of the context being studied, or if not, then they become part of that context. It would, of course be impossible for a researcher 'going in' to replicate exactly experiences held by true 'insiders'. Rossman and Rallis highlight the fact that 'fully representing the subjective experience of the participants...is an unachievable goal'; it is therefore the responsibility of the ethnographer, you, to 'strive to represent clearly and richly their understanding of what they have learned' (1998, 38). As Fetterman points out, 'an emic perspective compels the recognition and acceptance of multiple realities' and that 'documenting multiple perspectives of reality is crucial to understanding of why people think and act in the different ways that they do' (1989, 31).

Ethnography is now viewed as interpretivist research that accepts that the researcher enters the field with predefined values and beliefs; everything that is witnessed is influenced by those values and beliefs. A balanced ethnography should combine emic and etic perspectives, although there are many researchers who will always prefer to approach their investigation only from their own paradigmatic viewpoint. The emic view places the researcher 'at the ideational and phenomenological end of the ethnographic spectrum'. The etic view places the researcher 'at the materialistic and positivist philosophical end of [the] ethnographic spectrum' (Fetterman, 1989, 32).

Components of ethnographic study

It would be extremely misleading to set out a process here for ethnographic study as I do in many other chapters; it may imply that there is some form of linear progression through that process and with ethnography that is most certainly not the case. The term 'iterative' was used to describe the data collection-analysis-theory-development process within case study research. Here that iteration or cyclical process is taken even further. There are no defining lines between collecting data, analysing data, reflecting, interpreting and writing; generating theory is not the goal of ethnographic study although theory building may result on some occasions.

Ethnography is made up of a number of components or elements which, for the most part, run alongside each other but the most basic and most important is extended and uninhibited access to the location or field site: 'The two key terms for an ethnographer are context and pattern' (Fife, 2005, 1). As Fife points out, this may appear relatively simple when reading the theory from a text book but when it comes to the reality of *doing* there are two questions which confront the would be ethnographer: '(1) how much context do I have to cover, and (2) how will I recognize a pattern when I see it?' (Fife, 2005, 1). I try to respond to these questions by attempting to convince my students that 'letting go' is the key to full exploration, but the idea of 'letting go' usually terrifies them more than the initial questions did. The idea of having a predetermined, fairly rigid, research design provides security and a sense of 'control'; this is not possible in ethnographic research.

What follows is not a rigid research design, it is discussion of the basic components of this method which provide something to hang on to while learning how to let go and in so doing allow the research to grow and develop. This research method is concerned with real life settings and social interaction in all its forms, in order to investigate social interaction of any kind. Grills (1998, 6) claims there is no real alternative to ethnographic study:

> Quite simply, there is no adequate substitute for the direct engagement of activities and acts of the other if we wish to understand the practical accomplishment of everyday life. We cannot manufacture social worlds out of bits of text, regression equations, or responses to questions that divorce the account of action from the action itself. Of course it is easier to do this, and it is less troublesome for the researcher. The result, however, is a sociology in which the people are hard to find.

Ethnography relies on the following components.

The research question

It is generally accepted that all research should begin with a 'good' research question, but ethnography rarely conforms to this norm. In fact Hammersley and Atkinson (1995) point out that the research question usually changes during the course of an ethnographic study. We go in wanting to know one thing and as our knowledge of the context deepens our focus often shifts; therefore it is more useful to begin with an interest than with a rigid question. Of course, walking into a field site with no guidelines can be overwhelming even for the most experienced ethnographer. The chaotic multitude of stimuli that assails you on entering a 'new world', and the myriad of potential interpretations of this stimuli, demand some guiding principles, however flexible they might be. It is important to accept that we need to have a 'springboard', but the purpose of that starting point is to guide the observation, not to restrict discovery.

Prolonged fieldwork

The term 'fieldwork' in ethnography is used for two types of engagement in the field. Fife (2005) describes these as the 'macro and micro environments', where a 'macro level' of engagement is used to describe an investigation into the background and context of an environment before entering the field at a 'micro level', when the local community is investigated. Fife provides a wonderful example of this, and I strongly recommend this text to anyone really interested in engaging in this type of research. Before travelling to Papua New Guinea to investigate the issue of 'formal primary education and its relationship to formal expectations for economic development in that country' (Fife, 2005, 2), Fife spent three months in the missionary archives of the School of Oriental and African Studies at the University of London. Using primary historical sources available there he was able to establish the context and background to the current situation in that country before travelling there.

There is no suggestion that this could ever be a substitute for having lived through those experiences but it does highlight ethnocentric biases that exist within all researchers and adds to our ability to 'go native', at least to the extent of knowing something of the development of current social conditions in a region and culture that would otherwise be totally alien to the researcher. This could be termed 'acclimatization', developing awareness and an understanding of the macro environ-ment that has an impact on all micro environments. How this would translate into an ethnographic study of a user community in library and information science (LIS) may not appear too obvious at first but think about the community you may be studying.

Staying close to the subject of Fife's investigation, let us look at a school library. In order to understand our users we would have to understand its wider social, cultural and historical context, current legislation and the expectations of those who use the library. An understanding of these factors would establish context and background for the locally situated investigation. As an ethnographer this is part of immersing yourself into the reality of your research participants. As I said earlier, ethnographic studies in LIS tend to be conducted by researchers who are already situated within a particular context or at least approaching the research having existed within a similar social milieu. Even so, the use of historical and current primary sources is a must before you engage in empirical data collection. We enter a context with an open mind but that is not the same as an empty head.

On entering the field at a micro level the researcher has to become immersed in the context and the lives of the individuals within that context. This takes time, time to understand the social and cultural context, time to identify key players in the setting, time to become less of an *outsider*. There are some who claim it is possible to conduct ethnographies over a relatively short period of time. I would be very cautious about recommending short-term engagement unless the researcher was already an *insider*. Establishing the trustworthiness of an ethnography depends very much on the time spent in the field and the level to which the researcher can truly claim to have immersed themselves in the context. Prolonged engagement in the field is encouraged as this type of research 'involves establishing rapport in a new community: learning to act so that people go about their business as usual when you show up; and removing yourself every day from cultural immersion so you can intellectualise what you've learned, put it into perspective, and write about it convincingly' (Bernard, 1994, 137). If you can do that over a short period of time then you may not agree with me when I say extended time in the field is essential.

Researcher as instrument

> Ethnography exploits the capacity that any social actor possesses for learning new cultures, and the objectivity to which this process gives rise.
>
> (Hammersley and Atkinson, 1995, 8)

It is essential in ethnographic research that the researcher is the primary instrument of the research (see Part 1) and this is recommended in case study research. Human lives and their interpersonal relationships create complexities that need to be understood and the only way to understand and depict these complexities is if the researcher acts as the research instrument: 'These complexities . . . cannot be figured out, cannot be understood by one-dimensional, reductionist approaches; they demand the human-as-instrument' (Maykut and Morehouse, 1994, 27).

Ethnography combines the individual research participant, the researcher as research instrument and qualitative data collection techniques in a collaborative process of interpreting data and using that interpretation to present the description of the context, to tell the story. The researcher is the main instrument in this research. It is human experience and situations that are the subject of ethnography, therefore the human-as-instrument is 'the only instrument which is flexible enough to capture the complexity, subtlety, and constantly changing situation which is the human experience' (Maykut and Morehouse, 1994, 26). The researcher as instrument is also in a position to apply appropriate tacit knowledge to each situation and event as it occurs. The human as instrument is capable of *responsiveness* to situations as they arise, *adaptability* in collecting data from multiple sources and multiple levels at the same time, *holistic emphasis* on the entire context, *knowledge base expansion* using tacit knowledge, *processual immediacy* processing data immediately and generating and testing hypothesis in context, and *reflexive clarification* when data is complex or multiple interpretations present themselves (Lincoln and Guba, 1985, 193-4). Ethnography can be carried out using little more than a pen and a note pad, it is the researcher who gathers, interprets, analyses and presents the research. 'Relying on all its senses, thoughts, and feelings the human instrument is a most sensitive and perceptive data gathering tool' (Fetterman, 1989, 41).

Reflexivity is a vital element of ethnography, rather than attempting to 'stand away' from the subject of inquiry and lay claim to any *objective observation*. It is far more important to acknowledge and understand one's own ethnocentric biases and respond to these during the course of the study. As a researcher you should never step into the field to engage in ethnography unless you are prepared to 'ask questions, become aware of your own perspective (your assumptions) with its in-built interests, biases, opinions, and prejudices' (Rossman and Rallis, 1998, 26). You should question yourself as an ongoing process throughout the study, acknowledging who you are and how this colours your sight, rather than attempting to deny who you are and claim clear vision. We should be aware of the baggage we carry into the field, not in denial of it. However, a word of caution here, I agree with Fife that 'a little bit of reflexivity is a good thing, a great deal of it can be very distracting at best and at its worst can turn into an exercise in self-indulgence' (2005, 150).

Participative engagement with the study population

> If a person is to be understood as a person and not as a thing, then the relationship
> between the researcher and the other person must be a dynamic and mutual
> relationship.   (Maykut and Morehouse, 1994, 37)

It is important to remember that data collection in ethnographic research is all about 'participation'; you are involved in the context and observing from that inside place, not looking on from the wings. Gaining entry to the field site is a key issue here. Being accepted into an existing social context relies very heavily on identifying an appropriate *gatekeeper* who will allow you access to the community and has sufficient respect and trust to give credibility to your presence within that community. 'A strong recommendation and introduction strengthen the fieldworker's capacity to work in a community and thus improve the quality of the data' (Fetterman, 1989, 44).

Once you are 'in' you must not be surprised if occasionally the tables are turned; people are as likely to ask you questions as you are to ask them, so be prepared to answer them as truthfully as you can. Being evasive and mysterious can seriously damage any rapport you establish. There is nothing wrong with admitting you are there as a researcher, in fact I take the stance that it is essential to admit your motivation. There is a long running debate on the rights and wrongs of covert or overt research. When it comes to recommending an approach I always recommend overt research (when it comes to my students I insist on it). You are who you are and you have a purpose in this place; honesty will get you further than deception every time.

This may seem like a trivial statement but appearance counts. If you are attempting to immerse yourself in a situation it will do you no good at all to stand out like a sore thumb, or even worse, appear to be a threat. When engaging in research with young teenagers I was all set to meet a group of 13- to 14-year-olds who were classed as 'borderline exclusion'; they were all under threat of being excluded from school because of their 'anti-social' behaviour. I was so focused on making sure the headmaster of the school was impressed with me that I completely missed the point of my being there. I arrived dressed in what I assumed was appropriate attire, a smart suit, a smart coat, briefcase and hair neatly arranged; all was geared towards the headmaster trusting me as a professional. But it was not the head's trust I needed. To a group of young people who had experience, not always pleasant, of many authority figures, I appeared as just another 'suit'. To them I was 'a coppa' (police woman), 'from the social' (social worker) or 'a shrink'. I could see them putting up a 'barrier' as soon as I walked into the room. It was a mistake that took me some time to repair.

'Participating' means more than engaging in the same activities, discussions or events as your research participants, it is about blending in to the context. The important factor here is to establish and maintain rapport with your community; this 'may involve participation in an established role in the setting . . . or in a "visitor" or specially created researcher role' (Hammersley, 1990, 30).

Multiple perspectives

Ethnography is concerned with people and their everyday lives. It is important for anyone wishing to engage in this type of research that everyday lives also include multiple realities. Insiders as well as outsiders have multiple views of the context, 'every view is a way of seeing, not the way', there can be 'no monolithic insider view' (Wolcott, 1999, 137).

One of the fundamental tasks of this method is to accumulate as many perspectives as possible within the setting. This does not mean you should focus on a few key informants and tell the story from the viewpoint of these individuals, but you should provide a holistic picture of the setting; that means looking at that picture from as many angles as are available to you in the context. Who will make up those multiple perspectives depends very much on the focus of the study; the important point is to acknowledge that there are multiple realities running alongside each other within every setting, including those of the researcher. The task is to represent those views when it comes time to draw the whole picture, and in order to do this we must ensure that we have engaged with the community in a way that allows for diversity and convergence to be exposed and presented.

Diverse data collection

Ethnography is a method of research which 'includes as many options of collecting data as can be imagined and are justifiable' (Luders, cited in Flick 2002, 146). There is no doubt that the primary technique for data collection in this method is that of participant observation. As with all the other data collection techniques mentioned here, this will be discussed in much more depth in Part 3. Data collection techniques are not always easily defined and are usually conducted in a way appropriate to the method; this also will be emphasized in Part 3. For now it is sufficient to say that an ethnographer collects data from within the setting in whatever way presents itself and can be justified as credible and ethical. Investigation of the macro environment is likely to include documentary analysis, interviews and observation in order to establish context.

Once we have entered the micro environment we rely on 'emergent design' to guide the collection of data. It is almost impossible to establish what type of data is needed before entering the field and, therefore, how it will be collected. It is usually accepted that ethnographers begin with 'the big net approach conducive to participant observation' (Fetterman, 1989, 42). As the study progresses the focus will begin to emerge and may begin to narrow; as this happens other data collection techniques are identified and implemented in a manner suitable to the method. For example, interviews within ethnographies are more likely to be conversations than structured interviews. What really matters here is the diversity of data collection. To gain insight into multiple perspectives it is necessary to engage in multiple data collection techniques. 'Broadly conceived, participant observation thus includes activities of direct observation, interviews, document analysis, reflection, analysis, and interpretation' (Schwartz, 1997, 47). Autobiographies are frequently used as a means of allowing research participants to tell their own life stories, and asking children to write essays on a particular topic provides insight into their way of thinking (Fife, 2005). Researchers' logs are an essential tool in ethnography, used for data collection, analysis and interpretation. Data collection is restricted only by the imagination of the researcher and what is deemed to be trustworthy and ethical.

Cycle of theory building

> Pragmatically, theory is the matrix that creates 'facts' and gives us the framework from which we can have a meaning[ful] discussion with others about the evidence or information gathered through our ethnographic methods.   (Fife, 2005, 139)

Analysis and theory generation in ethnography is not something that happens once the data has all been collected; as with case study it is an iterative process, even more so in this type of research. It requires a lot of the researcher. It is a constant cycle of jumping in and out of the setting, metaphorically speaking of course: being able to take yourself away from the activity and read, interpret and reflect on what you have learned, usually each day. Field notes are the central data-recording activity of the ethnographer, as Fife (2005) highlights through many examples. It is possible to conduct an entire study using nothing but a note book and pen. Gathering data is followed almost immediately by analysing that data in relation to itself and to the ever increasing body of knowledge that is being accumulated. As each new element is gathered it is given a tentative place in the emerging theory as the researcher reflects on what is already known, what has been newly acquired and what remains a mystery but needs to be explored.

Grounded theory (the practice of developing other theories that emerge from observing a group) is a typical approach to the analysis and interpretation of ethnographic research and is discussed in greater detail in Part 4. The aim is not to create universal 'laws' but localized theory relating to the specific phenomenon. Theory emerges from local sites and the background analysis of the context; this adds to theory from other sites, other researchers and the theory building continues as an ever increasing understanding of concepts by repeated, in-depth exploration.

Descriptive 'story telling'

Many ethnographers see the writing of the narrative as the most 'artistic' element of their work. This highlights the very nature of this method; it is both a science and an art, just as interviewing is both a science in terms of systematic procedure and an art in terms of an individual developing their own artistic strategy for conducting an interview. Ethnographers rely on 'thick description' to tell the story of their investigation and share their findings with their audience. According to Mitchell and Charmaz, the aim is to hear 'a whole human being who lived the story, rather than an anonymous report of it' (1998, 236). Objectivity, in the traditional sense of the term, in reporting the results of an ethnographic study is not possible. We do not seek to control variables, therefore we cannot demonstrate internal or external validity, which is the traditional way to demonstrate objectivity. As this is not possible then the goal of ethnographic narrative should be objectivity in the sense of 'openness, a willingness to listen and "give voice" to respondents . . . it means hearing what others have to say, seeing what others do, and representing them as accurately as possible' (Strauss and Corbin, 1998, 43). The final story as it is presented to the reader will reflect the researcher's own personal interpretation of the individual and shared realities of the study. Written accounts will reflect your culture, interests, training and purpose (Agar, 1996), and this is not to be seen as a 'bad' thing. Wolcott claims there is 'nothing to stop researchers from putting themselves squarely into their inquires' (1999, 173), reporting what they have seen and experienced as part of the investigation. In Part 4 writing up is discussed in more detail; ethnography, as with all other methods, has an accepted tradition in terms of the finished work although that tradition has changed somewhat over the past few decades and continues to change.

Virtual ethnography

I have supervised research studies in a number of 'virtual' ethnographies in recent years and for the most part they are not that different from traditional studies in traditional settings. Essentially it is the setting that has changed shape, not the process. That said, there are issues which relate specifically to the nature of the setting and need to be considered. The process essentially remains the same, but in a virtual environment there are unique features that need to be highlighted, and I would like to look at those I feel are the most significant. If you are planning to carry out research in a virtual environment I would strongly recommended that you read Christine Hine's *Virtual Ethnography* (2000) as it provides invaluable insight into research in this setting. Virtual settings have some unique features: establishing the existence of a 'community', personal identity in a disembodied environment, and the nature of 'truth' in a transient reality.

The existence of 'real' communities in cyberspace is not as yet accepted 'fact'; a number of attempts have been made to define 'community' and empirically test for the existence of such a community based on predefined criteria. Jones (1997) proposed a 'virtual settlement theory' where there are a minimum of four conditions that must exist before a cyber-based environment can be termed 'community':

- a virtual public space containing significant interactive group computer-mediated communication
- a variety of communicators
- a minimum level of stable membership
- a minimum level of interactivity.

The use of these conditions as a technique for establishing a level of community has been empirically tested by other researchers and, in the absence of any other technique for establishing the existence of a virtual community, it offers researchers some boundaries of an acceptable 'norm' to work with. There are of course those who disagree with the need for any such techniques, stating that if individual participants feel part of a community then that community exists (Rheingold, 1993).

Another problem for researchers in virtual communities is that of personal identity. Disembodied communication makes it very difficult for a researcher to engage in participant observation. All the usual visual clues from social settings are missing and we become completely dependent on the words of the individual and the story they share with us.

The final issue I want to cover here is the question of whether 'truth' can exist in virtual spaces. 'Life on the screen makes it very easy to present oneself as other than one is in real-life' (Turkle, 1995, 228). This could be seen as both a problem for the researcher (how much can we believe of what we read on the screen?) and an advantage as it becomes infinitely easier to 'blend in' to a context when your own identity is restricted to the detail you choose to share.

Ethics in ethnography

The chapter on research ethics in Part 1 (Chapter 6) examined research ethics in a general sense; much of that chapter can be applied to an ethnographic context (see Example 10.1). It needs re-emphasizing here that there is a long running debate about ethical considerations in ethnography. This debate centres largely around the covert or overt nature of the investigation. There is still a strong feeling that a researcher has the 'right' to engage in research without the agreement, awareness or consent of the research population. As this is my story I will put forward my view, not as the 'right' view but as the view I 'feel' to be right from my perspective, my reality.

> **Example 10.1** Ethnography in LIS
>
> Seale, M. (2000) Project *Ethnography*: an anthropological approach to assessing digital library services, *Library Trends*, **49** (2), Fall, 370–85.
>
> This research project took an ethnographic approach to evaluating digital library services within a university. The various communities (micro-cultures) were identified and investigated using participant observation to reach a deeper understanding of the individual communities (engineers, educators, service providers), and how context impacted on service use and satisfaction. Seale argues that in order to truly evaluate a service it is necessary to reach an understanding of the micro-cultures that form the major stakeholders then determine 'satisfaction' based on the nature of the micro-culture, not based on generic standards and expectations that can be assumed to apply to all users in the same way.

All research should be overt, research participants should have the right to decide if they want to be part of an investigation and they should be fully informed about the nature, purpose and process of that research. In ethnography this becomes, in my view, even more important, as you are sharing someone's life in order to report on it and draw theory from what you learn. It is not always possible to obtain written consent from research participants for a number of reasons, but that doesn't mean that consent should not be sought; only when it is given in some agreed form can the research begin. Not only do we require consent at the outset but I recommend that we attempt to gain consent for the finished work. A seal of approval from those who are living the story can only strengthen a theory. The choice, outside specific institutional or association guidelines, ultimately belongs to you, the researcher. Make your choice in the light of your own values and beliefs.

Summary

Let us return to those two questions posed earlier in this chapter: '(1) how much context do I have to cover, and (2) how will I recognize a pattern when I see it?' (Fife, 2005, 1). These questions are impossible to answer theoretically. The practical exercise at the end of this chapter offers insight into how it feels to engage in participant observation and allows you to assess your ability to engage in the process. Ethnographical research is a craft that can only be learned by doing, it is impossible to become competent in the use of this method without actually getting out there and engaging. This research method is primarily concerned with 'going native', getting inside the context and being able to observe, analyse and interpret what you see, feel, hear and read. It is about immersing yourself totally in a field study site and still remaining 'critical' of all the data you gather.

 PRACTICAL EXERCISE

There is no quick and easy way to practise ethnography. This exercise is designed to make you think about participant observation and the nature of the insider–outsider view of a setting.

Take a notepad and pen and visit a local café at a busy time such as on a Saturday. Position yourself at a table that gives you a wide vista. Become familiar with the context, how busy the café is, how much seating space is available, the positions of windows, toilets and the nature of the seating (secluded tables, open tables in very close proximity, and so on). You are about to engage in a study of the community that visits this café. The focus of your study is the following:

'Are there any patterns to behaviour that can be related to gender?'

As a guide here are some 'signposts' to things you could be looking for, in the form of questions:

1 Is there a gender pattern to picking up the tray at the counter?
2 Is there a gender pattern to selecting and paying for the food?
3 Is there a gender pattern to selecting a seat?

(Adapted from Marvasti, 2004)

This is only a guide to some questions you could be asking as you watch what is going on around you. Engage in this observation for at least two hours, then take your notes and find a quiet place to review what you have seen and what you have written.

From your notes see how well you can describe the context of the setting and any patterns of behaviour you have identified.

Have you described the context in sufficient depth?
Did you notice any patterns of behaviour?

Suggested further reading

Agar, M. (1996) *The Professional Stranger: an informal introduction to ethnography*, Academic Press.

Fife, W. (2005) *Doing Fieldwork: ethographic methods for research in developing countries and beyond*, Basingstoke, Palgrave Macmillan.

Hallcom, F. (ongoing) *An Urban Ethnographic of Latino Street Gangs*, www.csun.edu/~hcchs006/gang.html. This is an excellent example of an ethnographic study.

Hammersley, M. (1992) *What's Wrong with Ethnography?*, London, Routledge.

Hammersley, M. and Atkinson, P. (1995) *Ethnography: principles in practice*, London, Routledge.

Hine, C. (2000) *Virtual Ethnography,* London, Sage.

Kottak, C. P. (2005) *Window on Humanity: a concise introduction to general anthropology*, New York, McGraw Hill.

Wolcott, H. F. (1999) *Ethnography, a Way of Seeing*, Walnut Place, CA, Altamira Press.

Internet resource

Library of Congress, Ethnographic Resources Related to Folklore, Anthropology, Ethnomusicology and the Humanities, http://lcweb.loc.gov/folklife/other.html.

Chapter 11

Delphi study

Introduction

The purpose of a Delphi study is to 'obtain the most reliable consensus of opinion of a group of experts . . . by a series of intensive questionnaires interspersed with controlled opinion feedback' (Dalkey and Helmer, 1963, 458). Helmer and Rescher were researchers employed by the RAND Corporation, the first organization ever to be called a 'think-tank', working for the US Air Force. The research project they were working on required the design of a method that would lead to predication of future events based on expert knowledge. Together they designed, justified and applied a method that was later to become known as the 'Delphi' method. In the first public dissemination of the development of this method, in 1959 Helmer and Rescher offered this explanation of why their method was best suited to prediction:

> The informed expert, with his resources of background knowledge and his cultivated
> sense of relevance and bearing of the generalities in particular cases, is best able to carry
> out the application of the quasi-laws necessary for reasoned prediction in this field. . . .
> For the expert has at his ready disposal a large store of (mostly unarticulated)
> background knowledge and a refined sensitivity to its relevance, through the intuitive
> application of which he is often able to produce trustworthy personal probabilities
> regarding hypotheses in his area of expertness.   (1959, 31)

The name 'Delphi' was first applied to this technique by Kaplan (Woundenberg, 1991), and the association with Greek mythology was no accident. The temple at Delphi was the supposed location where the oracle Pythia would consult the Gods and interpret their responses for the waiting public. There is a hint here that this was a somewhat less than complimentary reference but nonetheless the name quickly became the accepted term for this research method.

The original purpose of a Delphi study was to predict future trends but over the past 50 years this method has been applied to many studies that sought a consensus of expert opinion, not always concerned with predicting future events, but always concerned with 'expert opinion'. This method has been used extensively in the private and public sector for such things as policy analysis, planning and long-range forecasting (Gupta and Clarke, 1996). 'Delphi may be characterized as a method for structuring a group communication process so that the process is effective in allowing a group of individuals, as a whole, to deal with a complex problem' (Linstone and Turoff, 2002).

In information and communication research the Delphi method has been applied within a great many studies; examples include a study carried out by Ludwig and Starr (2005) into the future of a library as a place. This study used a panel made up of health librarians, architects, building consultants and information technologists. The panel was asked to reflect on over 70 possible changes in the use of the library space. Cole and Harer (2005) used a Delphi study to determine the importance of critical performance measures on measuring academic library quality. A postgraduate student of mine applied the Delphi method to a study of criteria for the evaluation of holocaust films; the study was also used as a means of evaluating the Delphi method as a form of qualitative research. The results of this evaluation demonstrated that this method is well suited to gathering 'rich' and 'deep' qualitative data (Cape, 2004).

The Delphi process

The key to conducting a good Delphi study is good planning, and traditional Delphi studies will go through the following steps.

1   Decide on the general aims of the study. As is usual at this stage with any research method, you begin with a statement of the problem then turn this into specific aims, which you organize into a set of sequential tasks and issues to be tackled. As the Delphi method is already so well defined the research design is established a priori. There are a number of studies that are referred to as *modified* Delphi studies; if this is the case with your study then it will be necessary to design the pattern of the research and be in a position to justify the modifications that have been made to the process.

2   Review all relevant literature and documentation (such as descriptions of service, mission statements, research or annual reports) following the process established in Chapter 2. You should also discuss your developing ideas with key informants or experts at this stage in the research.

3   Identify an expert panel who can inform the discussion on the issues at the heart of the investigation. Make contact well in advance of the data collection and be sure to explain exactly what it means to agree to be part of the panel; this will not be a 'one-time' affair. Provide any potential panel members with a detailed outline of what will be required and remember it is better to have fewer members on the panel who are prepared to engage in all stages of the study than to have a large panel to begin with, only to lose members as the research progresses.

4   You will now be in a position to describe your research question in detail and state your hypothesis if you have one. You may have several.

5   You will now need to design appropriate questionnaires. Delphi studies always

use questionnaires; it is the only acceptable form of data collection within traditional Delphi method. If this is not appropriate to your research question then you are obviously conducting a 'modified Delphi study' and you need to be explicit about this in your methodology.

6 Always pilot your data collection instrument, amend and try again. This is almost certainly the single most important step in the chain. You may think your questions are crystal clear, with no hint of ambiguity. You will be amazed at how many meanings can be given to an apparently straightforward question or instruction.

7 Round 1: Send out the questionnaire to all members of the expert panel at the same time. Collate and summarize the responses and return them to all panel members. In a traditional Delphi study this initial questionnaire will usually consist of a small number of open ended questions, the purpose here being to encourage the panel to present their reaction in a detailed and descriptive narrative.

8 Round 2: Send a list of ideas, comments and viewpoints taken from all responses to the panel members. There must be total anonymity in the list, no comment being attributed to an individual. Ask the panel members to review the statements and assign a rank of numerical value demonstrating their level of agreement or disagreement with the statement. Give an opportunity for panel members to make additional statements or comments.

9 Once you have processed this second round, decide if further rounds are necessary. If consensus is reached as early as in the second round then it is perfectly legitimate to stop there. This is fairly unusual as new comments are frequently added at this stage – the reaction from the panel when they receive the first feedback is usually to make some additional comments. Reading the thoughts and ideas of others drawn together in a collective list often triggers extended thinking on the issues. The next round, should there be one, will be a synthesis of the second list, ranked, and the additional comments; ask panel members to rank the additional comments in the same way as they did for the first list. This process continues until you feel consensus has been reached and no further information is being added.

10 Processing is ongoing as data will be processed between each round. It is usual for a Delphi study to include three to seven rounds; in modified studies the number of rounds may vary but it is necessary to provide robust justification for modifications such as this.

11 You will now be able to write up your research report. You will describe your results in words and pictures, interpret your data and draw conclusions. The ranking system used in traditional Delphi studies allows graphical representation; the aim is to reach consensus although most reports also include the 'maverick' comments that inevitably appear in any research study.

Rules of a Delphi study

Only experts are used on the panel

The whole point of engaging in a Delphi study is to make the most of expert opinion; it is therefore counterproductive to invite anyone onto the panel who is not an expert. It may often be tempting to 'make up the numbers' by attempting to involve someone who may have some knowledge of the subject but is not truly an expert; it is better to have fewer members but retain the expert integrity of the panel.

All data is collected in writing

Because of the nature of this method there is potential for the researcher (in the role of the oracle Pythia) to make assumptions, but interpretation of the data is essential, as it is with most research data. When the panel responds in writing there is evidence of their contribution and if their responses change during subsequent rounds of the investigation, the written evidence is there as an audit trail or to allow an independent analyst to examine the evidence and confirm the credibility of the interpretation. Of course the added advantage of this is that, generally speaking, people take a more considered approach to writing down their thoughts than providing a verbal response.

There is a systematic attempt to produce a consensus

There is a deliberate attempt to achieve some form of consensus from the panel; although not always achievable, it is a goal of this method. This is not concerned with manipulation and coercion; it is concerned with sharing views and being given the opportunity to reconsider views based on opposing arguments.

Panel member are given anonymity

In order to encourage honest and open answers to the questions being asked, much of the literature on the Delphi method states that the identity of individual members of the panel should never be disclosed. This is often very difficult in areas where all experts will be aware of other experts in their field. Anonymity has usually been a characteristic of Delphi studies but many modified studies do not place anonymity high on the list of priorities. Usually the reason given for this is that there is more to be gained by engaging in whatever activity relies on members 'seeing' each other than there is from keeping them apart. Turoff and Hiltz (1997) claim that there is more to be gained by revealing the identity of panel members to motivate them into giving serious thought and deliberation to the questions being asked. Knowing that contributions are being made by those in the best possible position to comment encourages more honest and better considered responses.

At least two rounds are used

The purpose of a Delphi study is to reach consensus. This means allowing experts to consider and reconsider their views and opinions in light of the views of others. This cannot be done by a single round of questioning. The researcher in this situation is both a researcher and a moderator, acting as a go-between as ideas are shared, modified and 'debated'. 'At least two rounds' is an absolute minimum, three or more is more common, and the goal is to reach consensus having allowed the panel maximum opportunity to contribute their thoughts and ideas.

Consensus is the most common outcome but occasionally divergence is the only result

A Delphi study seeks to achieve consensus but this is not always possible; where ideas continue to run at odds with each other this must be reported as part of the research findings. It is rare that an entire study would culminate in complete divergence but not unlikely that there is an element of divergence in the findings.

Modifying a Delphi study

In more recent applications of this method the term a 'modified Delphi study' is often used to describe the research method used when one or more of the 'rules' of a Delphi study was deliberately omitted from the study design. This does not mean the method is no longer valid. It simply means that the study design is based on Delphi principles, but modifications have been made to accommodate local requirements: panel members might be engaged in some form of face-to-face contact; definitions of 'expert' are perhaps more loosely applied; and so on.

Caution must be taken when modifying a Delphi study as the design was created for a specific purpose and any modification may well disrupt the process. An example of this could be calling a face-to-face meeting. The very point of a Delphi study is to ensure that all voices are heard with a guarantee of anonymity; in any face-to-face meeting there will be those who command a stronger presence than others and they may alter the thinking of the panel by no other means than force of character. This should be avoided at all cost. Justification for any modifications to the process will be presented and will include explanations of those modifications and any impact they could have on findings.

Delphi studies and new technologies

Delphi studies (see Example 11.1) are being increasingly facilitated by advancing technologies. The use of e-mail to deliver and return questionnaires, digital questionnaires online, posting of feedback in virtual discussion spaces and the potential for online virtual discussion forums are encouraging greater use of the traditional approach and increasing opportunities for variations in modified Delphi studies. As with other research methods the impact and use of technology can only really be seen in the data collection and analysis; the methods remain constant. The structure of a Delphi study will not be altered by the mechanisms adopted to collect data, providing that the research design remains constant. In Part 3 and Part 4 the use of technology to collect and analyse data will be discussed in more detail with reference to specific software.

Example 11.1 A modified Delphi study
As part of a much larger study (JISC, User Behaviour in Information Seeking: longitudinal evaluation of EIS), a modified Delphi study was designed:

- to provide an indication of trends and emergent agenda items
- to determine the relationship between relevant stakeholders
- to establish the needs of the stakeholders in relationship to the Framework requirements of the JISC stakeholders, leading to a definition of the JUBILEE evaluation activity.

Design of modified Delphi
Stage 1:   Identify and contact membership to secure participation.
Stage 2:   Send initial questionnaire to all members.
Stage 3:   Have face-to-face meeting (pre-meeting: provide members with detailed plan of the meeting and clear definition of the objectives of the day).

Proposed day-long event to include:

- introduction and presentation defining the purpose of the Delphi study and presentation of the results of the initial questionnaire
- group discussion and debate from questionnaire findings
- feedback from the groups after lunch
- discussion of toolkit and its role in the JISC Framework
- members completing the questionnaire again after they have discussed and debated the issues.

Stage 4:   Analysis of the findings from the day.
Stage 5:   Mapping the relationship between the stakeholders and identifying trends.

Online debate is set up to continue to discuss the issues identified and trends noted.

Source: Banwell et al. (2005)

Summary
The Delphi method offers a great deal in terms of exploring and developing practical issues within a wide variety of contexts. The formal structure of the method is also highly appealing to many researchers, not least neophyte researchers who see it as a way of removing much uncertainty in terms of design and justification. These are all

very positive reasons for using the Delphi method, and could go a long way to explain the increasing use of this method within LIS over the past few years. Since introducing it into my own teaching curriculum it has become almost as popular with my students as the traditional survey approach.

The Delphi method is highly structured and following an accepted design is very appealing, but that does not mean you have to be restricted by the formal structure. Modifications to the process can be made if well justified, and often modifications will result in deeper and richer insights. Although this method was developed as a means of prediction this does not necessarily mean that it is the only suitable application it has. Policy development, or indeed any form of planning, can benefit from the consensus approach.

One of the major drawbacks of the Delphi method is the level of commitment required from research participants. As a number of rounds are involved and a considerable amount of thought and often self-reflection is needed, participants are being asked to make a fairly substantial commitment to the research. Essentially a Delphi study takes the concept of discussion, confrontation and multiple views and constructs a carefully planned and executed series of debates and exchanges that encourages individual viewpoints, while striving towards a core consensus. How much modification is applied to the standard tradition is in the hands of the researcher, but modifications should not be so extreme that the true purpose of the method is lost.

 PRACTICAL EXERCISE

You have been asked by your head of department to identify the most important elements of information skills training needed by your users for the development of future training packages. You decide that a Delphi study would be the best way to identify these elements. To begin designing your study you need to answer the following questions:

1 What do you need to know?
2 Who would be the best individuals to provide you with the information you need?
3 What is their current level of understanding of information skills?
4 How will their existing understanding affect the way you design your data collection?
5 Which is most appropriate, a traditional or a modified Delphi study?

Suggested further reading

Cape, B. (2004) Gathering Opinion and Initiating Debate: the success of the Delphi method in purely qualitative research, *Library and Information Research News*, **28** (89), summer, 35–43.

Gupta, U. G. and Clarke, R. E. (1996) Theory and Applications of the Delphi Technique: a bibliography (1975-1994), *Technological Forecasting and Social Change*, **53** (2), 185-211.

Linstone, H. A. and Turoff, M. (eds) (2002) *The Delphi Method: techniques and applications*, www.is.njit.edu/pubs/delphibook/ (also includes extensive bibliography).

Ludwig, L. and Starr, S. (2005) Library as a Place: results of a Delphi study, *Journal of the Medical Library Association*, **93** (3), July, www.pubmedcentral.nih.gov/articlerender.fcgi?artid=1175798.

Turoff, M. and Hiltz, S. R. (1997) *Computer Based Delphi Processes*, http://eies.njit.edu/~turoff/Papers/delphi3.html#AI.

Chapter 12

Action research

Introduction

Action research is rapidly becoming one of the most popular research methods in information and communication research among practitioners. Increasingly they are recognizing the value of this approach in improving service provision, encouraging reflective practice and structuring and disseminating experience to the wider community. Action research has been used to investigate organizational functions such as the role of the library and library staff in the provision of distance learning programmes (Bailey et al., 2004), for educational research investigating individual solutions to differing learning needs such as tackling student referencing errors (Kendall, 2005), and to improve students' information literacy skills over a longitudinal series of interventions (Pickard, 2005). As Rowley points out:

> Action research encourages practitioners to acquire the habit of researcher in the workplace, and provide them with an approach that teaches them to critically evaluate their practice. Action research differs from other research approaches in that it assumes a tight coupling between research and action. In traditional research, findings and theories may serve as a basis for recommendations for future action. With action research, action and research proceed in parallel. In addition, action research depends upon a collaborative problem solving relationship between the researcher and the client with the aim of both solving a problem, and generating new knowledge.
>
> (Rowley, 2004, 212)

Kurt Lewin is the sociologist who first used the term 'action research', to describe his work in the field of human dynamics with individuals affected by post-war social problems. He believed that in order to truly make a difference some form of change or action had to be embedded in the research design from the outset. An investigation leads to some form of action, which is followed by an evaluation of that action: 'The research needed for social practice can best be characterized as research for social management or social engineering. It is a type of action-research, a comparative research on the conditions and effects of various forms of social action, and research leading to social action. Research that produces nothing but books will not suffice' (Lewin, 1948, 202).

Lewin devised the 'action research cycle', which has remained the basic model for applying this research method. However, there have been some significant changes in the way the research is conducted. Initially action research was devised as a method of research that allowed the researcher to identify a group of research subjects, devise an intervention strategy and apply that strategy to the 'subjects'. The researcher remained very much an outsider, independent of the group and with no vested interest in the intervention.

During the 1960s action research declined in favour among sociologists; when it began to regain favour during the early 1970s action research had a new form, having undergone a subtle, but significant, change. Influenced by the work of Paul Freire, who challenged the 'teacher–student' relationship, claiming it should be replaced by a more participatory approach to education (Freire, 1972), the new form of action research placed the researcher firmly within the research context. The usual notion of the 'objective observer' is replaced in this method by the researcher who is an active participant in the process before, during and after the research activity. Not only is the researcher an active participant in the research context, this method also encourages research 'subjects' to become actively involved in the process: 'As an evolving approach to enquiry, action research envisages a collaborative approach to investigation, that seeks to engage 'subjects' as equal and full participants in the research process' (Stringer, 1999, 46).

Action research is best suited to practitioners seeking to improve their practice by development and analysis; this method embraces change: putting action at the core of the research process and seeking to create change, then investigating the outcome of that change. This is an interventionist approach to research taken with the explicit intention of improving practice, and understanding that practice and the situation in which it takes place. Action research is the process by which practitioners attempt to study their problems scientifically in order to guide, correct and evaluate their decisions and actions: 'Action research is simply a form of self-reflective enquiry undertaken by participants in social situations in order to improve the rationality and justice of their own practices, their understanding of these practices, and the situations in which the practices are carried out' (Carr and Kemmis, 1986, 162).

The action research cycle

This method is characterized by the researcher examining current processes, taking action to improve those processes, then analysing the results of the action. It is most common in educational research but can be found in many professions where improvement to practice is being sought. The action research model takes an approach that is described as either cyclical or spiral, and includes the following stages.

Identifying problems

Action research usually begins by identifying a problem or issue, or when there is a desire to improve practice. The topic in question is often a subject of concern before the idea of conducting research emerges. As with any research activity, you should review all relevant literature and documentation at this stage (for example descriptions of service, mission statements, research or annual reports). You should also discuss your developing ideas with key informants or experts either in the workplace or from other, similar working environments. Maybe there is a colleague in another organization who has already faced an issue or problem similar to your own. If you are part of a team whose members are also responsible for, or have a vested interest in, your project, you will want to include them in any discussion and gather as much knowledge from them as possible. This is usually formalized by holding interviews or focus group meetings to allow you to analyse other people's input in a more rigorous fashion.

At this stage it is easy to see why action research is very close to professional practice; many people will say 'well we do this all of the time, this is how we work'. That is probably the case; the difference with action research is that the usual daily practice is formalized into a research project that can be written up and presented in order to share your findings. It is often difficult to separate the research from normal daily routine; you must remember that this is a research study that will be subject to all the usual scrutiny of robust research.

Record everything and demonstrate rigorous analysis of the findings. From this very early stage, casual conversations with colleagues must be formalized into interviews or focus groups. You don't have to alter the way you interact with these people but you must ensure that you record what is said and that you are able to present evidence to support decisions you make throughout the process. In Example 12.1 (page 138) data gathered included a focus group with other academic tutors, interviews with library staff and interviews with tutors from other academic institutions.

Another form of data that will be needed at this stage comes from your users. Before designing an intervention it will be necessary to establish the current context from the perspective of those who will be the target of the intervention. This can be done in a number of ways, such as using questionnaires for large groups to establish their current behaviour or opinions, interviews with individuals, focus groups, observation of behaviour in the chosen context and analysis of existing documentary evidence. This data will also be very useful as a benchmark for evaluating the intervention later; establishing the current situation before making any changes is the only real way to gauge the success of the intervention.

In Example 12.1 (page 138) the data gathered at this stage included questionnaires to the first year undergraduates asking questions about their use of electronic information resources, two focus group meetings discussing how participants felt about using those resources, and a bibliographical analysis of assignments the students had submitted in their first semester.

Action planning

The design of the programme of intervention (new teaching method, induction programme and so on) is based on analysis of the data gathered in the first stage. There is no predetermined formula for the length and nature of this intervention; it will depend on a number of factors. The analysis of the first stage will provide the evidence needed to design an appropriate intervention.

This intervention is the product of a diagnosis and interpretation of the evidence provided in the first stage, current practice within the subject area and analysis of the literature. This will suggest possible improvements in relation to the needs of the target group. The planned action could take the form of a single event (such as a practical training workshop with a specific focus), a series of events over a period of time (such as a training programme on the use of electronic information resource services within the institution during a semester) or a more 'fixed' change to a system already in place (such as reorganization of the layout of a collection). The nature of the intervention will in itself be a product of the research process.

Implementation

Once the intervention has been identified and designed it must be implemented within the context of the research. The process now moves from the empirical and theoretical arena of other research methods to the practical. Systems analysis is the only other research method that comes close to the practical nature of action research and the actual creation and delivery of a solution, although even in systems analysis the solution usually goes no further than the prototype stage during the research. This may lead to the creation of a complete solution, but this is not a formal step in the process. Only in action research is the delivery of a solution implicit to the method. The form of the solution is completely dependent on the context and the nature of the problem.

A word of caution: if this is part of an academic research study leading to the award of a degree time is a critical factor. Ensure that there is sufficient time allowed to enable you to implement the solution and go on to evaluate and reflect on the research, thereby completing one full cycle of the action research process. This does not have to be the end of the process and indeed if this is part of your usual working practice you will no doubt go on to review the situation continually, but you have to be in a position to produce a research report of the activity, including the evaluation and reflection. The reflection will lead to your conclusions and recommendations for ways forward. Both the timescale and the nature of the solution are critical.

A change in everyday working practice, such as rearranging a service area or offering a completely new service, may be a possible solution, but will there be enough time to monitor and evaluate the difference this has made to the research subjects? If the solution is an intervention, say for example a user education programme, how long will this last and how will you evaluate the success of the programme? Can this be done in the timescale you have allowed for the study? The answer to all of these questions will be specific to your own context and the nature of the research, but you must be aware that in order to evaluate you have to have sufficient time to allow research subjects to engage with the solution and you must have a suitable evaluation mechanism in place. All of these issues should be resolved at the research proposal stage.

Evaluation

The success of the intervention then needs to be examined. This can be done in a number of ways, for example by sending questionnaires to participants to see how they have reacted to the intervention or by analysing outputs as a result of the intervention (has information-seeking behaviour improved as a result of new information retrieval workshops?). Interviews or focus groups can be carried out, documents collected (for bibliographies or evidence of other output) and journals that have been maintained throughout the process can be analysed (journals can be used by all research participants not only the researcher).

An example of action research that students will be familiar with is that of a module or course evaluation. Academic tutors usually ask students who have studied with them to complete an evaluation of some form. The results of that evaluation are then collected; usually questionnaires are used but sometimes focus groups and individual interviews are carried out and an evaluation of assignments which can go beyond the usual marking process can also be used.

This is an example of action research which is actually an integral part of professional practice but remains a research activity. Very often this time of action research practice is not written up in the usual research report format, although it is used to inform the development of teaching and learning practice by the tutor. There will usually be some form of presentation of findings; a course review would include evidence from students about the success of the course or module.

No matter how formal or informal the presentation of findings are from this activity, the tutor has evidence to examine practice and decide if that practice needs to alter in some way. Evaluation is often seen as the final stage in a research activity, and leads to the presentation of findings, conclusions and perhaps recommendations. With action research the evaluation is the first stage analysis; in order to make the most of discoveries from the evaluation the researcher or practitioner must engage in serious reflection.

Reflection

Action research is a cyclical research method. As a result of the analysis, the success of the intervention can be assessed and, more than that, it is possible to go beyond the evaluation of what happened and how it happened to consider 'why' it happened. The researcher (very often the practitioner also) reflects on the results of the intervention and the evaluation; this may or may not result in more action, but usually more action will follow. Reflection is a human activity in which people purposefully 'recapture' their experience, and think about that experience in order to evaluate and make sense of it (Boud, Keogh and Walker, 1985). This is synonymous with meta-cognitive activity, which includes making inferences, analogies and evaluation, and affective activities such as feeling, remembering and reacting. Reflection is a challenging activity if carried out with sufficient conviction. In order to be truly successful we must be prepared to acknowledge and question our own beliefs and perceptions. Self-criticism is difficult but it is only through rigorously and consciously questioning our own beliefs, biases and convictions that we can reconsider those preconceptions and transform practice (Mezirow, 1991).

'Action research is characterised by the use of autobiographical data' (Herr and Anderson, 2005, 23). The research journal has a vital role to play in data collection for this particular research method. As with ethnography, the need to maintain a log as the research progresses is central to the reflective nature of the activity. Although the journal can provide very useful data for evaluation, it is at the reflective stage that it becomes the primary source of data for the researcher or practitioner. We will discuss the research journal later but for now it will suffice to say that it is as vital a data collection instrument in action research as it is in ethnography or case study research.

Example 12.1 Action research
Undergraduate use of electronic information resources
As part of a much larger, longitudinal study of students' use of electronic information resources [Banwell et al., 2005] I engaged in action research with my own undergraduate students. This project began in their first year of study and continued until they graduated. There were two major interventions during this time, two full cycles to the action research model. Although much of the activity I was involved in could easily be claimed as my normal working practice, the difference with this group and this three-year study was the formalization of the activity and the record of analysis. The overall research model for this study was case study research but within the wider case there was structured action research at two specific stages of the case study. The first intervention involved structured information skills training over a ten-week period; the second was a year later and was delivered as a core teaching model dealing with literature searching and preparing literature reviews. The results of both interventions were analysed using questionnaires, interviews, focus groups and bibliography analysis. A more detailed account can be found in Pickard (2005).

Pickard, A. (2005) The Role of Effective Intervention in Promoting the Value of EIS in the Learning Process, *Performance Measurement and Metrics*, **6** (3), 172–82.

Trustworthiness in action research

Action research as a method is identified by a number of characteristics which, for the most part, are exclusive to this method and single it out from all others. The greatest criticism of this research method comes from the positivist notion of *objectivity*. Although action research differs very significantly from ethnographic research, one similarity between them is that the research is *emic* or 'insider' research: the researcher is part of the context being researched. In ethnography the researcher usually makes a conscious effort to enter the context and become part of it; in action research the researcher is already *inside* the context and has considerable tacit knowledge of the situation. Far from having a negative impact on the research, this is what gives the investigation credibility in terms of problem solving and solution testing. Because knowledge is generated through the interest of the mind, knowledge and human interest are inseparable (Habermas, 1991). The notion of objectivity was discussed in Part 1 and will not be repeated here; there is little doubt that it would be futile to argue that an action researcher or practitioner could be completely objective during the research activity. If that were the case then the research would lose a great deal of what is useful and insightful in this method. When it comes to establishing the trustworthiness of action research the criteria used are slightly different from those usually associated with qualitative methodology. To begin with it must be understood that action researchers are not attempting to produce results that are immediately transferable to other contexts; the findings are 'true' only within the immediate research context and no attempt is made to generalize from these findings. The purpose is not to produce a definitive answer to a universal question, but to improve practice within a given context, move reflective practice into a systematic framework and share the findings with a wider audience.

Anderson and Herr point out that 'practitioner research should not be judged by the same validity criteria with which we judge "positivistic" and naturalistic research. This is not to say that there is no overlap or that it is less rigorous, but that a new definition of rigour is required that does not mislead or marginalize [the] practitioner researcher. As practitioner research is disseminated beyond local sites, we believe there is a need to deepen conversations about these issues' (1999, 15).

Herr and Anderson (2005) go on to provide five criteria that can be applied to measures of trustworthiness in action research: democratic validity, outcome validity, process validity, catalytic validity and dialogue validity.

Democratic validity is demonstrated by the extent to which the researcher and research participants were involved in the process. This means that you would have to be in a position to demonstrate that collaboration took place and the research outcome, solution, evaluation and reflection were relevant to the setting and context.

Outcome validity is demonstrated by the extent to which the intervention resolved the problem that was identified. This judgement is based on the quality of the data on which the action was planned and the evaluation of the action after implementation.

Process validity is concerned with the degree to which process can be aligned to outcome. There is a need here to demonstrate that evidence gathered can sustain assertions made in the design and implementation of the action. Triangulation of data collection techniques is applied to ensure that evidence can be corroborated from multiple sources.

Catalytic validity is the degree to which the research activity focuses, reorients and energizes all participants, including the researcher, towards really knowing and understanding their reality in order to change it. This emphasizes the transformative nature of action research; action research is a power for change and this should be clearly demonstrated throughout the process.

Dialogue validity focuses on communication with peers to establish the relevance and significance of the data collection, design and implementation of the action and the evaluation. This is a form of peer review; there is still some debate as to the nature and extent of the dialogue. There is no consensus on whether critical and reflective dialogue should extend to beyond the 'critical friend' or the 'community of collaborative inquirers' to wider research communities.

Remember, the real purpose of action research is not to offer generalizations based on the findings of localized studies, it is to produce and deliver a solution to a 'real life' problem and measure the success of the solution. Subjectivity in this context is a positive aspect of the research in the sense that tacit knowledge is essential if solutions are to be appropriate to and fitting for the specific context.

Action research as reflective practice

Action research is a dialectical interplay between practice, reflection and learning; the recursive nature of this research method implies that action research and reflective practice is one and the same thing. Although there is little doubt that most professionals engage in reflective practice to some extent, the distinction here is the level of formality attached to the process. A review of working practice and service provision takes place on a number of different levels; individual reflection and action goes on almost continuously as we all learn and adapt as a natural outcome of our professional behaviour. Peer and performance review offer a more systematic account of reflective practice, which is often accompanied by some form of documentation.

Action research takes this all a stage further; the intention from the outset is to engage in systematic research, which can be shared and disseminated to the wider population as well as used to improve local practice. Each stage in the process is formalized and designed to provide documented evidence that will withstand critical review. It may appear extreme to suggest that action research could be a continuous component of professional practice but, accepting that it will not always be possible to engage in systematic research, initiating the process with one study provides you with the baseline for all subsequent developments to practice. The depth may differ but the process can become a continuous one, contributing not only to improved service provision but also to more rigorous, evidence-based appraisal and review.

Summary

Action research is a cyclical process involving problem identification, action planning, implementation, evaluation and reflection. Not only is it an ideal method for practitioner research, it could be said to be an extension of professional practice into the formal research arena. Design, collaboration, documentation, rigorous analysis and critical self-evaluation and reflection are vital in this approach to research. Data collection techniques best suited to action research are focus groups, interviews, observation, questionnaires, research diaries and 'in-house' documentation.

As a method, action research is ideally suited to the researcher or practitioner. Brookfield (1995) describes critical reflection as a 'stance and dance' attitude, the stance being the openness of the researcher or practitioner to further investigation and constant learning, the dance is the experimentation and willingness to take risks. Extending this metaphor, if reflective practice is the 'stance and dance' then action research is the choreography, the deliberate scripting of the 'dance' in a recognizable research format that can be shared within and beyond the professional community.

 PRACTICAL EXERCISE

Identifying action research potential

1   Within your current workplace (full time students may have a part-time job they could use as the context for this exercise; if not think about your own study routine and analyse how you organize and engage in your learning activities) identify an aspect of the service you provide, not the entire service, but a small, bounded element of the service. (This could be a particular document delivery system, online resource or tutorial.) You can do this by completing one of the following sentences:

'I would like to improve..'
'Some people are really unhappy with......................................'
'I really don't like the way I...'
'I really wish we could..'.

2   Write a brief description of this particular aspect of your service or study routine.
3   Identify the potential research participants who would be involved in this study.
4   What post-intervention data could you collect that would help you to identify improvements and would also act as a baseline for evaluating success?

Suggested further reading

Herr, K. and Anderson, G. L. (2005) *The Action Research Dissertation: a guide for students and faculty*, London, Sage.
Rowley, J. (2004) Researching People and Organizations, *Library Management*, **25** (4/5), 208-14.

Somekh, B. (2006) *Action Research: a methodology for change and development*, Maidenhead, Open University Press.

Stringer, E. T. (1996) *Action Research: a handbook for practitioners*, London, Sage.

Zuber-Skerritt, O. (ed.) (1996) *New Directions in Action Research*, London, Falmer.

Chapter 13

Historical research

History is a meaningful record, evaluation, systematic analysis and synthesis of evidence concerning human achievement. It is not a list of chronological events like we remember at school. It is an integrated account of the relationship between persons, events, times and places.

(Burns, 2000, 481)

Introduction

Historical research plays a vital role in the development of theory and practice; it has relevance as a research method in all subject disciplines and although very different from the other research methods discussed in this section, it is still a 'scientific' method, which must conform to standards of practice. The most notable difference between historical research and all other methods available to the researcher is the nature of the 'evidence' used to generate theory or test a hypothesis. Historical research relies on data that already exists in one form or another, unlike other methods, which are designed to create or generate data as a part of the research process. This is not to say that historical research cannot create or generate *some* data but this is likely to constitute a relatively small part of the data set to be analysed and will depend on the research topic. History, after all, starts with the minute that has just passed; the sentence you have just read has now become a part of your history, however recent. Historical research is essentially qualitative because of the interpretation that is inevitably involved; there are uses for quantifiable data in some investigations but because this approach depends so much on interpretation, by definition it becomes qualitative. Most historical studies deal with natural behaviour in real life situations and the interpretations the researcher brings to the evidence. Quantifying evidence can be provided where suitable data exists but it can be difficult to justify quantification of anything other than tangible evidence, such as reported statistics or records.

This research method is concerned with reconstructing the past, identifying pieces of a puzzle and putting them together to provide insight and understanding of a situation, event or process. In the field of information and communication studies historical research can be used to investigate processes, behaviour, individual events or patterns of use. For example, an investigation into a particular collection, the purpose for which the collection was created, how it developed and patterns of use over time, could provide valuable insight. This could inform future collection management as well as provide insight on the past.

It could be claimed that historical research is a core professional competency for many information and communication practitioners. Many of the tools of historical research are the same tools that librarians, information managers, archivists, curators and records managers use daily. This method is also referred to as 'desk research' simply because the majority of the data already exists and the task is to identify that data, locate and retrieve it, then analyse it in light of all of the other data that has been collected. It is important to remember that the term 'history' means far more than a chronology of a series of events; it is usually a historian's interpretation of events constructed from primary sources. Whenever we read 'A history of . . .' it is an interpretation of a series of events based on primary sources, but still an interpretation not necessarily a definitive 'truth'. It is also important to bear in mind that history is always changing; new evidence and new interpretations often lead to new reconstructions of the past. The term 'history' can apply to both actual events and interpretations of those events (Tosh, 2002).

Many practitioners engage in this type of research every day as part of their normal working practice. The most obvious example of this would be those who work in local studies libraries or archives; a great deal of their time is spent tracing and recording historical documents, sometimes using them in the study of a specific topic or structuring, classifying and storing them for retrieval by others. Without a doubt the most popular form of historical research is genealogy. Tracing family history is a phenomenon which has grown massively in popularity over the past two decades; the growth of internet resources and access has contributed to an increasing number of individuals going in search of evidence of their ancestors. It is easy to assume that, because this is often done by individuals who are not 'expert' researchers, it does not fall into the same category of research as would say a dissertation or a large scale funded project. It is a mistake to make this assumption; the process involved in tracing family history is not so far removed from the process of any historical research.

Uses of historical research in information and communication studies include both the obvious and the not so obvious, remembering that everything before this moment is *history*. In examining the complex issues associated with the development of open source software Nuvolari (2005) suggests that 'nineteenth centuries experiences [sic] of technical change can provide some useful insights for the investigation of these issues'. Using documented evidence of software development this study provides an *interpretivist* history of patterns of behaviour and resulting design choices. This research provides valuable insight into a tradition and offers potential solutions for problems which continue to perplex designers today.

Examining the use of terminology and definitions over time can extend our understanding of meanings and reduce misunderstanding. Other areas where historical research can document the past and suggest policies for the future include tracing procedures and practices of information management within organizations

(Lal, 2005), tracing the development of legislation (Warren and Dearnley, 2005), trends in information science (Bensman, 2005; Hjorland, 2005), and histories of institutions and organizations (Bakowska, 2005; Choldin, 2005; Muddiman, 2005). Potential applications of historical research are many and varied; the past has many tales to tell and there is a great deal to be learned from the mistakes and successes of former times.

The research process

> Historical research must involve a penetrating analysis of a limited problem, rather than a superficial examination of a broad area. The weapon of the research historian is like a target pistol, not a shotgun.
>
> (Burns, 2000, 488)

It is the task of the historian to gain access to the past through primary and secondary evidence along with personal interpretation of that evidence; how history is written depends entirely on how the researcher engages in the research process. The threat of 'subjectivity', if indeed this is seen as a threat, is highly prevalent here. The earlier discussion on the nature of qualitative research highlights many of the potential pitfalls associated with individual interpretation. As with all other research methods, historical research follows a general process but the nature of the method is such that this process will depend very much on the researcher and the topic under investigation. It is in the nature of the evidence and the transparency of the interpretation that historical research demonstrates trustworthiness. During each step of the process it is up to the researcher to use whatever means possible to demonstrate trustworthiness without attempting to deny some level of subjectivity. These steps are presented here in a linear fashion, but as with all qualitative research you are reminded that this is an iterative process, moving between steps, sometimes taking a step back. Theory emerges from the investigation and is moulded as the investigation proceeds; you must always allow for consideration of new developments and be prepared sometimes to alter your stance.

Identifying a topic

As with all research we begin by identifying a topic of interest. What is it you want to know? It is vitally important that you begin your research with the formulation of a very specific purpose; there is too much scope for distraction within any historical investigation to begin with vague or broad questions. There are a number of ways to formulate a good research question; most historical research is concerned with 'why' and 'how' questions, using evidence to interpret a series of events. A good research question is a 'critical' question, one that will lead to further questions and provoke discussion; it is also one that has well defined boundaries. Defining the scope and coverage of any historical question can be done using chronological limits, geographical limits, and primary source restrictions, or in fact anything that appears to be a natural boundary to your investigation.

Saying something meaningful and relevant about a particular is far more useful than broad statements relating to generalities. Examine your topic and identify precisely what it is you want to explore. One way to do this is to ask yourself a number of questions about the topic. First, *where* did these events occur? Is there a geographical boundary to the events you wish to explore? For example, you could be interested in the development of a particular service; can this be 'bounded' in some way? The location of your investigation could be anything from an individual organization to a particular country; on an international scale, obviously the broader your location the less depth you provide. The next question you need to ask is *when* did the events occur that interest you? Are you interested in a very specific time frame or are you more interested in establishing a longitudinal timeline? Third, *who* is involved? Is there a particular individual or group of individuals that have played a very significant part in these events? By asking yourself these questions you will be in a position to define a critical question that continues to cover your topic but has gained a very specific focus.

Using the examples of historical research given earlier we can see how the researchers formulated their critical questions using some of these limiting factors. In tracing the development of legislation, Warren and Dearnley (2005) defined their research questions in a number of ways. They responded to the *where* question by locating the study in the UK; they further restricted the study by adding chronological limits, responding to the *when* question by focusing the study 'from the late 1960s through to the enactment of the 1984 Data Protection Act' (238). Muddiman (2005), in his study of the Association of Special Libraries and Information Bureaux (ASLIB), had already responded to the *where* question by locating the study firmly within a specific organization. He went on to respond to the *when* question by focusing on the 'first quarter of a century of the Association' (402). A further limitation was added that could be said to respond to the *who* question but is essentially concerned with defining the primary sources to be used; the study focused on 'two collections of primary documents: ASLIB's own records, held at Aslib Headquarters, London; and the papers of Edith Ditmas, held at the National Library of Wales' (402). These two examples demonstrate how it is possible to take a topic of interest and define that topic to construct a critical research question with a precise focus.

Locating data

Historical research for the most part relies on data that already exists. Occasionally a historical study can also include 'new' data gathered from participants in an event by way of personal reconstruction, but more often it is concerned with primary sources that already exist. For this reason identifying the existence of data usually contributes to the formulation of the research question; you must sometimes be prepared to alter your question based on the availability of primary sources.

This is yet another way of focusing the topic; the three questions already discussed must be accompanied by a fourth question, which asks, *what* is available?

Historical research typically relies on five types of data: documents, oral records, artefacts, photographs and quantitative records. These are referred to as your 'primary sources':

> A primary source is a document, image, or artifact that provides evidence about the past. It is an original document created contemporaneously with the event under discussion. A direct quote from such a document is classified as a primary source. A secondary source is a book, article, film, or museum that displays primary sources selectively in order to interpret the past. (Williams, 2003, 58)

We will look at primary sources in more detail later. Secondary sources are used in historical research but only to complement primary sources or to help fill any gaps left by a dearth of primary evidence. The authority of any interpretation is weakened by the absence of primary sources so secondary sources should be used sparingly. One of the most productive uses of secondary sources is as an aide to forming your hypothesis or defining your topic. At the outset of an investigation it is extremely useful to read as many secondary sources as you can to provide an overview of the wider topic and determine what others have done. This is often the core of your literature review, providing the background and context that leads to deeper exploration of the topic using primary sources. Secondary sources are written accounts of events such as history textbooks; the author of a secondary source has written an account based on their own interpretation, moving another step away from an actual record of an event.

When formulating a research question it is vital to identify potential primary sources that will provide sufficient data to allow you to place your own interpretation on events. The actual collection of this data is the next step but you must identify what data exists and how accessible that data is. Secondary sources are often readily available at a number of different locations; access to these sources rarely poses any particular difficulty other than the usual problems of finding the textbook you need or ordering a dissertation or thesis. Primary sources on the other hand are, by definition, unique; access to this data is a very different story. At this stage in your research you must ensure that you have the resources necessary and the appropriate access rights to view this data. This could mean a number of things depending on the nature of the primary source; the key is to locate the data then establish accessibility. Public and private archives will usually have clearly defined policies of access; familiarize yourself with them and take the necessary steps well in advance of data collection. Applying for permission to view data can take time, so think ahead and prepare the groundwork. You may need to contact individuals to access personal papers or small private collections; again this needs to be done well in advance of data collection.

The internet has without doubt increased our access to primary sources but there are pitfalls, it is not the great panacea we are often led to believe it is. There is a great deal of unique primary evidence that remains in only one form: the form in which it was created. This evidence often remains housed in a single location with extremely restricted access. One major benefit of using the internet is to identify what actually exists; it may not all be accessible remotely but you can discover a great deal concerning the existence and whereabouts of potentially useful data. Many of our largest archives make their catalogues available online, and some permit access to digital images of originals. There is no generic rule here so it is vital you identify what is accessible and do not assume that an online catalogue also implies there is online access to the original source. Unless you are very familiar with the type of data you will be accessing it is always better to err on the side of caution when relying on 'virtual' records; authority cannot always be guaranteed if you are using a recognized gateway or institution. There are some links to useful internet sites provided under the 'suggested further reading' section but please remember the nature of the internet: things do not remain constant; change is a basic characteristic of the medium.

Collecting and recording data

Collecting and recording data is different from creating new data. Surveys, case studies, ethnographic research, action research, experiments and systems analysis all create new data sets for analysis; historical research is predominantly concerned with collecting and analysing data that already exists. This is not to say that you will be aware of all the data that is available; part of the research process involves discovery, following a lead and seeing where it takes you and what data you uncover in the process.

The first stage in your data collection is to establish the authenticity of the evidence; in many cases this will have been done, depending on where the source was located, but it may not have been done in relation to your investigation. Being authentic is one thing but how that relates to your question is something only you can decide. Examine the source initially with these questions in mind:

- What type of source is it?
- Is it authentic?
- What is its provenance?
- Who created the source?
- Is the creator trustworthy and knowledgeable?
- What did the source mean in the time it was created?

This is a fairly standard procedure for evaluating sources but you must be prepared to ask these questions in relation to your research question. Many primary sources were never intended to be used as a testimony to events; personal accounts such as diaries are often unintentional or unwitting testimony, written for a purpose but not written as an historical account. This does not necessarily devalue the source but you do need to be conscious of the fact that detail contained within such a source will be influenced by the agenda and social milieu of the author (Marwick, 2001).

Once you have determined the usefulness of the source you will need to record it in precise detail. Remember you may only have one chance to examine this evidence. You may have travelled a considerable distance to visit an archive, an organization, a family. Photocopying may not be possible and a second visit could be out of the question; you have one opportunity to take as much from this source as possible. Establish a routine for scrutinizing and taking all that you need from the evidence; this will be the basis of your analysis, therefore it is vital to take away as much from the source as you possibly can.

There are a number of highly systematic ways of doing this. Preparing note cards in advance with predefined fields to be filled out as the data is scrutinized is one way; this technique can also be applied to database software if you have a laptop to record your notes. How you collect and record the data is up to you; the important thing is to be systematic and thorough. Even if you are fortunate enough to retain copies of the original, this process is still necessary as part of your analysis. Very often having copies can encourage sloppy note taking, never a good thing as you will always have to go back and do it again. Begin to develop a systematic habit of data interrogation from the outset; this is the first step in your analysis. Knowing when to stop collecting data is very important but it is rarely possible to predetermine this point. As with case study research, information saturation is the usual goal but this is rarely achievable in historical research. Remember the techniques of triangulation discussed in Part 1; the more sources you use the more thorough your analysis, the more diverse your sources are the more trustworthy will be your hypothesis or theory.

Initial analysis and drafting of discussion

Analysis of historical data is iterative; analysis begins with the first piece of data collected and continues throughout the process. Analysing and writing history 'is a continuous process of interaction between the historian and his facts' (Carr, 1961, 30). As it is unlikely you will have in your possession the original, your notes and bibliographic record are usually the basis of your analysis. Data collection has already taken you 'into' the data and allowed you to begin the iterative thought processes associated with qualitative analysis. Although historical research is far more than a chronology of events, the interpretation should be framed within a sound and clear chronology.

When dealing with descriptive or narrative primary data many of my students have successfully applied grounded theory to the analysis of historical data, some using the very formal approach designed by Anselm Strauss (1987; Strauss and Corbin, 1998), others using the more 'open' technique propounded by Barney Glaser (1992). Regardless of your preference, taking this approach to analysing primary sources for historical interpretation is the approach I would strongly promote to allow for systematic analysis that will demonstrate trustworthiness. This approach is of course only appropriate when dealing with certain types of data – written accounts, letters, personal diaries and so on – more quantifiable primary data will require a different approach but the basic process remains: systematic, iterative analysis that allows for new evidence to be integrated into developing theory.

A history is rarely written once; the final interpretation is usually the result of a number of preliminary discussions written as the data is collected and added to the existing framework. It is important that you write when analysing in order to piece together the ever growing collection of details; it may be you prefer to write short pieces as each new data element is added or you prefer to wait and draft out your impressions as they begin to emerge. The choice is down to individual preference. The point is to *write*; integrate the evidence and your interpretation as you go along, always being prepared to adjust your stance as new evidence comes to light.

I would also highly recommend you to use a researcher's journal throughout the process; this is discussed in detail in Part 3 and can be used for historical research in much the same way as an ethnographer would use a journal, as a reflexive mechanism for constant discussion of emerging themes and a detailed logbook of events. These can be combined into a single journal although many researchers prefer to maintain two 'diaries', one in which they discuss emerging theory and 'test' ideas and thoughts, the other as a log of where they have been, what they have found and how they found it.

Completing interpretation

You will reach a point in the research when you have examined all relevant sources, or at least you will in an ideal world. More usually you will reach a point when you have examined all the relevant, *available* sources. The majority of researchers work within predefined boundaries, physical, geographical, financial and/or durational. Such constraints are normal and will in themselves restrict the amount of data you have access to. Of course it is up to you to design a study and formulate a topic that reduces the impact of these constraints as much as is possible, but realistically there is always something you may have to do without; it is up to you to recognize what this is and to judge any potential impact it may have on your final interpretation.

Once you have reached the point where no new data can be added it is time for you to formalize and complete your interpretation based on the work you have done. This will be a combination of the preparatory work you did in constructing your literature review, the wider context you have presented based on secondary sources concerning your specific topic or areas closely related to it, and your primary analysis. Remember that you are constructing and *interpreting* the facts, not giving a factual account of events. Listing activities as they occurred may provide a useful chronology but it is not the essence of historical research. As with the majority of qualitative research, you are the research instrument, it is you who will present the final theory based on the facts you have gathered. In order to do this you need to be aware of a number of important factors.

1 You are interpreting facts out of time and context. Historians need to develop an empathy with the context in which the investigation is situated; this will require more knowledge than detailed facts drawn from the evidence. An understanding

of the social milieu is essential if you are to present a fair and balanced theory in response to your research question (Rael, 2004).

2 As with all qualitative analysis you must be able to look wider than the data, to think in the abstract and identify themes and relationships (Strauss and Corbin, 1998).

3 The use of humans as research instruments always demands an awareness of yourself, your beliefs and values. It is essential that you recognize this as your own value system will influence how you interpret what you read and see (Guba and Lincoln, 1989).

4 Historical evidence almost always has gaps, 'black holes' where no evidence exists to interpret. Leaving them out is not an option for the historian; the alternative is to use imagination, prior knowledge and logic to present a *possible* explanation or link. This is not about *guessing*, it is about logical estimations of the reality.

This is your interpretation of the facts based on evidence, knowledge and understanding. Once you have established your theory or tested your initial hypothesis it is time to present it to your audience.

Writing up

As with all research, the way that researchers share their findings largely determines the impact of the research. In Part 4 we will look at this final and vital stage in the research process in more depth. There are, however, some points which are specific to the writing of history that need to be pointed out here.

Establishing trustworthiness

As with all qualitative research, historical research must demonstrate trustworthiness. This can be done by applying the relevant criteria discussed in Part 1 but in addition to this there are a number of issues specific to historical research that must be addressed. The first of these is to do with the nature of data used. 'Is there sufficient primary data available for analysis or is there an over dependence on secondary data?' There is nothing to prohibit the use of secondary data such as other reconstructions of the event, but this should only be used to complement primary data such as a diary written at the time, records or visual evidence recorded at the time.

Dependability of data is vital as there may be no way of confirming the 'truth' of what was recorded other than the known reputation of the source. An example of this is the British census. There is widespread belief that since 1831 the census recorded information about all individuals in a household. The census return does include some information of this nature but in reality this was collected purely at the discretion of the officer gathering the data; there was no specific requirement for additional information until 1861. The source is dependable in so far as it is an 'official' source and is often the best record available for some information. The truth is that the information is only as good as the individual charged with gathering it and up until 1861 there is no consistency of recording data outside of the minimum requirement. As a single primary source the census would provide only tenuous support for any claim; any discovery made from within the census at this time would need to be substantiated by other information. It may be a good place to start carrying out research but usually a lot more evidence would be needed, depending on the subject under investigation.

Another question that must be answered, is 'Does the researcher demonstrate sufficient insight into the data?' This is to do with the depth and nature of the critical analysis carried out when interpreting evidence; often this means identifying conflicting possibilities. Rigorous and systematic analysis must be demonstrated if interpretations are to have real significance; there will always be alternative interpretations but that does not make any of them *wrong*. What makes them untrustworthy is lack of detailed investigation, using data to *prove* a point without considering alternative explanations. Insight into the data is not always about depth of analysis alone, it is also concerned with the level of knowledge the researcher brings to the data. This could be knowledge of the subject, knowledge of the source or personal experience.

Summary

Historical research is often criticized for lack of 'scientific' method because of the absence of control the researcher has over events that have already taken place. Variables cannot be manipulated in any controlled fashion and there is no way of knowing what variables affected a situation and how they were influenced. Written accounts of witnesses will be based on individual interpretation and if these accounts were retrospective there is no way of knowing what was lost in the process of *remembering*.

The puzzle that the historian must attempt to put together will undoubtedly have missing pieces; the gaps created by these missing pieces can only be filled by interpretation or inference. It is obvious how closely related these criticisms are to the criticism of qualitative research in general; by taking a systematic approach to the investigation and providing an overt and detailed description of the process, the value of the research becomes easier to assess. 'Finality of knowledge is impossible in all areas of study, and all contain uncertainties and inaccuracies' (Burns, 2000, 483). It is misleading to assume historical research is any different. Reconstructing past events, piecing together a puzzle from the past and adding interpretation, makes a significant contribution to new knowledge. This helps us to move forward in a constructive manner, and to avoid past mistakes and 'reinventing the wheel'.

 PRACTICAL EXERCISE

Select one of the historical research papers mentioned in this chapter. If you are unable to locate them then select another historical account. Read it and analyse the paper by answering the following questions:

1 What is the central argument or hypothesis of the paper?
2 Are the questions raised sound and relevant?
3 What primary and secondary sources are used?
4 Is sufficient authoritative primary evidence presented?
5 Does the primary evidence support the argument?
6 How sound are the conclusions, based on the argument and evidence?
7 How clear is the author's voice?

Suggested further reading

Reading historical accounts is one of the most useful activities you can engage in when attempting to become a successful historian. The references to particular studies provided in this chapter would be a good place to start.

Marwick, A. (2001) *The New Nature of History: knowledge, evidence, language*, Basingstoke, Palgrave Macmillan.

Tosh, J. (2002) *The Pursuit of History: aims, methods and new directions in the study of modern history*, 3rd edn, London, Longman.

Williams, R. C. (2003) *The Historian's Toolbox: a student's guide to the theory and craft of history*, Armonk, NY, M. E. Sharpe.

Internet resources

Internet Modern History Sourcebook
    www.fordham.edu/halsall/mod/modsbook.html.
National Archives
    www.nationalarchives.gov.uk/default.htm.
Rael, P. (2004) *Reading, Writing and Researching for History: a guide for college students*,
    http://academic.bowdoin.edu/WritingGuides/.
US National Archives and Records Administration
    www.archives.gov/.
World Archives
    www.hartford-hwp.com/archives/index.html.

Chapter 14

Grounded theory: method or analysis?

Over the years after its inception in 1967 the term grounded theory has been packed with multiple meanings, but also fraught by numerous misunderstandings, and complicated by competing versions.

(Charmaz, 2006, 177)

Introduction

I am not completely convinced that this is the right place in this book for a discussion of grounded theory; it is here as it is so often referred to as a 'research method'. Grounded theory (see Example 14.1 on page 162) is an approach that uses 'simultaneous data collection and analysis' (Charmaz, 2006, 20) and as such can be applied in ethnography, case study, historical or action research. It is more about how data is collected and analysed than about the entire research design. Grounded theory is a process of qualitative analysis not a research method; it is a 'general method of comparative analysis' (Glaser, 1978, 116). Although taking a grounded theory approach will influence the design of a research method, for example, in pure grounded theory the literature review very often comes *after* the analysis of empirical data (Charmaz, 2006), it is *not* a research method in its own right.

Grounded theory is described as 'a strategy for handling data in research, providing modes of conceptualisation for describing and explaining' (Glaser and Strauss, 1967, 3). This is supported by Barney Glaser who consistently refers to 'grounded theory analysis' and when making reference to the ways in which data can be gathered makes no reference to this as a research method (Glaser, 1998). *The Discovery of Grounded Theory* (Glaser and Strauss, 1967) offered a systematic approach to qualitative research practice, emphasizing that qualitative research had a logic of its own and for the first time practical guidelines were offered in applying that logic.

Since 1967 the two originators have taken very different paths. Strauss (1987) and Strauss and Corbin (1990, 1994 and 1998) present a systematic and what some describe as 'rigid' approach to grounded theory analysis. Many claim their approach has moved too far from the original concept of grounded theory and suggest that the constant comparative method of Strauss and Corbin has changed the way data is used, from the concept of emerging theory, to theory being forced: 'the technical tail is beginning to wag the theoretical dog' (Melia, 1996, 371). Barney Glaser (1978, 1992 and 1998) has continued to urge caution in the use of any rigorous system of analysis and maintains that the research should be open and receptive to data, not struggling to fit data into existing categories, even though those categories may have originally emerged from data: 'Anselm's (Strauss) methodology is one full of conceptual description and mine is grounded theory. They are very different, the first focusing on forcing and the second on emergence. The first keeping all of the problems of forcing data, the second giving them up in favor of emergence, discovery, and inductive theory generation' (Glaser, 1992, 122).

There are many published grounded theory studies which contain obvious mistakes (Skodal-Wilson and Ambler-Hutchinson, 1996); this and the clear conflict between Glaser and Strauss can often make neophyte researchers wary of attempting this type of analysis. Although the differences between the two approaches are very distinct, errors usually occur more in the application of the principles than in the actual analysis. A researcher needs to be very sure that grounded theory fits the purpose of the research and the nature of the research question. Before we look at the actual process in Part 4, we can examine the underlying principles that related to grounded theory. For a more detailed discussion of the conflict that developed between Glaser and Strauss in relation to LIS research see Selden (2005). Examples of LIS research using grounded theory include developing theories of information-seeking behaviour (Ellis, 1990, 1993 and 1996; Ellis and Haugan, 1997), identifying the major issues that influence academic library development (Badu, 2004), studying children's information literacy (Filipenko, 2004), and investigating how young people interact with electronic information (Pickard, 2002). Taking a grounded theory approach allows for 'the generation of theories and models' which are developed 'inductively from empirical data' (Ellis, 1993, 473).

Although I do not see grounded theory as a method, the principles of grounded theory may influence the design of a method. In this chapter we will examine these principles and look at how they may influence our research design, regardless of the method we adopt. The roots of grounded theory lie in symbolic interactionism; Blumer's (1937) development of the interactionist approach together with investigation in natural settings was a major influence on grounded theory (Hammersley, 1989). Grounded theory, although developed as an approach for analysing social phenomena, is particularly applicable to LIS research involving users. This approach is 'concerned with discovering *process* – not necessarily in the sense of stages and phases, but of reciprocal changes in patterns of action/interaction and relationships with changes of conditions either internal or external to process itself' (Strauss and Corbin, 1994, 278).

Defining grounded theory

What defines grounded theory is not a particular research method but a set of components and principles that need to be included in the research design (that could be the design of an ethnographic study, a case study or action research). Going back to the origins of this approach from 1967 and looking at the work of today's most prominent grounded theorists we can see what it means to engage in grounded theory research. The major principles of grounded theory are:

- the research question
- simultaneous data collection and analysis
- sampling towards theory construction
- constructing data categories from empirical data
- developing theory during each step of the data collection and analysis
- memo-writing as way of advancing theory (Charmaz, 2006).

In this chapter we will focus on the principles behind these components and in Part 4 (Chapter 21) we will explore grounded theory analysis. We will look at two distinct versions of this process, the 'constant comparative method' of Strauss and Corbin (1998) and the more open (and some claim more true to the original concept of grounded theory) approach: the 'theoretical sensitivity' of Glaser (1978): 'To take a *grounded theory approach* to research is to combine theoretical sampling, data collection, design of data collection, data analysis and theory generation, in one wholly interactive, iterative and interdependent process. The approach is an assemblage of all of these activities, which then allows a theory to emerge that is grounded in the data' (Pickard, 2002, 17).

The research question

A grounded theory approach to research is solely focused on discovery. It is a process of analysis that is intended neither to answer specific questions nor to test an existing hypothesis. 'Grounded theory methods are suitable for studying individual processes, interpersonal relations and the reciprocal effects between individuals and larger social processes' (Charmaz, 1995, 28). We usually go into the research with no more than a very open, and often broad, question with grounded theory; the focus is usually on social processes or interaction. In LIS the information-seeking process has been the focus of a number of research studies; the question most of these studies begin with is something like 'How do people engage in the information seeking process?'; the only focus is the process and the particular user group. The purpose is discovery, to engage in research to find out what is going on and why; the research begins with a very broad question and it is not until the researcher begins to observe and collect data that a focus starts to emerge. Charmaz provides a number of ways in which we can engage in questioning without restricting our investigation:

- Watch for actions and processes as well as what people say.
- Delineate the context of actions carefully.
- Record what was done by whom and why.
- Identify the conditions under which actions, intentions and processes emerge (2006, 21).

This provides the rich depth of data that is necessary to produce theory; in relation to the information-seeking process these guides for watching, listening and recording are particularly pertinent. We begin with a single, open question then explore that question in all of its potential forms; the salient issues emerge as we begin to interpret what is going on. Grounded theory cannot begin with rigid, a priori assumptions concerning the context, the process or the issues. Specific, detailed questions rarely exist at the beginning of research taking a grounded theory approach; these questions emerge as we begin to observe the situation or process that interests us.

Simultaneous data collection and analysis

In grounded theory it is important to emphasize the 'simultaneous involvement in data collection and analysis phases of the research' (Charmaz, 1995, 28). Inductive data analysis is an ongoing process from the outset; the method of analysis is essential to the formulation of a theory grounded in the raw data. The 'data collection and analysis go hand in hand to promote the emergence of substantive theory grounded in empirical data' (Marshall and Rossman, 1989, 113). Regardless of how a data collection begins, whether by an interview, an observation or a discussion with a group of research participants, this initial data is the first step in our analysis. It is impossible to conduct this type of research by engaging in a data collection phase and then move on to a data analysis phase; the process does not allow for this linear approach. We have to take an iterative approach, constantly moving between data collection and analysis. Analysing our initial data serves a number of purposes. First, it gives us our initial, however tenuous, categories; second, it guides our next steps in data collection, which include decisions about both the 'type' of data we may need and the people we are likely to get it from. This means that these decisions are based on what we learn from sampling and designing the data collection as well as from empirical data.

Grounded theory relies on rich data – detailed and full descriptions of events, emotions, reactions and so on. This usually means we must carry out intensive interviewing and observation. We will look at data collection in Part 3; the important thing to remember here is that grounded theory involves simultaneous data collection and analysis. When engaging in grounded theory research I have always scheduled intensive interviews based on the time I would be with the participant, the time it would take me to transcribe the interview, and the time it would take me to complete my initial analysis of the interview, where possible doing this as one timetabled activity. This is not always possible and is very demanding on the researcher; what matters is that analysis is carried out before you move on to the next data collection activity.

Sampling towards theory construction

The logic and power of purposeful sampling lies in selecting information-rich cases for study in depth. Information-rich cases are those from which one can learn a great deal about issues of central importance to the purpose of the research, thus the term purposeful sampling.   (Patton, 1990, 169)

In grounded theory the approach to sampling is always purposive and always *theoretical*. Many texts discuss theoretical and purposive sampling as if they were the same thing; they are not, theoretical sampling is a type of purpose sampling. Theoretical sampling is driven by the data; there can be no a priori identification of precise participants, as we do not know what it is we need to know until we begin to interrogate our data. 'Theoretical sampling involves starting with data, constructing tentative ideas about the data, and then examining these ideas through further empirical inquiry' (Charmaz, 2006, 102). The size and structure of the sample cannot be known in advance; the only guideline is to 'sample a category until confident of its saturation' (Glaser and Strauss, 1967, 70).

Constructing categories from empirical data

Coding is the pivotal link between collecting data and developing an emergent theory to explain these data. Through coding, you define what is happening in the data and begin to grapple with what it means.   (Charmaz, 2006, 46)

Developing categories begins with coding the data; the categories will emerge from the rules we create for our codes as the higher level conceptual form of the codes. Codes are created as shorthand descriptors of each data element; categories are developed as descriptions of the codes. This process ensures that the categories did emerge from the data and were not created by the researcher without any empirical evidence. Some purists maintain that use of existing theories in grounded theory research belongs only as a final stage in the research, reviewing the literature at the end of the empirical analysis as a way of identifying any relationship with emerging theory. This is not usually the case; the use of prior theories that are themselves grounded firmly in the raw data of previous research has always been seen as an important part of grounded theory (Glaser and Strauss, 1967; Lincoln and Guba, 1985; Guba and Lincoln, 1988; Glaser, 1992; Charmaz, 1995; Walsh, 1998). However, such prior theory should not in itself influence the data collection and analysis of the new research, although it may act as a set of signposts for the researcher: 'The design of all research requires conceptual bridges from what is already known, cognitive structures to guide data gathering, and outlines for presenting interpretations to others' (Stake, 1995, 15).

Grounded theory relies on the creation of codes and categories that have emerged from the data and are not preconceived hypotheses. These are then tested in real world situations. We will examine the process involved in Part 4.

Continuous theory development
The purpose of grounded theory is to produce theory based on empirical evidence:

'grounded theory is derived from the data and then illustrated by characteristic examples of the data' (Glaser and Strauss, 1967, 5). Theory emerges from the data and grows as we confirm and add to it through further empirical investigation. The theory is interpretivist as it relies on the interpretations placed on the evidence by the researcher. The point is that there is evidence to support the interpretation. There are no massive leaps of faith in grounded theory, no huge assumptions based on scant evidence. This is not about 'absolute truth', it is about interpretation of actions, interactions, process, thought and feelings discovered in the field and given meaning by the researcher. The evidence is there: the players, the context, and the entire social milieu that makes up the environment. The point is that we do not go out, collect copious amounts of empirical data, lock ourselves away in a garret and attempt to draw a formal theory from the data. This is a process that begins very early in the research, with the first analysis, and grows as the research moves on, constantly shifting and developing.

A grounded theory 'must correspond closely to the data if it is to be applied in daily situations' (Glaser and Strauss, 1967, 238). That means intimate and constant interaction with the data allows theory to emerge, not looking for specific data to confirm a preconceived idea or assumption. There are two major stages in theory development, the first is to produce *substantive theory*, which is directly related to, and situated in, the substantive area of investigation. This theory comes first and is directly relevant to the context of the research investigation dealing with very specific and 'real' events. From substantive theory *formal theory* is developed which takes the theory to a higher level of abstraction. Formal theories rarely emerge from a single study; single studies tend to produce substantive theories relating to the specific situation, which is usually exactly what the researcher wants, particularly if it is practitioner research that is focused on their own situation. They are asking questions to understand their own world, so substantive theory can provide the insight they need. Formal theories tend to develop as an accumulation of empirical knowledge from more than one study; very often the formal theory could come from researchers other than those who developed the initial substantive theory. The example given in the chapter shows how theory grows and develops; in this example the theory is a model of information-seeking behaviour. The research began within a very specific research context with very specific players in the social milieu. Over time this theory was extended and developed; the empirical evidence used to support this theory not only increased in depth but also extended in breadth, to cover wider contexts but losing nothing in terms of rich data.

The significance of theory that has emerged directly from the data means also that researchers, practitioners and lay people alike can understand it because it has been arrived at from real world evidence not abstract conceptualization (Glaser and Strauss, 1967). Theory develops during the research as a result of the constant analysis of new and existing data, and depends entirely on the researcher engaging in extensive interaction with the data. Memo writing is the usual way of encouraging this level of interaction.

Memo-writing to advance theory

'Memo-writing is the pivotal intermediate step between data collection and writing drafts of papers' (Charmaz, 2006, 72). Theory emerges as a process of constant inter-action with the evidence and emerging categories; this means continuous commentary by the researcher on that data in the form of memos (Glaser, 1998). Usually memos are written as attachments to the data or kept in a well maintained researcher's diary or log. In Part 3 we will look at the various uses of a research diary and discuss those uses in more detail; here we will look at the purpose of memo writing. Essentially it is a written commentary on the data, an interpretation of data as it is gathered.

Memo writing has a number of benefits for grounded theory. Primarily it is the process of visualizing your analysis, thinking aloud about what you are seeing, reading, feeling and understanding in your data. It forces you to stop and think about the data, to make sense of it and give it some meaning in the context of your research question. This constant writing allows you to develop your own rhythm in terms of emerging theory and it helps to initiate ideas about relationships within the data. Because you are writing about real data this process helps to keep you grounded in the evidence and not force your data into extant concepts that may be far removed for the actual evidence in front of you. Memo-writing is a very useful way of identifying gaps in your data, showing up areas which appear to have been overlooked or need further investigation. In qualitative research it is very important that you find your voice as a researcher; constant writing encourages you to do that. Memos are close to the data, even when they begin to go beyond individual categories and start discussing evidence across categories. This helps to ensure that your final theory will also be close to that data. Memos link the whole process of data collection, analysis and research reporting. They are your own private dialogue with the data, as you think about the words, actions, feelings and relationships you have witnessed and attempt to make sense of them in rhetoric.

'Memo-writing forms a space and place for exploration and discovery. You take the time to discover your ideas about what you have seen, heard, sensed, and coded' (Charmaz, 2006, 81). Memos change in nature as the research progresses and move from usually short and very directed statements about individual data, to more intricate discussions concerning relationships and patterns. This is a private space for interaction; ultimately it is up to you how much of this you share. I always encourage people to be as honest and open as possible in memos, not wasting time trying to make grand statements, but speaking about the data in words that make sense to you. A memo is a private diary; you are using your words to make sense of the research setting, just as many people use diaries to make sense of their private worlds. Memo writing is part of the data analysis. Although we will discuss it more when we talk of Glaser's 'theoretical sensitivity' it also plays a part in the constant comparative method of Strauss and Corbin. Because memos are regarded as 'data' we will look at 'collecting' this type of data when we discuss diaries.

Example 14.1 Grounded theory research

Research carried out over a number of years by Ellis (1989 and 1993), Ellis, Cox and Hall (1993) and Ellis and Haugan (1997) demonstrates how the grounded theory technique can lead to the discovery of theory and the subsequent testing of that theory.

Initially Ellis (1989) carried out an investigation to determine the information-seeking process of academic researchers in the social sciences, using the elements of grounded theory; a model emerged from this research that began to identify patterns in behaviour. This produced the initial substantive theory. Later this theory was used as the starting point for another investigation into the information-seeking process of physicists and chemists (1993). This study was then extended to focus on researchers outside the academic arena, investigating engineers and research scientists in industry and business (Ellis and Haugan, 1997). Although all subsequent studies had an established theory to work with, this still fits the grounded theory approach as 'emerging' remained central to the investigation. At each stage, each new research project applied open interviewing as a data collection technique; a priori assumptions were not allowed to control the direction of the questioning and as data was collected it was used comparatively with data from previous studies. This led to the formulation of a *formal theory* which has relevance and significance on a broader scale.

This series of studies demonstrates the nature of theory that emerges from grounded theory research. Social theory is never static, it remains subject to change and shift. The models that emerged from the work of Ellis et al. provide a broad framework, not a rigid representation of behaviour.

Summary

Glaser and Strauss define a grounded theory as being one that will be 'readily applicable to and indicated by the data' and 'be meaningfully relevant to and be able to explain the behavior under study' (Glaser and Strauss, 1967, 3). Grounded theory is not a research method, it is a process for the logical analysis of qualitative data. However, there are a number of 'guiding principles', which need to be followed if any researcher wishes to claim they have used grounded theory in their work. Glaser (1998) tells us that rather than talking about it we should get on with it, engage in active discovery allowing the data to speak and not be forced.

In Part 4 you can look at the two approaches to data analysis, now widely used under the same 'grounded theory' banner. The important thing is that grounded theory is a cognitive process. We all have very different cognitive styles and deciding which approach best suits your own natural way of thinking and processing data is the best advice I can offer. What really matters is that the research as a whole follows the principles discussed in this chapter. We have to walk into the research setting with an open mind but, as Dey points out, 'there is a difference between an open mind and an empty head. To analyse data, we need to use accumulated knowledge, not dispense with it' (Dey, 1993, 65). To carry out grounded theory analysis it is necessary to be open to all eventualities and not allow prior theory to drive the data collection nor the analysis. The emphasis must always remain on theory emerging from the data.

PRACTICAL EXERCISE

Grounded theory is essentially a process of analysis; the practical application is concerned with handling data, how to harvest appropriate data and how to conduct analysis that allows the data to lead the theory building process. In Chapter 21 we will look at a structured approach to generating grounded theory, the 'constant comparative analysis' of Strauss and Corbin (1998) and the 'theoretical sensitivity' approach of Glaser (1978). Practical exercises in that chapter will deal with handling data.

Here we will try a simple exercise that looks at the principles of grounded theory. Identify a topic that interests you, either in your workplace or something you have touched on in your studies.

1 Construct an open question about the topic that includes no preconceived ideas.
2 Identify your first task in exploring this question.

This is as far as we will go for now. This sounds very simple but the major question you need to ask yourself is, how much am I prepared to 'let go' and trust in the process? One of the most difficult aspects of grounded theory research is the ability of the researcher to follow where the data leads and not be forced by preconceived ideas about the topic. Could you be a grounded theory researcher?

Suggested further reading

Charmaz, K. (2006) Constructing Grounded Theory: a practical guide through qualitative analysis, London, Sage.

Glaser, B. (1992) *Emergence Versus Forcing: basics of grounded theory analysis*, Mill Valley, CA, Sociology Press.

Glaser, B. G. and Strauss, A. L. (1967) *The Discovery of Grounded Theory*, New York, Aldine.

Selden, L. (2005) On Grounded Theory - With Some Malice, *Journal of Documentation*, **61** (1), 114-29.

Strauss, A. and Corbin, J. (1998) *Basics of Qualitative Research: techniques and procedures for developing grounded theory*, London, Sage.

PART 3

Data collection techniques

PART 3

Data collection techniques

This section will deal with individual techniques for collecting empirical data. As I said in the opening section of this book, data collection techniques are not necessarily directly associated with specific research methods. Very often particular techniques for the collection of empirical data are presented as if they are synonymous with particular research methods, for example a questionnaire or a survey. I do not regard these as the same and hope that the distinction is made clear in this text. Your choice of research method does not necessarily restrict you to a particular technique for the collection of your empirical data, although sometimes this may be the case. This is usually because a particular technique is the most commonly applied, not because it is the only choice available. As I have pointed out in earlier chapters, research is a constantly evolving process, just because something has 'always been done that way' is not a good enough reason to continue doing it that way. We learn by trying and adapting what tools we have. I am going to discuss the most common of those tools here. How you apply them and in what context to choose to apply them is up to you within whatever constraints are imposed on you by academic or organizational requirements. Remember, success and failure in research are very tenuous concepts; finding out what *does not* work can be as useful as finding out what does.

Here is my understanding and interpretation of a selection of data collection techniques. Consider your research question, your research focus, your data sources and your own life experience and make your selection based on 'best fit for purpose'. I would urge you to take the occasional risk and sometimes take the less common approach, but that does not mean I would want you to jeopardize the success of your research in an attempt to be overly adventurous. Weigh up your experience and your goals, seek advice from your supervisors or mentors then go out and collect your data in the most appropriate way for you. This can often be the most challenging element of the research process but in my opinion it is also the most exciting and rewarding. It is amazing what you see when you start looking.

Each chapter will examine a particular technique in detail, discussing the purpose, format, design and delivery of the technique. One stage that you will find is repeated over and over in each chapter is the piloting of your research instrument. Regardless of the nature of that instrument, be it a printed questionnaire, an interview guide, or an observation map, I cannot over emphasize the need to test your instrument before you approach your research participants. There is nothing that can replace testing. Even a pilot interview may not reveal all the potential problems, but it is the closest you will get to the real thing without wasting time and energy asking the wrong questions, asking them in the wrong way or asking them of the wrong people. I have yet to see a research instrument that has not been improved based on the results of a pilot study. It is the surest way of knowing how your research instrument will perform and is as vital to your data collection as the instrument itself.

A single research design may include one or more data collection techniques. If you are aiming for methodological triangulation then you will be engaging in a number of data collection techniques. There is no rigidly prescribed combination, it is up to you, your topic and your study population. People may tell you what they do in an interview but you may want to watch them do it to see if their interpretation of a certain behaviour matches yours so you will observe the situation as well as ask questions about it. The possible combinations are what makes a research design your own.

Remember that data collection and data analysis often go hand in hand; think carefully about selecting and designing your data collection tools and remember that whatever is gathered needs to be analysed. Try to plan ahead and be aware of the nature of the data you will be harvesting and exactly what you plan to do with it. Regardless of which data collection techniques you decide to use in your research design there are a number of general points which apply in almost all cases.

1 Be very sure of what you are doing before you enter the field. The truth about real world research is that it is very much 'the art of the possible' (Robson, 1997). Access to a field site is very often only possible because of prior relationships and connections; sometimes we have to engage in fieldwork before we have had time to do all of the detailed preparation that I have outlined in preceding chapters. We go in because we can and we go in when we can. Few researchers will discuss this when they write up their final account but it happens more often than you might suspect. You may not have had time to complete an exhaustive literature review, but take heart, as long as you know *why* you are there and you know *how* you intend to collect your data then you have a sound start. Many research studies will be iterative, moving between empirical data collection and the literature; what you do need is to be very sure of what you are there to see, hear and feel.

2 If you do not have connections within the field site then you will need to negotiate access. Don't leave this until the week before you want to engage in your data collection. Novice researchers are inclined to put this stage off, as they are rather nervous about contacting officials. Arrange your access as soon as possible. It can take time and don't be down hearted if you feel you get passed from one potential 'gatekeeper' to another. Persevere but do it politely. Read the

chapter on case study research for a detailed discussion concerning entry to the field.

3 Make sure you have informed consent before you begin collecting data. This could range from the very informal to the very formal signed consent form. Be aware of what you need and use the correct channels to get it.

4 Always pilot your data collection instrument before you apply it to your research subjects.

5 Prepare a detailed timetable of your fieldwork for yourself and your research subjects.

6 Don't be surprised if things don't go exactly as you planned. I'd be more surprised if they did. This is the real thing, not theory and rarely will it proceed without you having to 'think on your feet'.

7 Enjoy it, or at least look as if you are enjoying it. Nothing cuts off the flow of data more swiftly than a researcher who looks bored or irritated. Remember you will be asking a lot of people for their time and effort; without them you have no research, so treat them with the respect they deserve.

8 Thank your participants in whatever way is appropriate, whether with a letter, a simple verbal 'thank you' or an acknowledgment in the final report. Don't just walk away.

Chapter 15

Interviews

Conversation is a basic mode of human interaction. Human beings talk to each other. . . .
Through conversations we get to know other people, get to learn about their experiences,
feelings, and hopes and the world they live in.   (Kvale, 1996, 5)

Introduction

The research interview can take a number of different forms, from the very
structured, formal interview which is usually a researcher-administered
questionnaire, to the very informal, purposeful conversation (Dexter, 1970; Lincoln
and Guba, 1989), usually led by the participant with the researcher not taking
control of the process until it comes to the analysis and interpretation (Tagg, 1985).
Between these extreme poles it is possible to design an interview that is appropriate
to the topic of the research, the nature of the participant and the experience of the
researcher. I would never recommend that a neophyte interviewer attempted a totally
unstructured conversation as their first ever experience. Not only is the prospect a
daunting one but also lack of experience could lead to very little being taken away
from the interview situation.

The only way to become a *good* interviewer is to practise; there is no secret formula
to becoming an expert interviewer if there is such a thing. It is all down to knowing
your topic and knowing yourself and how you react in the interview situation.
Knowing your topic is the easy part; your literature review should have you 'steeped' in
the topic. Knowing yourself is a different matter. If you decide to use interviews in your
research then spend time practising your technique. The best way to start is to choose
a topic you are very familiar with, then choose a friend who is also familiar with this
topic. Design a set of questions, keep it as informal as you wish then engage in a
purposeful conversation. The difference between this and any other conversation you
might have with this friend on this topic is that this time you will collect data, and have
evidence of what was said in the form of answers to your questions. We will look at
formal piloting later; this interview practice is more concerned with gauging your own
ability as an attentive, interested, alert and responsive interviewer.

Interviews are used frequently in information and library research. Recent
examples include a study by Hartley and Booth (2006) to discover 'how users use

and view union catalogues and to consider the views of librarians towards union catalogues'. Crumley (2006) used interviews to investigate 'the role of health care professionals and librarians involved with complementary and alternative medicine (CAM)'. There are many more examples of research studies that have used interviews to gain in-depth understanding of individual perceptions.

Before you decide what form of interview will suit you best you have to decide if indeed the interview is the most appropriate technique to use. In order to help you make this decision you have to understand the purpose of the research interview: what can an interview contribute to your research? What can an interview do that no other technique could do, or at least not do as well? Is the interview 'fit for purpose'? Once you have made this decision then you can go on to decide on the form the interview will take and the details of the process.

What is the purpose of an interview?

The purpose of an interview is to access what was in, and on, the interviewee's mind, (Stenhouse, 1984). We interview when that is the most appropriate way to access the data we need. Other constraints will always drive decisions about data collection but the predominant factor should always be the nature of the data we seek and the type of questions we need to ask to access that data: 'A major advantage of the interview is that it permits the respondent to move back and forth in time – to reconstruct the past, interpret the present, and predict the future, all without leaving a comfortable armchair' (Lincoln and Guba, 1985, 273).

Interviews are usually used when we are seeking qualitative, descriptive, in-depth data that is specific to the individual and when the nature of the data is too complicated to be asked and answered easily. This does not apply to researcher-administered questionnaires but all other interviews allow for some degree of interaction between the researcher and the subject. Interviews can be used for reconstruction of events, descriptions and feelings about current events and predictions of future developments. You are discovering individual opinions; the information you get from interviews is different from pure factual data. If you want precise dates, times or measurements, or indeed any type of quantifiable data, interviews are not really the most appropriate tool to use. It is very rare that individuals can instantly recall any great quantity of precise factual data without consulting records of some kind. The interview situation is not particularly conducive to the reproduction of complicated and exact data; you talk to people to discover what they think, feel and remember about events. Interviews allow people to respond on their own terms and within their own linguistic parameters, providing them and the interviewer with the opportunity to clarify meanings and shared understanding (Bertrand and Hughes, 2005).

The seven stages of the interview process

Kvale (1996) sets out seven stages of the interview process: thematizing, designing, interviewing, transcribing, analysing, verifying and reporting. The process is not always as linear as this suggests, however. Depending on the nature of the interviews analysis could begin as soon as the first interview is complete; in the case of the purposeful conversation this should most definitely be the case. We can use these stages as a broad outline of the process but be prepared for iteration, particularly in the final three stages when engaging in unstructured interviews.

Thematizing

'The "*why*" and "*what*" of the investigation need to be clarified before the question of "*how*"' (Kvale, 1996, 88). Before even thinking about particular interview types or formats, you need to be clear about the purpose of your research and the topic you are investigating. You need to establish themes within your topic and make sure these themes are appropriate to each interviewee; in many studies you may be asking different people different things. Once you have identified your themes you should attempt to structure them in a natural order that allows the interviewee to follow a logical thought process and allows you, the interviewer, to gain a growing understanding of their feelings, behaviour and beliefs.

Designing

The purpose of using an interview guide is to 'ensure that each interview covers basically the same ground but gives the interviewer considerable discretion in the conduct of the interview' (Ellis, 1993, 475). The degree to which the guide 'controls' the interview depends very much on the type of interview. The guide can range from a strict 'script' not only providing predetermined questions but also providing a limited number of response categories, to a list of topics the interviewer wishes to cover. Example 15.1 on page 180 is a 'semi-structured' general guide designed to be used with young teenagers (Pickard, 2002). For those of you new to the interview process I would suggest that this is as far as you go in terms of keeping the interview open. For many of you it may be too open. Be sure of the extent of structure you require before you enter the field. This example was actually the first interview in a series of interviews with the same group of respondents; as time went on the interviews became increasing less structured and many took place during observations. This interview was designed to identify salient issues and formed the ground work for the 18 months of fieldwork that followed.

Your design will depend very much on the type of interview you decide to engage in. For the very structured, formal interview you would be better advised to read the next chapter and design the guide as you would a questionnaire.

Interviewing

> Conduct the interviews based on an interview guide and with a reflective approach to the knowledge sought and the interpersonal relation of the interview situation.
>
> (Kvale, 1996, 88)

I find it rather strange to be writing this section as I have spent so many years telling my students that they can read all the theory available on conducting an interview and it will never totally prepare them for the real thing . . . and here I am adding more theory that will never be as useful as sitting opposite a research participant and engaging in that all important conversation. I will give my interpretation of the theory of the interview but I will also share some mistakes I have made; some things that all the theory in the world could not have prepared me for.

Interviewing depends very much on the rapport built between the interviewer and the interviewee; it is the responsibility of the interviewer to make the interviewee feel comfortable and relaxed. This is not an easy task for inexperienced interviewers, not least because they are likely to be rather nervous themselves. This is why I always recommend that although piloting for structure and question style is extremely important you must also practise your technique.

There are a number of things you can do to make the interviewee and yourself feel more comfortable. If you appear relaxed your interviewee is much more likely to open up and relax too, but please remember there is a difference between 'relaxed' and complacent. You really need to know your questions, and I mean 'know' in the sense that you are completely aware of why you are there, not that you can recite a list of questions rigidly. You need to be able to flow with the situation, listen carefully and follow up on what you hear and learn. Interviews demand preparation, so prepare thoroughly.

First impressions count: when you arrive at the interview make sure you are dressed appropriately. A good example of this – in reverse – is described on page 117, and shows how easily people make judgements based on your appearance!

Timing is also very important. When you request an interview you must indicate how much time you will be taking up and it is important that you do not exceed the time you have asked for. Finishing early, but not too early, is always better than over staying your welcome. Try to estimate as accurately as possible the time the interview will take. This should be easier after the first real interview but the pilot test will help you before you enter the field.

Types of interview

The type of interview you decide on depends first on the nature of your research topic and the sort of data you need to collect to respond to your research question. After that there are the more practical considerations such as your own experience, the time you have available, the number of respondents you want to reach and also your analysis. Think very careful about gathering data. Analysing 100 questionnaires or closed, fixed-response interviews is a lot less complicated than analysing 20 unstructured, in-depth conversations.

> Traditionally this has been associated with a mutual reading of presentation of self. In any social situation there is a swift appraisal of age, gender and ethnicity; of accent, dress and personal grooming; of conventionality, eccentricity and subcultural marker; of confidence

levels, physical attractiveness, friendliness or restraint. In addition, oral dimensions of language (pitch, tone and so on) might identify whether what was said was spoken from a position of confidence, doubt, irony and so forth. (Mann and Stewart, 2000, 126)

Structured interviews

'*Structured interviewing* refers to a situation in which an interviewer asks each respondent a series of preestablished questions with a limited set of response categories' (Fontana and Frey, 1994, 363). This is often referred to as the 'researcher administered questionnaire' as it is highly structured and follows many of the same guidelines as a questionnaire. You will be very limited here in terms of acting as the research instrument; the structured interview framework is actually the instrument here and you must resist the temptation to react, respond or expand on the contents of the framework. Many would claim that this type of interview 'wastes' the majority of the benefits of interviewing, namely the ability of the researcher to become part of the conversation (more about this in the next section on unstructured interviews).

There are two forms of structured interview. In a *standardized, open-ended interview* all interviewees are asked the same, open-ended questions but allowed to respond in any way they feel is appropriate and with any information they choose to share. In a *closed, fixed-response interview* interviewees are asked the same questions and choose from a predetermined set of alternative answers. It is also possible to use a combination of the two methods.

Although this type of interview is very similar to the questionnaire the major benefit is the visual and oral clues you can pick up by listening to and watching your respondent. Although the content of the interview remains standardized, your role as the research instrument can still be useful in terms of interpreting the nature of the response. For example, is the answer given ironically? Does the interviewee look nervous or confident? You can learn a lot from *how* something is said; it is not only *what* is said that contributes to your research. Of course there is also the increased control the research has over response rates; you leave each 'interview' with your data complete and you can measure as you go how much data you are gathering. This eliminates the risk of poor response rates so common with typical questionnaire distribution. There is also the added benefit of being able to pre-code as you would with a questionnaire; this saves time during the analysis. I would recommend the structured interview approach to anyone who is new to the interview process.

Unstructured interviews

Unstructured interviews are used to gain a holistic understanding of the thoughts and feelings of the interviewee: you are there to learn about their point of view. Very often this type of interview is used in the early stages of the research to explore salient issues for further investigation (see Example 15.1 on page 180). Unstructured interviews are concerned with open-ended questions that allow the interviewee to tell their own story in their own words.

Patton (1987, 113) describes two approaches to conducting unstructured interviewing: the informal conversation and the general interview guide. The *informal conversational interview* is the 'purposeful conversation' mentioned earlier. It is important to allow questions to flow from the immediate context; you must listen carefully and respond to the interviewee. You will have to be very familiar with your topic and very comfortable with the interview situation to engage in this type of interview. It demands a very high level of concentration and the ability to be very reflective and reflexive. Listen and respond as you would in any conversation, taking care to steer your interviewee along your lines of interest. People can be very passionate about certain areas of a topic and although you need to know this you may also need to ask them about other areas that are not their primary concern. There is an art to steering a purposeful conversation as well as a craft. You need to appear to hang on every word even when the conversation turns a corner you were not anticipating; this corner may or may not be very beneficial to the research, you have to decide. Remember, you came here for their point of view; if that provides you with something unexpected, many would say 'all the better', but you have to know how to react to this. This is not an easy activity; many view it as the most difficult form of data collection and for that reason I would never recommend it to someone new to the research process. There is an alternative, the *general interview guide approach* (commonly called the *guided interview*).

In a guided interview the researcher prepares a basic checklist to make sure that all relevant areas of the topic are covered. You are still free to explore, probe and ask a question not previously specified when something interests you. This type of interview approach is useful for eliciting information about specific topics. Example 15.1 (on page 180) is just such a guide; the areas that need to be covered are there but there is opportunity to follow any strands that were not expected. The example guide was used with 16 young teenagers and although the data gathered varied considerably, the guide was never altered during the first round of interviews (although I did replace the word 'information' with 'stuff' after the first few interviews).

Recording

How you record your interview depends on a number of external variables as well as personal preference. Audio recording brings with it a lot of security; people feel much better if they think they will leave the interview with a full recording of everything that was said and this is true, or at least it usually is. I travelled a considerable distance once to interview members of a parent teachers' association; after a day of interviews and a long drive back I arrived home and eagerly switched on my tape machine. To my absolute horror the tapes were blank! I discovered later that I had accidentally flicked a switch on the side of the machine as I was getting it out of my briefcase which had disabled the record facility, a switch I did not even know was there. Fortunately I had taken copious notes so the interviews were not wasted but it could have been a disaster. Since then I have always become very familiar with my equipment before conducting any interviews.

Recording may provide a secure way of keeping all of the data but it can sometimes have a negative impact on the interview. Many people feel inhibited by the fact that their words will be recorded; it makes them very conscious of what they are saying and how they say it so you may choose to make a trade-off and opt for no recording in order to make your interviewee feel more comfortable. Of course some interviewees could simply refuse to be recorded; this is their right and you should always respect this. Unless your intention is to transcribe every single word of the interview there may be no real need to record at all. You could always choose to take notes; the problem here is that you could be so busy writing things down you miss important data. There is a fine balance between noting important information and remaining actively involved in the conversation. If you enter the interview with a note pad ready prepared, topics listed and a space for relevant verbatim quotes then this could make life a lot easier. I use a small A5 perforated note pad. I list the topics on the verso side of the first page; that way I have access to my list at all times. I write down anything I may want to use as evidence in the form of verbatim quotes opposite on the next page. This is marked with the code I am using for that interviewee. Once I move to the next interview I simple remove the response notes and I'm ready to start the next interview with a clean page.

Each technique for recording has advantages and disadvantages; you have to decide on the most appropriate technique for you, or the most convenient in the situation. The important thing is that you leave the interview with all the data you need in a form that you can understand. I often attempt to discourage the use of audio recording as I feel it can sometimes lull the interviewer into a false sense of security and they cease to be as active in the process as they would otherwise be, not paying close enough attention because they think they can listen to it all later. This is fair enough if your only role is to ask a set of questions but that is not why you engage in a purposeful conversation. Your role here is to *listen*, *reflect* and *respond*. You need to remain fully engaged in the interview at all times. Once again, it is practice as well as available resources that will guide your choice.

Transcribing

I always suggest that transcription be done as soon after the interview as possible. Whenever I schedule an interview I always allow the time for the interview then two hours immediately after for initial transcription. In qualitative research this means initial transcription and analysis as you should be interpreting the data as you process it, noting themes as they emerge or making notes in the form of memos to yourself. More detail is provided in Part 4 when we look at qualitative analysis, but for now I would ask you to consider seriously the interview and the initial transcription as a single activity.

I am frequently asked about the detail needed in transcription: 'Do I need to transcribe every single word?' is the usual question I get asked, asked with an underlying sense of despair by the researcher! Interviews can produce vast amounts of unbounded data. Open-ended, unstructured interviews allow the interviewee to talk at length about the topic, and very often this is at length, not all of it being pertinent to your research question. You may decide to transcribe every word. In ethnographic studies and often case studies this should be the case. You are there to understand the experience of the research subject, that means everything they tell you. In surveys it is more usual to be listening or reading for specific themes. In this case then you may only choose to transcribe the relevant sections or particularly significant sections that you intend to use as evidence. This is not possible if you are taking a grounded theory approach as the theory emerges from the data and you are not in a position to decide what is pertinent and what is not in the early stages of the fieldwork.

What you transcribe depends very much on the way you recorded the interview; audio recording allows for full transcription, note taking does not, but if you write up the interview immediately after leaving the interview you will be in a much better position to remember how things were said and more detail around the notes you have taken. Be careful when adding your own comments to hand-written notes; make sure you are not tempted to 'pad out' what was said.

If you are engaging in qualitative research I would strongly recommend that you do not fall into the trap of conducting ten to 20 interviews before you begin the transcription process. First, that is not the way to engage in emerging qualitative research; each interview can inform the next, there is no reason to stick to a rigid set of questions if this will not achieve your research goals. You can learn from one interview before you move on to the next. Second, the amount of work and time involved in transcription is extremely daunting, particularly if you are the sole researcher on the project, which you will be if this is dissertation research. If you are asking the same questions and looking for a few significant themes then you may use the same interview with all respondents. Even then I would suggest you transcribe the interview after it takes place. Only with researcher administered questionnaires would I suggest collecting all the data analysing it; precoding will make this much easier.

Analysing
Analysis of interviews will be discussed in Part 4, but for now it is important to stress that in qualitative research analysis is a constant, ongoing element of the research process; it begins during the interview, and each time you reflect on what you hear and ask a follow-up question you will have engaged in initial analysis.

Verifying
Kvale (1996) uses the verification stage to refer to the extent to which the interview asked what it was intended to ask: did it answer the research question? I would agree with this but add another, very different, interpretation of the verifying stage. I see it as a form of 'member check' (Lincoln and Guba, 1985). After the interviews have been transcribed and analysed it is possible to return to the interviewee and confirm that your interpretation matches theirs: did you understand what they had intended you to understand? There is the possibility that the interviewee might deny something you thought they had said, but I have yet to be faced with a problem like

this; each time I have verified my interpretation of an interview it has usually been confirmed by the interviewee, in some cases it has even harvested more data, more detail on a particular subject.

Reporting

Again this stage is discussed in Part 4. In your research report your evidence from interviews will form the foundation of your emerging theory; remember that the spoken word is evidence. Quite often a lot of work goes into transcribing and analysing, then when it comes to reporting for some reason researchers forget that those verbatim quotes are evidence. Your interpretation of what was said is an essential part of your report, but the actual evidence on which you based that interpretation is also important.

Online interviewing

There is still significant debate surrounding the use of computer mediated communication (CMC) in the researcher process. Interviewing online is no exception to this debate. I have already discussed the importance of establishing rapport with interviewees and the visual clues we pick up during an interview. This 'sense of other' (Mann and Stewart, 2000) can be lost when the interview situation changes from a physical meeting to a synchronous or asynchronous exchange of words on a screen. In this case is it possible to conduct a qualitative interview without all the visual and verbal clues we are familiar with from everyday social interaction?

There are arguments both for and against using CMC as a means of interviewing (read Mann and Stewart, 2000, Chapter 6, for a detailed discussion). This medium provides sufficient benefit to encourage its use in many research studies. There are two approaches available to online interviewing: the synchronous or asynchronous approach.

Synchronous interviewing

Synchronous or 'real-time' interviewing involves the use of internet relay chat (IRC) software which facilitates a 'live' chat area allowing for real-time conversations between two (or more) people. The conversation takes place on the screen with both parties taking part at the same time, it is a *virtual* conversation, the only difference from a conventional conversation being that the questions and responses are typed rather than spoken. As well as becoming familiar with the necessary software the online interviewer must also be aware of the 'paralanguage' now commonly used within IRCs. This includes abbreviation and emotional reference, which adds a slightly more 'human' element to the typed conversation.

Asynchronous interviewing

Asynchronous or 'non real-time' interviewing involves the use of e-mail and sometimes discussion threads within a designated area. Questions are sent or posted into the designated space and respondents can add their reply at any time.

Of all the data collection techniques available it is possibly the online interview and online observation (for different reasons) that are the most controversial. You will need to weigh up the benefits and disadvantages of using CMC in your research and decide for yourself if this is appropriate for your research study and research participants.

Example 15.1 A semi-structured interview
This is a guide designed to be used in a semi-structured interview with young teenagers.

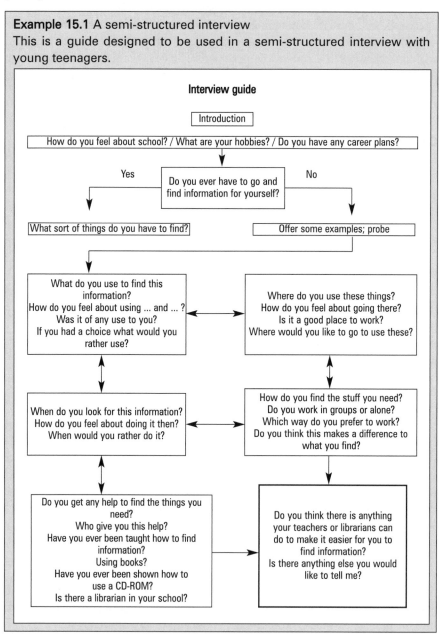

Summary

Interviewing is a well established and well used technique for data collection. The interview can take any form, from the highly structured researcher-administered questionnaire to the highly open purposeful conversation. Choice of type depends on issues such as the researcher's experience, the nature of the research topic and questions, access to research participants and the time available for data collection. You need to think very carefully about your choices before you design and engage in the interview process.

Interviews are appropriate when the purpose of the researcher is to gain individual views, beliefs and feelings about a subject, when questions are too complex to be asked in a straightforward way and more depth is required from the answers. People will nearly always write as little as possible when asked a question; if they are asked to reply verbally they are far more likely to talk at greater length and depth about the topic. Interviews can be used to confirm or refute data gathered from other tools such as observation or diaries; they can be used to identify salient issues that need to be followed up, possibly using another data collection technique.

Interviews usually produce rich and detailed data that can often be very complex when you come to analyse the responses. This needs to be factored in to the research design or you run the risk of being unable to make the best use of data simply because you do not have the time or the facilities to give it the attention that it needs. Considerable thought and preparation is needed when using interviews as well as an understanding of your ability and experience. Although potentially a rich source of data, there are a number of factors that can have an impact on the quality of the data.

 PRACTICAL EXERCISE

Interview questions are usually said to fall into one of six categories:

- **'here and now' facts:** 'What are your hobbies?'
- **facts about the past:** 'Did you use the public library when you were revising for your GCSEs?'
- **predictions about the future:** 'Do you think internet access will increase the number of users in the open access area of the library?'
- **feelings and emotions:** 'You said the internet makes you angry sometimes. When you are searching for information online what makes you angry?'
- **attitudes and opinions:** 'How do you feel about the new issue system?'
- **beliefs:** 'Do you think the internet is a useful resource for people living in rural communities?'

Using a topic that you are very interested in, for each of these six categories construct a question or maybe two. Using this as your interview guide engage in a practice interview with a friend or acquaintance. For the purposes of this exercise take only a note pad and pen to record the responses. After the inter-view reflect on what you heard and what you recorded; write up the responses as best you can straight after the event, without the interviewee present. Take your transcription of the interview back to the interviewee and confirm how much accurate data you have gathered from the interview.

You may also want to consider what is actually meant by 'accurate' in terms of the data you harvested. Interviews are about personal perception; this could mean that answers may not always be factually accurate but they are the per-ception of the interviewee.

Suggested further reading

Fontana, A. and Frey, J. (1994) Interviewing: the art of science. In Denzin, N. K. and Lincoln, Y. S. (eds) *Handbook of Qualitative Research*, London, Sage, 361–76.

Kvale, S (1996) *InterViews: an introduction to qualitative interviewing*, London, Sage.

Mann, C. and Stewart, F. (2000) *Internet Communication and Qualitative Research: a handbook for researching online*, London, Sage, Chapter 6.

Spradley, J. (1979) *The Ethnographic Interview*, New York, Holt, Rhinehart & Winston.

Chapter 16

Questionnaires

Survey data are usually obtained by means of a questionnaire, a series of pre-determined questions that can be either self-administered, administered by mail, or asked interviewers. When the questionnaire is to be administered by interview, it is often called an *interview schedule*. The use of questionnaires in research is based on one basic underlying assumption: that the respondent will be both willing and able to give truthful answers.

(Burns, 2000, 571)

Introduction

Questionnaires are without doubt the single most popular data collection tools in any research involving human subjects. I usually begin any lecture on questionnaire design by saying that so much of what you are about to hear (or in this case read) would appear to be 'common sense'. It's amazing how common sense can fly out of the window when a researcher becomes so steeped in his or her subject and is eager to gather data that they lose their objective eye when it comes to critically analysing data collection instruments. A lot of the discussion in this chapter may appear to be 'common sense', if that is indeed the case then try to ensure that you use your common sense well.

There are a number of reasons for using questionnaires in your research: you can reach a large and geographically dispersed community at relatively low cost, you can harvest data from a larger sample than would be possible using any other technique, anonymity can be offered as well as confidentiality, and the data analysis can be determined from the outset, even as far as coding before the questionnaires have been distributed. Having said all of that the most usual reason I am given by new researchers for the choice of questionnaire for data collection is, 'I won't have to talk to anybody'. This may well be a very good reason in the eyes of the neophyte researcher; it is not a good enough reason in terms of research credibility. Identify the purpose of your investigation and what you hope to do with your data once it has been analysed; base your choice on the aim of the research (although we all know personal preference will enter into the decision-making process). Strange as it may seem, the apparent biggest attraction of a questionnaire is also one of the greatest limitations of the instrument: the lack of opportunity to talk directly to respondents (Foddy, 1993, 8).

Designing questionnaires

Despite being the most popular research technique, questionnaires produce a notoriously low response rate unless the researcher administers them personally. One of the most important things to remember is that a questionnaire is required to stand alone; the researcher is rarely looking over the respondent's shoulder while he or she completes the questionnaire. You won't be there to confirm that the respondent understands the questionnaire or to provide additional information. Appearance and content are extremely important if you want to encourage responses: your questionnaire has to look good and read well, your instructions need to be clear and plausible. Questionnaire design is a very serious business and can mean the difference between a high response rate that provides you with detailed data or a sad lack of data which puts you in the position of being able to say very little about your research question. Inadequate design will not only discourage respondents from taking part but could also increase measurement error (Oppenhiem, 1992).

Figure 16.1 shows the steps involved in designing a questionnaire. However pressed you are for time, never be tempted to omit any of these steps.

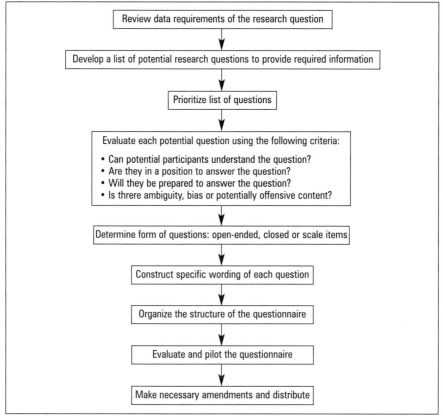

Figure 16.1 Steps in designing a questionnaire

An effective questionnaire should:

- be designed as a holistic tool; the overall picture should be clear
- begin with a brief introduction providing clear and simple instructions
- be concise
- ask questions clearly, without ambiguity, bias, use of jargon or technical language (unless you know that your particular subjects would expect certain technical terms, and leaving them out could imply you don't know your subject very well)
- be short enough to be completed in a reasonable time
- avoid leading questions
- avoid asking potentially offensive questions
- be logical in the order of questions - this means providing an obvious pathway through the questionnaire and avoiding complex instructions on where to go next depending on a previous answer
- appear uncluttered and inviting - don't scare people off with tightly packed questions that are almost impossible to read without a magnifying glass
- provide data that is easily processed - make sure you know how you intend to analyse your data before you distribute your questionnaires.

These are some general points to remember when compiling and sending out questionnaires. The details will depend on the nature and context of your research.

- Give your questionnaire an appropriate title (not necessarily the title of your research project as the questionnaire may only be designed to address some of the study focus).
- Send a covering letter of introduction providing some detail about the topic, the purpose of the research, how the data will be used, contact details (and where appropriate contact details for your research supervisor) and a statement of confidentiality (which should be honoured). I recently heard of a researcher who had begun their covering letter with a freedom of information request statement. I was appalled by this for two reasons. First it trivializes the entire underlying ethos of the Act; second, it would seem to me to be the most obvious way of closing off access to data that I can imagine. Encouraging someone to contribute to your research is difficult; to do anything that could antagonize them seems to me preposterous. Putting recipients in a position where they may feel 'forced' to respond will certainly not create goodwill. I am inclined to think it would encourage them to be as disobliging as possible whilst staying within the requirements of the Freedom of Information Act.
- Include a stamped addressed envelope for postal questionnaires.
- Include some form of tracking number for anonymous questionnaires (be sure to destroy your tracking code book if you have promised anonymity and be prepared to see this number removed or erased on returned questionnaires as some people may not be comfortable with it).

- Never ask questions unless you really need the answers; for example if age or gender are not variables in your study don't ask about them.

Developing questions

The questions in a questionnaire need to be easily understood and easily answered, if they aren't then you run a very high risk of low response, a risk already present for numerous other reasons. However obvious, clear and appropriate the questions seem to you, this is no guarantee of how someone else will interpret them. Sometimes explanations that appear to be repetitive and unnecessary can make a considerable difference to your response rate. 'Questions that began with a repetitive or redundant introduction . . . induced respondents to give more information than briefer versions of the same questions' (Laurent *in* Foddy, 1993, 48).

Generally speaking it is useful to structure your questionnaire by asking unthreatening, friendly questions first, questions that are relevant to the subject but relatively easy to answer. So often questionnaires open with basic demographic questions first. This is not a very good idea; who wants to give details about themselves before they have provided any other answers? Keep these questions until the end, the point at which the respondent may be sick of 'thinking' and will appreciate very basic questions. The important thing about asking questions concerning gender, age, location and so on is to consider the usefulness these questions serve in your analysis. So often I see research reports with a sample questionnaire in the appendix; on that sample are a list of demographic questions yet there is nothing in the analysis that appears to have used this data. If demographic variables have no place in your analysis they should definitely have no place in your questionnaire.

Start with friendly, simple questions about the topic; move on to the more complex questions after you have engaged the respondent. Leave all questions that require your respondent to express a view or an opinion until at least a third of the way through the questionnaire. It is really important to include a variety of question types; nothing is more mundane than a list of dichotomous questions. Not only does it lead to boredom but it may also appear superficial, as if you don't really want to know your respondents' views in any depth or detail. On the other hand if you prepare a list of open-ended questions all requiring a detailed response then you are wasting your time, as answers will not be forthcoming. If you prepare a list like this then you really should be considering conducting an interview as opposed to using a questionnaire.

It is notoriously difficult to encourage respondents to complete great sections of blank lines in their own words, it demands too much thought and therefore too much time. It is far easier to give a verbal response to an open question, but when it comes to putting your thoughts down on paper we all take more time and are more concerned about what we are writing. Remember that descriptive responses will take considerably longer to analyse than replies to simple questions, which is why we never conduct as many interviews as we do questionnaires. We go for depth or breadth. Questionnaires provide breadth with some detailed description; for real depth we need interviews or observations. Think about the holistic picture not a list of individual questions. Design your questionnaire with an overall function so you can use techniques such as *funnelling*, which 'starts off with a very broad question and then progressively narrows down the scope of the questions until it comes to some specific points' (Oppenheim, 1992, 38).

Try to make your overall design as simple and straightforward as possible; one way to avoid confusion is to limit the amount of *filtering* you do. Filtering is 'used to exclude a respondent from a particular question sequence if those questions are irrelevant' (Oppenheim, 1992, 39), but using this too often can confuse people and leave them feeling very unsure about which questions to answer and which to ignore. This is yet another potential risk that could lose you a response. It takes very little to put someone off completing a questionnaire; if you make life difficult for your respondents you are giving them the perfect excuse to opt out of the exercise.

Closed questions

These questions fall into three major categories: the dichotomous question, the multiple dichotomous question and the rank order question (see Example 16.1, page 189). The *dichotomous question* allows the respondent to choose from two possible responses (usually a third neutral response will also be offered such as 'Don't know'), or questions with a set of fixed alternatives. These must be exhaustive so the respondent can find something on the list of choices to address their condition.

There is also the *multiple dichotomous question,* which provides a list of possible responses and allows the respondent to select any number of choices from the list. Remember to consider analysis as well as data harvesting when you construct individual questions. Decide how you will analyse responses and whenever possible code questions so the framework is established before the data are returned.

Another form of closed question is the *rank order question* when respondents are asked to rate or rank each option that applies. This allows the researcher to obtain information on relative preferences, importance and so on. 'Long lists should be avoided (respondents generally find it difficult to rank more than 5 items)' (Trochim, 2005). Closed questions can be 'attitudinal as well as factual' (Oppenheim, 1992, 112), although attitudinal measures are usually referred to as 'scale questions'.

Scale items

Scale items are often included in questionnaires although they are a data collection technique in their own right. They are attitude measures, which perhaps should have had a separate chapter. I have chosen not to do that as so many researchers include an attitudinal scale in a questionnaire among other closed questions and open questions. I think to some extent this may have 'watered down' the actual procedures involved. You must remember that preparing a scaled attitude measurement involves a lot of work and is rather more than just another closed question in your list of questions. All too often I see something referred to as a Likert scale, when it is really little more than a question asking respondents to identify the extent to which they agree or disagree with a given statement. A Likert scale is a lot more than that if constructed correctly.

Scaled questions offer greater uniformity of response and therefore they are easier to code. However, they can often appear superficial and may force respondents to answer inappropriately. You may need to explain your choices if you produce a questionnaire that is intentionally made up of scaled questions. This can happen if you are carrying out an attitudinal study based on a fixed design.

There are two broad groups of scale questions: unidimensional and multi-dimensional. *Unidimensional scales* are measurements taken along a single dimension; only one thing is being measured and it is either more or less. *Multidimensional scales* are much more complex as they attempt to scale responses along three different dimensions: cognitive, behavioural and affective.

The attitudinal measure can take a number of forms; the most common unidimensional measure is the Likert scale but there are other examples such as the Thurstone scale and the Guttman cumulative scaling (Trochim, 2005). I will provide a brief discussion here of these three types of attitudinal measure but I stress that if you intend to use any of these in your research and you are not already familiar with them then you will need to read more extensively. (Oppenheim, 1992, and Robson, 1997, both provide detailed discussion on attitude measures.)

The Likert scale

The Likert scale (Likert, 1932) is a bipolar scaling technique, which allows a respondent to select a choice that best demonstrates their level of agreement with a given statement (see Example 16.2, page 190). There is an inherent order to a Likert scale but no indication of the interval measure between each choice. Because of this the Likert scale does not *measure* attitude, it gauges intensity of attitude in relation to other respondents. It provides ordinal data; this can be manipulated but essentially you have an ordinal measure. We will look at analysing results of a Likert scale in Part 4 but it is important to note that you should be considering your analysis as you are drawing up the scale. It's too late after the data is in to decide that you don't want to engage in certain forms of analysis; sometimes your data dictates that. For this reason it makes sense to say a little about analysis here, as it is particular to this type of scaling.

The stages in developing a Likert scale are discussed below.

- Construct a list of attitude statements relating to your research question – done as with everything else using your literature review and research objectives.
- Structure a response system – the most common is the five-point scale of 'strongly agree, agree, neutral, disagree, strongly disagree'. These choices are weighted 1, 2, 3, 4 and 5.
- Arrange your list in a random way, mixing positive and negative statements to prevent people falling into a habit of ticking one column.

Example 16.1 Different types of interview question

The dichotomous question
'Have you used Information Central within the last week?'

❑ Yes   ❑ No   ❑ Can't remember

The multiple dichotomous question
'Which of the following resources do you use to produce your reports?'

❑ Reference texts
❑ The internet
❑ Databases
❑ Newspapers

Other, please state ....

Fixed alternative question
'Which is your designated study day?'

❑ Monday   ❑ Tuesday   ❑ Wednesday   ❑ Thursday   ❑ Friday

Rank order question
'Please rank the following online resources in order of preference, 1 being your favourite, 5 your least favourite.'

❑ BUBL info services   ❑ CSA   ❑ ERIC   ❑ JSTOR   ❑ BEI

(Please note you would only use acronyms where respondents are familiar with them and would expect to see them.)

- Select a random test sample from your target population to test your list and scoring system. Oppenheim (1992) suggests 100 people for the sample group; I would suggest this could be rather high for dissertation research. Ask each member of your test group to rate the statements based on interest and relevance to the topic, not relating to their own opinion.
- Score the list obtained for each respondent based on your weighting, then rank the respondents' highest score to lowest score.
- Select the items you intend to use in your final list, the list that will be given to your actual research sample. To do this you must carry out a statement analysis and calculate the *discriminative power* (DP) for each, or correlate each statement with the overall score. To calculate the DP you have to work out which statements discriminate best between the respondents' totals in the upper

quartile and those in the lower quartile. You ranked your respondents earlier. For each statement you calculate the score from all respondents in the lower and upper quartile, calculate the total weighting, then the weighted mean. The DP is the difference between the weighted means for each quartile. Those statements with the highest DP are selected for inclusion in your final scale.
- You are now ready to construct and administer your Likert scale to your research sample. It is recommended that you have between ten and 15 statements for your questionnaire, all of which have now been tested for importance in relation to your topic. Remember to mix positive and negative statements to avoid respondents randomly ticking boxes down a single column.

Once you have your received your completed questionnaires you can calculate the attitude of each respondent but this is only attitude in relation to other respondents, not an actual measurement. You can rank respondents' replies in relation to each other but you are not in a position to 'make assertions about the equality of underlying attitude differences, and that identical scores may have very different meanings' (Oppenheim, 1992, 200). Likert scales produce ordinal data, which means that only non-parametric tests can be used with this data because they do not assume normal distribution between respondents.

Example 16.2 Likert scale

INSTRUCTIONS: Please rate how strongly you agree or disagree with each of the following statements by placing a tick in the appropriate box.

	Strongly agree	Agree	Neutral	Disagree	Strongly disagree
The new self-issue system is easy to use					
I don't understand the system on-screen help facility					
I feel confident about using the self-issue system					
The self-issue system saves me time					
I would rather go to the desk to return my books					
There should be a member of staff close to the self-issue machines to help					
I am confident that my books are off my library card when I use the self-issue system					

The Thurstone equal appearing interval scale

The Thurstone scale (Thurstone and Chave, 1929) is a way of adding measurement to attitude ratings. Where the Likert scale can only rate respondents' attitudes against those of other respondents, the Thurstone scale (see Example 16.3) is an interval measure which allows a value to be placed on each choice with an equal appearing interval scale between values. This implies that the scale will reflect the absolute attitudes of respondents rather than their relative attitude.

The process for constructing a Thurstone scale follows a similar pattern to the Likert scale but with significant differences.

- Construct a list of attitude statements relating to your research question - done as with everything else using your literature review and research objectives. You will need around 80-100 statements in this initial pool.
- Enlist the help of a panel of judges, usually 50-100. This is the most difficult step to complete and is usually the reason so few researchers apply this scale. These judges should be experts in the field of attitudes being investigated.
- Judges are then given the list of statements (sometimes they are given them as a pile of single slips, one statement on each slip). Judges are asked to rate each statement on an 11-point scale based on the favourableness demonstrated towards the attitude in the statement, 11 being the most favourable, 6 is the neutral statement, and 1 the least favourable. They are also asked to avoid making personal judgements on the statement, but to score it only in terms of favourableness.

Example 16.3 Thurstone scale
INSTRUCTIONS: Please state whether you agree or disagree with each of the following statements by placing a tick in the appropriate box.

	Agree	Disagree
The new self-issue system is easy to use		
I don't understand the system on-screen help facility		
I feel confident about using the self-issue system		
The self-issue system saves me time		
I would rather go to the desk to return my books		
There should be a member of staff close to the self-issue machines to help		
I am confident that my books are off my library card when I use the self-issue system		

- The median value for each statement is then calculated based on the judges' scoring. If the scoring for any statement is scattered over the 11-point scale, then discard this statement. There is clearly no way of measuring its degree of favourableness.

- Calculate the variability in rating for each statement.
- Select the statements that are spread evenly along the 11-point scale, allowing you to construct a scale of equal appearing intervals. Depending on how many statements you want this could mean selecting statements with a median value closes to the scale points 1, 1.5, 2, 2.5, 3, 3.5 and so on to 11.
- Now construct your questionnaire providing only a dichotomous response option of agree or disagree.

You now have a yardstick you can use to measure respondents' attitudes towards the topic of your investigation. When completed questionnaires are returned you can calculate the attitude measure of each respondent, which will be the median of the scale values that the respondent agrees to. Thurstone scales produce interval data, which means that parametric tests can be performed on the data as normal distribution is assumed, based on the equal appearing intervals of the scale.

The Guttman cumulative scale

The Guttman cumulative scale (Guttman, 1950) is the most difficult attitudinal scale to construct (Kumar, 1999, 134), and is also the least used of all the attitude measures – perhaps for that reason. This scale (see Example 16.4) relies on a one-dimensional focus on a topic. In the examples above there could be a variety of dimensions to the topic – individual confidence, costs, cognitive and affective attitudes towards electronic systems, and so on. The Guttman scale is concerned with cumulative scores, a one-dimensional continuum for the topic you wish to investigate. The basis of a cumulative scale is that statements become increasingly more focused. For example if a respondent agrees to the fourth statement on a list you would expect that they had agreed with all preceding statements up to that point.

The process of constructing a Guttman scale or a *scalogram* begins in the same way as the previous two attitude measures, but then varies.

- Construct a list of attitude statements relating to your research question – done as with everything else using your literature review and research objectives. You will need around 80-100 statements in this initial pool.
- This list is then given to a test group (judges) and they are asked to tick all statements they agree with.
- You will then carry out a scalogram analysis, which means you will arrange responses to give you the best triangular shape (Robson, 1997). This can involve a lot of manipulation and the removal of some statements (see Example 16.4, but in reality there will be many more than this).
- This best triangular shape gives you the list of statements for your scale) to be used to give to respondents.

Example 16.4 Guttman scale

Analysis of returned test statements

Statements are arranged in order of total number of 'agree ticks' given by your judges. We arrange them in the best possible 'triangle' formation (X = agree: the example shows the ideal scenario; it is unlikely to form such a perfect pattern in reality):

Judge	S	B	F	A	J	W	M	D	O	K	Total for statement
Statement 1	X	X	X	X	X	X	X	X	X	X	10
Statement 6	O	X	X	X	X	X	X	X	X	X	9
Statement 9	O	O	X	X	X	X	X	X	X	X	8
Statement 16	O	O	O	O	O	O	X	X	X	X	4
Statement 3	O	O	O	O	O	O	O	O	X	X	2
Statement 4	O	O	O	O	O	O	O	O	X	X	2

(Adapted from Robson, 1997)

Our rank order may appear something like this after our judges have rated the statements. This is your Guttman scale:

S1: I know there is a new self-issue system in the library (Statement 1)

S6: The new self-issue system is easy to use (Statement 6)

S9: I understand the system on-screen help facility (Statement 9)

S16: The self-issue system saves me time (Statement 16)

S3: I am confident that my books are off my library card when I use the self-issue system (Statement 3)

S4: I would rather use the self-issue system than go to the desk to return and take out my books (Statement 4)

When you prepare your questionnaire you will mix up the statements giving no hint of any cumulative degree of attitude measurement; your question will look like this:

INSTRUCTIONS: Place a tick next to each statement you agree with.

I am confident that my books are off my library card when I use the self-issue system	
The new self-issue system is easy to use	
I would rather use the self-issue system than go to the desk to return and take out my books	
The self-issue system saves me time	
I know there is a new self-issue system in the library	
I understand the system on-screen help facility	

The semantic differential scale

The semantic differential scale (Osgood, Suci and Tannenbaum, 1957) is a multi-dimensional measure between two bipolar adjectives; respondents must select a point along this scale that represents the direction or intensity of their feelings. (For an excellent discussion of semantic differential scales see Heise, 1970.) The semantic differential scale (see Example 16.5) is used to assess the subjective meaning to a concept. The data is analysed using factor analysis, which involves a large number of correlations between variables. This measure is designed to identify an individual's beliefs about a concept or object over three dimensions: *activity*, the extent to which the object or concept is associated with action; *potency*, the strength or importance of the object or concept; and *evaluation*, the overall positive meaning associated with the object or concept (Heise, 1970).

Constructing a semantic differential does not include the various stages associated with other attitude measurements. The outcome is based on the factor analysis or a simple calculation and comparison between respondents. Factor analysis is only used if you want to take the analysis further and examine correlations between dimensions. The process of constructing the scale is relatively simple: you decide on the object or concept you wish to assess and construct a list of bipolar adjectives related to that object or concept.

Example 16.5 Semantic differential scale

INSTRUCTIONS:
1 For each pair of adjectives please place a tick at the point between them which best reflects the extent to which you feel the adjective best describes the new **self-issue system.**
2 Work through the items fairly quickly without worrying or considering them too much, your first reaction is wanted.
3 Resist the temptation to look back over your previous response.

	1	2	3	4	5	6	7	
valuable								useless
helpful								unhelpful
easy								difficult
reliable								unreliable
fast								slow
flexible								rigid

Open-ended questions

Open-ended questions provide no indication of possible answers and rarely define any parameters to restrict the respondent. These are essentially *descriptive* questions that require a more detailed and personal response. Very often I see them being described as the *qualitative* element in a questionnaire. This is something of an over-statement; they are descriptive but rarely are they truly qualitative. The depth of narrative needed to label something as qualitative data is almost impossible to harvest from a questionnaire. The descriptive data that open-ended questions may produce can add detail to the closed questions and can often bring a totally new perspective to an issue, one even the researcher had not considered, but please do not rely on them as a source of qualitative data. If your purpose is to harvest both quantifiable data and individual detail then I would urge you to employ more than one data collection technique in your research design. That is not to say open-ended questions are unsuccessful, they can be, but it's what they are successful at that is the issue. Relying on respondents to fill out vast empty spaces on a questionnaire is not something I would ever recommend except in the case of a Delphi questionnaire, which is something quite different aimed at a very particular audience. So, enough about what open-ended questions can't do, what can they do?

Open-ended questions (see Example 16.6 overleaf) provide your research subjects with an opportunity to make their own comments about an issue, to tell you precisely what is important to them about this topic. These questions follow the same format as questions designed for an interview schedule, although you must remain aware that, unlike an interview, you will not be there to clarify the meaning of any question. It is important to resist making the questions too complex. It is all too easy for a respondent to skip a question on a questionnaire or to answer in the easiest way possible. The last thing you want from an open-ended question is a response like 'Yes'. However, if your question is phrased in a way that the respondent can answer 'Yes' or 'No' to, then you can make a comfortable assumption that that is exactly what they will do.

Think about your own experience with filling out questionnaires: how often have you left a question blank because answering involved too much thinking or too much writing and you simply did not have the time or maybe even the inclination to do it? If you ask too many open-ended questions at best you may get your questionnaire back with some sorrowful looking white spaces, at worst the respondent may just decide not to bother returning it at all because it involves too much effort. Think carefully about using this type of question, think about why you are using it, think about the people you are expecting to answer it, think about how easy it is to answer, and most importantly think about how you are going to analyse the answers. Use open-ended questions when:

- you need more extensive or more individual data
- you have no way of knowing the range of possible answers
- it is not a particularly sensitive subject area.

Once you have decided that this type of question is really necessary and appropriate then consider how you ask it. These are some points to remember when phrasing open-ended questions.

Example 16.6 Open-ended questions

1 Preventing a Yes/No response:
Question: 'Do you collaborate with other webmasters/moderators? If so, in what way?'
Actual response: 'It all depends on the attitude of the moderator. Some site owners simply do not want to share information. In fact, they are actively against it. They view other sites as rivals to be denounced and discredited. They jealously guard their information and want to be the first to harvest a specimen. Other groups realize that more can be achieved by working together and sharing information.'

Here a follow question was included to encourage respondents to expand on the obvious Yes/No they could provide.

2 Asking a totally open question about personal behaviour; no response suggested:
Question: 'How do you decide if information is reliable or not?'
Actual response: 'Usually there is a set pattern. The person is not going to be very outward. Most people do not want to report a Bigfoot sighting, but deep down they know what they saw and eventually it eats away at them if you will and they have to tell someone. Also, we do some field research on reports that are received near our database.'

Examples taken from: Dmytriw, D. (2003) *Information Acquisition and Exchange Within Cryptozoological Virtual Communities*, unpublished dissertation, Northumbria University. (Winner of the LIRG prize for best student dissertation 2004)

- Be sure that it is almost impossible to give a one word answer to your questions.
- If they are used on a paper-based questionnaire make sure there is sufficient room for the length of response you are anticipating.
- Be aware of where they are placed in the questionnaire. Opening with this type of question is not a good idea; having a long list of them is not a good idea. Place them at intervals throughout the questionnaire. The most popular use of this type of question is at the end with the statement 'If there is anything you would like to add please do so in the space below' – usually this comes back blank! People will need to have fairly strong opinions about the topic to go to the trouble of constructing a response without any guidelines whatsoever.

- Keep the question simple; you don't have the space for lengthy explanations and if you need them then the question isn't working.
- Ask one question at a time.
- Think about how you intend to analyse your responses. Robson (1997) suggests leaving the coding until you have at least two-thirds of your responses back. Look at the responses in Example 16.6. How would you begin to code them?

I hope I haven't been too negative about the use of open-ended questions in questionnaires. They are used frequently and very often provide useful data, but they can also be the source of a great deal of disappointment as it is so easy to get it wrong (see Example 16.7). I have stressed the importance of piloting in all data collection but here it really is essential. Find out how a question performs before you even think about sending it off to participants.

Example 16.7 Ways of 'getting it wrong'
These examples are exaggerated to make the point but it is very easy to make these mistakes when constructing questions; piloting the questionnaire usually shows up this type of error but not always.

Ambiguity

Question:	'When did you start using the new issue system?'
Possible responses:	'In January 2005' (an objective date)
	'When I was 30' (a personal age)
	'Last month' (a relative answer)
	'Before we met' (shared private knowledge)

Personal or offensive questions

Question:	'How much do you earn a month?'
Possible responses:	'None of your business' (angry respondent, possible distortion of all subsequent answers)
	'£2,000,000' (angry and sarcastic or just very wealthy?)
	No response given.

Double questions

Question:	'Do you have cereal and exercise in the morning?'
Possible responses:	'Yes' (Yes to one or both? If one, which one?)
	'Sometimes' (think about the number of variations available here!)

Biased phrasing

Question:	'Most research methods lecturers are social misfits, aren't they?'
Possible responses:	This question is presupposing a common state of mind and most respondents (unless, like me they are research methods lecturers) will want to appear to be privy to the common state of mind.

Forms of questionnaire

There are a number of options available for administering and distributing questionnaires; you need to think very carefully about your target group when you decide how to reach them. Here is a checklist of the questions you need to ask before deciding on the format of your questionnaire:

• What form of questionnaire would best suit your subjects?
• What are your own capabilities?
• What resources do you have?
• How much time do you have?
• Is your sample group geographically dispersed?

Paper-based postal questionnaires

The most common form of questionnaire is the paper-based, printed instrument. The most typical forms of distribution are by post, handing them to individuals at group events or leaving them in a prominent position where people are encouraged to complete and return them to the distribution point. The latter of these is by far the least successful, as you can imagine. Postal questionnaires are the most costly as you will have to enclose a stamped addressed envelope in each for return; you will also be relying heavily on the willingness of the respondent to complete and return the questionnaire. Distributing paper questionnaires to a group when they are gathered together in a particular location is usually the most successful approach.

Electronic questionnaires

The term 'electronic questionnaires' is generally used to cover both online questionnaires and questionnaires contained within an email message; it does not cover questionnaires produced in a word-processing package then sent to participants as an attachment; this is still a 'paper-based' questionnaire using a different mechanism for distribution. Coomber defines an online questionnaire as one which is 'located on a Web page which respondents can "fill-in" online at a terminal. . . . Behind the questionnaire there will be a program (preferably on a secure server) that will store the data being sent through. This may be a database or an appropriate statistical package' (1997).

Online questionnaires offer many advantages but there are potential drawbacks to them. One major drawback is limiting your sample population; online questionnaires usually allow an individual to submit multiple responses and it is particularly difficult to restrict submissions from individuals outside your designated sample. Another problem is the technology itself; different browsers mean it can be difficult to be totally sure of how your questionnaire will appear to everyone who opens it.

A major consideration is the nature of your sample population. It is very easy to make assumptions about your sample's levels of access to the internet as well as their skills to use online facilities. Before you decide to design and construct an online questionnaire make sure your sample will have access to it and be comfortable using it. Questionnaires contained within emails may reduce some of these potential drawbacks but asking for return via email removes any anonymity as the respondents' address will be included in the response. Consider very carefully which type of questionnaire best addresses your needs and the needs of your sample population.

Researcher-administered questionnaires

Researcher-administered questionnaires usually generate the highest response rate of any questionnaires, because you approach your subject and you complete the questionnaire by asking the questions and filling in the document according to what they tell you. The most obvious example of this is the market researcher working in the street – if all of your avoidance techniques fail! As you can probably guess from your own response to people who approach you unsolicited in the street, this method is not the best way to win people over; it may not even be legal unless you have applied for and received the relevant permission. The most ethical and practical approach to this type of questionnaire is to select a location where your study population can be found, request permission to engage in the data collection and wait patiently for your designated sample to appear. You usually have to make more than a single visit to the location and you will have to work out when you should visit in order to reach your optimum sample size and composition.

Summary

Questionnaire design involves a great deal of common sense and personal experience. It is only by attempting to harvest data on specific research questions that you will come to understand the intricacies of designing effective question-naires. Always remain aware of the purpose of the investigation and make sure each question you ask relates to it specifically. Remember that a questionnaire depends entirely on the ability and willingness of respondents to answer the questions you are asking. Make sure you ask them questions they can answer in a format they can understand. It takes very little to turn a respondent off; that is the reason so many questionnaires end up in the waste bin never to see the light of day again. It is also a very good idea to be aware of how you intend to analyse the data and how it will be used to inform the investigation. Be sure to pilot your instrument with a reasonable number of test subjects before you release it to your sample population. This instrument has to stand alone and you need to know it will work as it is intended to work; you need to know that questions read the way you think they read and the only way to know this is to pilot.

Like any other data collection technique there are both advantages and disadvantages to questionnaires. Advantages include their relatively low cost and the potential to offer greater anonymity; respondents are free to answer in their own time. There is a reduced risk of the researcher's appearance influencing responses. Some disadvantages are the low response rate, self-selecting bias, complex questions leading to confusion, that levels of truthfulness cannot be measured only assumed, and lack of opportunity to clarify issues (Kumar, 1999, 114). Good question design and piloting can ensure that clarification of questions is not necessary. You can employ a number of tactics to increase your response rate but you will always be relying on the honesty and accuracy of self-reported data; this is the nature of the questionnaire.

 PRACTICAL EXERCISE

The following questions are not suitable for a questionnaire. Discuss the nature and purpose of each question, then rewrite them in a more appropriate form:

1 What do you eat for lunch?
2 How long did you spend travelling last week?
3 What is your educational attainment?
4 Do you agree that the new layout of the computer lab is better than it was before?
5 Are you fat, thin or average?
6 What did you do on your holidays last year?
7 Do you think it is fair to keep wild animals incarcerated in cramped, dirty, smelly cages in a zoo?
8 Are you happy with the course you are studying at university?

Suggested further reading

Burns, R. B. (2000) *Introduction to Research Methods,* 4th edn, London, Sage, Chapter 30.

De Vaus, D. (2002) *Survey Research,* London, Sage.

Foddy, W. (1993) *Constructing Questions for Interviews and Questionnaires: theory and practice in social research,* Cambridge, Cambridge University Press.

Heise, D. R. (1970) The Semantic Differential and Attitude Research. In Summers, G. F. (ed.) *Attitude Measurement,* Chicago, Rand McNally, 1970, 235-53, www.indiana.edu/~socpsy/papers/AttMeasure/attitude.htm.

Oppenheim, A. (1992) *Questionnaire Design, Interviewing and Attitude Measurement,* London, Pinter.

Robson, C. (1997) *Real World Research: a resource for social scientists and practitioner-researchers,* Oxford, Blackwell.

Chapter 17

Observation

A major advantage of direct observation . . . is that it provides here-and-now experience in depth.   (Lincoln and Guba, 1985, 273)

Introduction

Observations are carried out in order to provide evidence of the 'here and now', to discover how people behave and interact in particular situations. Almost all research involves observation of some sort, from the most formulaic laboratory experiment to the most natural ethnographic observation. In this chapter I want to focus on observation as a direct and stated technique of data collection, not as a casual observation of the activity taking place. In this sense the observation needs to be designed, constructed and implemented as you would any other data collection instrument. Casually watching what takes place in a research setting is unlikely to lead to any real evidence that can be analysed and interpreted. The human memory is extremely selective; even the most experienced observer needs some form of aide memoir to counteract the possibility of selective remembering.

It is difficult to say when it is appropriate to use observational techniques in data collection. 'As the actions and behaviours of people are a central aspect in virtually any enquiry, a natural and obvious technique is to watch what they do, to record this in some way and then describe, analyse and interpret that we have observed' (Robson, 1997, 190). There are very few research situations that could not benefit from some form of observation, but your decision isn't really 'is it appropriate?' but more 'is it the most appropriate?' Once you decide it is the most appropriate technique then you need to decide on the form and structure.

Patton (1987, 81) describes five dimensions of variation in approaches to observation:

- the role of the observer
- portrayal of that role to others
- portrayal of the purpose of the research
- duration of the observations
- focus of the observations.

These five dimensions provide a useful framework for discussing your option choices when considering how to observe, your role in the process of observing, and what to observe.

The role of the observer

The first and most fundamental distinction that differentiates observational strategies concerns the extent to which the observer will be a participant in the setting being studied.

(Patton, 2002, 265)

'The more you function as a member of the everyday world of the researched, the more you risk losing the eye of the uninvolved outsider: yet, the more you participate, the greater your opportunity to learn' (Glesne and Peshkin, 1992, 40). Glesne and Peshkin point out the major dilemma of whether to carry out direct observation in any research. The level to which the researcher becomes involved or immersed in the context is one of the central debates surrounding observation.

There are two main arguments. *If you become too involved you will lose your objectivity* – but who is to say that objectivity is the desired condition in your research? Sometimes it is the tacit knowledge of the researcher that allows for a more in-depth understanding of the situation. The more involved you are the more insight you may be able to bring to the analysis. *It is impossible to observe as a complete outsider and not influence the situation* – this is very true. People behave differently when being watched; the best way to minimize any impact the observer has on the context is to become as 'interesting as wallpaper' – easier said than done.

Accepting the impossibility of assuming and maintaining a role of complete outsider, then the researcher must be placed somewhere along the continuum from total outsider to full participant. There are three basic choices: are you going to be a participant observer, a semi-participant observer or a non-participant observer? The debate about the researcher being an 'insider' (emic researcher) or an 'outsider' (etic researcher) (Pike, 1954) will no doubt continue. There are sound arguments on both sides, it is up to you to decide which is the best role to assume for the purpose of the research then to attempt to engage in your data collection in a systematic and structured manner, gathering evidence, processing and analysing that evidence, then interpreting what you find.

Observation is *real*, and as in any real situation things will happen that are out of your control at the outset; you will have to think on your feet and react in a way that you feel is appropriate. More times than not you will be watching real people going about some part of their normal everyday life; remember at all times that they are real people, not objects of your observation, and try to act accordingly.

During one observation I was watching a teenage boy searching for information on photosynthesis for a homework project; this particular teenager had already told me in an interview that he felt he was 'really good at finding stuff on the net'. It was after school, we were in the learning resource centre and after searching for an hour he still hadn't found any useful material. My role in this observation was that of semi-participant observer; I was there to watch and maybe ask a few questions but not to 'interfere'. Half an hour before the centre was due to close the boy still had nothing; he told me the homework was due in the next day (yes, there was something I could have said but it wouldn't have made him feel any better, he knew he'd left it too late). He was beginning to get rather distressed about the whole thing and it was obvious it was time for me to make a decision about my role. I could have continued to watch the boy struggle and record his behaviour as he became increasing more distressed, but in reality I already had enough evidence of that; his searching had become increasingly more erratic as he began to panic. I decided to stopped the observation and we spent the next half an hour trying a new search strategy. The boy went home in a much better frame of mind although he had a long night ahead finishing his project.

This type of thing may not happen often, indeed this is rather mild in comparison with some experiences researchers have had in the field, but it does illustrate the point that observations are real. You have a responsibility to your research but you also have a responsibility to yourself and to your research participants. There are a number of ethical dilemmas facing the observer; I would recommend that you consider very strongly what you are, and what you are not, comfortable with from the outset. 'The participant observer attempts to enter the lives of others, to indwell . . . suspending as much as possible his or her own ways of viewing the world (Maykut and Morehouse, 1994, 69). The extent to which you enter the lives of others depends on your own situation, the purpose of the research, and the duration of the research and accessibility of the research site.

Participant observation

'A participant observer shares as intimately as possible in the live and activities of the setting under study in order to develop an *insider's view* of what is happening' (Patton, 2002, 268). There is a level known as the *complete observer*, which is the most extreme form of participant observation and a very controversial stance. It is the line that is crossed when a researcher seeks to infiltrate the lives of others and become part of their world without their knowledge. This form of participant observation is rare now but there was a time when it was fairly widely used, particularly in anthropology. There are many reports of research studies where the researcher 'went native' to the extent of joining a group and living in their world, often without the knowledge of the people being studied. I would never recommend this nor would I support the use of this technique as I feel there is no ethical defence for this level of covert, insider research. It is not just the debate of covert versus overt that disturbs me about this approach, it is also the pretense that becomes a necessity of the research. The researcher assumes a 'role' outside their own character, taking on a personality that is something other than who they are (Robson, 1997). There is a strong sense here of 'cheating' but you may feel otherwise; there are many studies documented that involved complete, covert observation.

The level of participant observation I would advocate is that of the researcher being actively involved in the subject of the study. That could mean joining a group and making it clear why you are there, or investigating a group you are already involved in. Many action research studies are carried out by practitioners evaluating or investigating their own system or programme; they are participant observers. This opens the discussion of *subjectivity* and the use of tacit knowledge in the research process. The argument against the researcher investigating their native environment makes the assumption that we are incapable of examining what we see in a rational and systematic way. This is not to say the situation is without difficulties; there could be many problems related to the researcher's role in the setting – relationships that already exist, or reactions of the other actors in the setting to being 'investigated', to name but a few. These potential problems need to be addressed in order to carry out an honest observation, but it is possible and indeed often very successful.

Gaining access to a research site and moving from outsider to insider can be very much more difficult and is only ever really possible in a longitudinal study. If your time is limited then your only real option is between semi- and non-participant observation. It is wrong to claim an insider view if you are only able to carry out short term observations lasting a few hours.

Semi-participant observation

The presence of any observer in a situation is highly likely to influence that situation to some degree, but the same can be said of any data collection method. The aim is to limit this impact and keep the situation as close to normal as possible. Observer effect can diminish over time as the observer develops a comfortable and trusting relationship with the observed, but this takes time and can only happen in a longitudinal study. A balance is needed between participant and observer in order to understand the situation as an insider and be able to describe it as an outsider (Maykut and Morehouse, 1994).

Semi-participant observation depends on the researcher being able to visit a location on a number of occasions and over an extended period of time. As time goes on the initial impact of the researcher on the situation will diminish but of course will never go away completely. Being able to interact with research subjects enables the researcher to build rapport and make the subjects feel more comfortable being 'watched'.

The most difficult aspect of this type of observation is knowing when to hold back and resist the temptation to become too immersed in the context. In the example I gave you earlier I had to make a decision to close the observation as I felt morally bound to offer assistance to the person I was observing. This impeded my ability to watch and learn. That particular situation began as a semi-participant observation but my level of involvement increased to a level where it was no longer creditable to claim semi-participation. Essentially in this type of observation you are watching, interacting and recording, but interaction should be kept to a minimum, usually only going so far as to ask questions to confirm what it is you think you have seen.

Non-participant observation

This type of observation requires the researcher to be as 'interesting as wallpaper' and have nothing at all to do with the setting being observed. You watch, record and later interpret what you have seen in the context of your research question. For many this is by far the easiest form of observation, as it requires nothing from the researcher in terms of interaction with research participants. You are a passive observer who makes no attempt to access the context.

Portrayal of the observer role to others

> The extent to which participants . . . are informed that they are being observed and told the purpose of the (research) ranges from full disclosure to no disclosure, with a great deal of variation along this continuum.   (Patton, 1987, 76)

This is a particularly sensitive issue and there is a great deal of disagreement among researchers as to the ethical and moral obligations facing the observer. You can read many research studies based on a researcher 'infiltrating' a particular group in order to observe their behaviour, assuming the role of an insider and hiding their role as a researcher. The arguments for and against this approach continue. I sit firmly on the 'against' side of this argument; watching people is a common enough activity but as soon as we begin watching with the intention of analysing and interpreting then we assume a responsibility to the individual lives we are interpreting. The degree to which you inform participants that you are conducting research depends very much on the individual setting and the practical issues involved but disclosure at some level is necessary. Naturally if you were observing activity in a public area or an area open to large amounts of individuals then it would be impossible to inform every person using that space of your role. What would be necessary is that you have informed the person or persons responsible for that area of your purpose and been granted permission to be there.

Portrayal of the purpose of the research

As with any data collection technique the researcher has to decide how much detail to share with research participants. In many cases they may not be too concerned about the intricate planning details of a study but at the very least they will want to know why you are watching and maybe even what you are looking for. One thing I will say from my own experience is that people feel much more comfortable if they are given some degree of 'ownership' of the research, even if this only means having an understanding of why the research is being done and what are the potential benefits. For the purposes of this book I will not go into the debate concerning covert research activity, that is a matter for individuals to decide, based on their own moral stance and the constraints placed on the research by any organization that is associated with it. My own view is that covert research has no place in academic study; if you are engaging in research as part of a degree award then I would think very carefully about even considering covert behaviour.

Duration of the observations

The duration of an observation should be determined in the planning stages. This includes both the length of individual observations and the duration of the fieldwork. How long will you be watching and how often will you be watching? These two decisions depend very much on the nature and purpose of the observation. If you are a participant observer seeking to understand how a group functions over time then you will need to be with that group over an extended period. This could mean anything from six weeks to years. If you are a non-participant observer you may only need to witness a single activity on a single day. It is important that you build this into your research design, not least so you can inform your research participants but also so you can schedule fieldwork and analysis.

When scheduling an observation I recommend that you build in time immediately after you leave the setting to consult any notes you may have made and expand on them while your memory of the event is still fresh. Allowing this time after leaving the setting avoids the need to take copious notes during the observation and allows time for field notes to be made soon after the observation (Denzin, 1978). Once you have tried out the observation exercise you will realize the level of concentration that is necessary during an observation, this must be taken into consideration when deciding on the duration of each session. There comes a point when you cease to take in the detail of what you are seeing and hearing; beyond this point there is little to gain so it is better to leave and process what you have than stay and lose your focus.

Focus of the observations

In order to organize the complex realities that are witnessed during fieldwork, observations can be oriented by the use of sensitizing concepts (Denzin, 1978). These assist in 'the systematic description of events, behaviours, and artefacts in the setting chosen for the study' (Marshall and Rossman, 1989, 79). Entering a setting with an open mind is essential but there is a world of difference between an open mind and an empty head. Regardless of the scheduling of your observations, whether they are the first or last elements of your data collection, you will never walk in empty headed. At the beginning of your fieldwork you have the literature review; even in a true constructivist inquiry you will have read something that helped you to focus your research question. If your observations are your first or even your only data collection technique, you will still be aware of potentially salient issues, something you are *looking* for. It may be that by the end of your fieldwork your focus has shifted considerably because you saw things you weren't expecting or others issues became more predominant as the inquiry moved on. The point is you enter the setting with a focus, a clearly defined topic that will guide what you watch and why you watch it. Observation in a natural setting is a complex activity; there is bound to be a lot going on. Make sure you can stay focused and have a clear idea of who the focus of your observation is and what categories of behaviour you really want to explore.

Recording what you see; going in with signposts

While observing any situation it is important to maintain the greatest level of normality possible. The researcher taking copious notes in front of research participants will not help this. If observations are scheduled to last 30 minutes to one hour then they should be timetabled as a two-hour exercise to allow you to write up field notes as soon as you leave the setting (Mellon, 1990). The field notes are descriptive, not interpretative, accounts of the phenomenon (Patton, 2002). Lincoln and Guba (1985) suggest that there is room in field notes for interpretation but they must be recorded as such. There must be no possibility of these asides becoming confused with the description of what you actually witnessed. Transcribing the notes immediately after vacating the field allows the interpretative notes to be added as memos inside the observation description. Most situations will occasionally allow for some notes, for example, verbatim quotes, to be written down without becoming obtrusive and closing off access to new information. However, it is necessary not to 'allow data collection procedures to cut [you] off from access to additional data [you] may need' (Erlandson et al., 1993, 103).

There are a number of ways to do this. One is to enter the setting with a briefing sheet (see Example 17.1 overleaf), a list of behaviours or activities you want to record, or simply a check list. This can be very restricting and may close you off to unexpected data but that will depend on the topic of your observation. If you use a briefing sheet be prepared to add to it when things happen you weren't prepared for. Another useful tool is a 'site map'. If possible you can map out the location before entering the setting and this will give you a framework, for example if you are observing how people move between desks or storage areas, map out the floor plan and prepare a set of codes for movement around that floor plan. I have read of a technique known as the 'de-briefing questionnaire' which is prepared in advance, to be completed after the setting is vacated. My main concern with this is that the preparation of the questionnaire may actually compromise what you see; the level of detail necessary to prepare such a questionnaires assumes a lot of a priori knowledge. There may be problems with field notes but in my opinion they are the most successful form of recording mechanism as long as you process them as soon as possible after the event. It is of little use to leave a pile of field notes in a folder to be processed at a later date; too much of the context will be lost.

Summary

Observations are a common data collection technique in many disciplines. Ethnography is based almost entirely on observation; case studies can rely heavily on observation; laboratory experiments use observation; it is also a useful technique

Example 17.1 An observation briefing sheet
This will depend very much on the nature of observation and the topic of the research; this is an example of how you could structure an observation.

CODE NAME OF SUBJECT...
LOCATION...
DATE..
TOPIC..
(e.g. What was the subject searching for?)
SETTING (e.g. What was the position of the subject in the room? How many people were using the room? Was it quiet or noisy? Level of activity?)

OBSERVATION (e.g. What did the subject do? How was it done? Was there any interaction with others? What did the subject say? Was there any change in mood during the observation?)

Facts written in blue; interpretations written in pencil.

in surveys and action research. The nature and form of the observation will vary greatly depending on the research method and the research question. It is important that you do not underestimate the difficulty of this technique; 'just watching' is not as simple as it sounds and there is a lot of pressure on the researcher to be alert and responsive to what is seen and heard. Never walk into a setting unprepared; this means having an understanding of your topic and having had some practice observing before the actual event. Having the cooperation of research subjects is vital; be sure you do not alienate your subjects before you start or as you conduct your fieldwork. Encouraging them to feel as if they have some degree of ownership can go a long way to securing your presence in the setting.

 PRACTICAL EXERCISE

There are two exercises here. First the exercise given in Chapter 10 – Ethnography – which is an example of semi- to non-participant observation. The second exercise is in participant observation. This involves a similar activity but this time the location is your place of work or study.

Participant observation

1 Decide on a particular day and time to take on your role as a participant observer.
2 Construct a set of signposts to guide your observation; these will depend very much on the setting but here is an example of the sort of things you may be looking for:

   • levels of physical activity (walking between locations, changing desks, carrying items from one location to another)
   • verbal communication between work/study colleagues
   • use of particular systems.

   Remember that while doing this you will still be maintaining your usual role in the setting, performing your usual functions and engaging in the usual way with your colleagues. For this reason I would suggest that you keep your observation time to a maximum of two hours depending on the level of activity.

3 As soon as possible at the end of the observation period attempt to transcribe your notes and write your descriptive narrative of the events you have recorded.

How much were you able to reconstruct?
What level of tacit knowledge have you applied to 'filling in' any gaps in your notes?
How difficult was it to maintain the dual role of observer and participant?

Suggested further reading

Erlandson, D. A., Harris, E. L., Skipper, B. L. and Allen, S. D. (1993) *Doing Naturalistic Inquiry: a guide to methods*, London, Sage.

Gray, D. B. (2004) *Doing Research in the Real World*, London, Sage.

Hine, C. (2000) *Virtual Ethnography*, London, Sage.

Mellon, C. A. (1990) *Naturalistic Inquiry for Library Science: methods and applications for research, evaluation and teaching*, London, Greenwood.

Patton, M. Q. (2002) *Qualitative Research and Evaluation Methods*, London, Sage.

Chapter 18

Diaries

Only good girls keep diaries. Bad girls don't have time.
(Tallulah Brockman Bankhead, 1903-68, from Lobenthal, 2004)

Introduction

The use of participant diaries as a data collection technique within LIS research has been largely overlooked, and where they are mentioned they are not looked on approvingly. Slater (1990) regards them as recorded self-observations and because of this places less value on their role in research in comparison with researcher observations. It is precisely the 'systemization and editing by their creators, at the conscious or unconscious level' (123) that Slater claims as a disadvantage, which provides the added data that may be valuable to the research. Ellis warns that diaries or logs rely 'on the willingness and ability of the [research participants] to complete the diaries' and that it is 'questionable whether they would [be] able to [do] so comprehensively and accurately' (Ellis, 1993, 475). Asking the participants in the research to keep logbooks or diaries of their behaviour can add to data collection in two ways: these records can provide confirmation of observations made by the researcher, and they can fill in gaps when the researcher can not be present. Diaries can offer insight into the behaviour, feelings and thoughts of research participants. However, it is not easy to encourage participants to maintain diaries; you are asking for quite a commitment in terms of time and effort. Participants need to be convinced there is a good reason for giving this much of their time to your research.

Participant diaries are not the only form of diary in the research process; researchers' diaries have long been used as a tool, although it is not strictly a data collection technique. I will discuss the use of researchers' diaries in this chapter as I feel it is an essential part of the research process. It is rare to find researchers' logs discussed in the methodology of any study but again this form of data collection has not received much attention in LIS research. Even in action research, which is heavily dependent on reflective thinking, we rarely find any real discussion about the use of a researcher's diary.

The purpose of diaries in research

As with any other data collection technique you have to be very clear about the purpose of the instrument and be very sure you have chosen the instrument that best fits that purpose. Researchers' diaries (or logs) will be discussed later as the purpose of this type of diary is somewhat different from that of participant diaries. Participant diaries are essentially a way of obtaining information specific to the individual and a way of recording events when the researcher cannot be present. Diaries also allow for autobiographic data to be recorded and shared with the researcher; the participant can decide on the depth and detail of this information but you will need to provide them with some guidelines on how 'personal' you want the information to be.

Participant diaries

One experience I have had of using participant diaries came very close to being a complete failure but actually ended up being a source of rich and enlightening data once I had changed my approach. In the beginning I prepared hard copy diaries in A4 format. This was a bound notebook containing an introduction to what information I was looking for and a series of identical pages, each providing a framework for data entry under a number of predefined headings. Each data page included a space for date, location, resource used and purpose of search. This was followed by a number of rows asking for details of the search and results, as well as feelings and reactions. I gave these out and asked participants to take the diaries with them at all times and complete a page every time they engaged in a search for any information.

After the first month I asked how the diaries were going. I was mortified to discover that only three of my participants had actually made entries in the diaries. I arranged a focus group of all participants to discus the diaries and see how we could change them in order to make them easier and more practical to maintain. During the focus group it became evident that what I saw as an ideal form of data collection did not fit with the views of my participants. Working together we identified a number of alternatives to collecting of this particular data. Not only did this assist the data collection process, it also increased the participants' sense of ownership of the study. It was necessary to make it very clear that the research was not concerned with *right* and *wrong* answers but with reality as they saw it.

Being involved in the design of the study alerted the participants to the fact that I was not conducting controlled experiments, it was an exploration not an experiment. The participant diary remained in its original form for a number of the participants; they were happy with the arrangement and wanted to continue using them. A database was designed by one participant and was used throughout the remainder of the fieldwork; the design was compatible with the arrangement of the hard copy version which assisted in the analysis. A number of participants kept personal diaries of their search activity; these were unstructured, the entries were in whatever form suited the participant. These diaries were maintained in either hard copy notebooks or as word-processed documents according to the preferences of the individual. This final method proved to be the most difficult to analyse. There was little, if any, structure to these diaries and they had to be read and re-read in order to identify the data content. However, the additional time involved was vindicated by the richness of data obtained, data that would have been lost if there had not been some degree of flexibility in the original design.

There was a lot of time and effort invested in these diaries by myself, the researcher, and the participants; in this case it was well worth the effort but I would stress that unless you are in a position to dedicate considerable time to the process, this is not a particularly straightforward technique for data collection. I would never recommend the use of diaries in a small-scale study; it is essential to build up rapport with the subjects of your investigation if you plan to ask them to keep diaries.

Structure of participant diaries

As the earlier example demonstrates, the format of a diary can be predetermined but very often you will need to amend this based on the reaction of participants to your design. The example I gave of my experience was unique in that I had an opportunity to discuss the diary format with participants and I had time to amend and reconstruct the diary to suit individuals. You will not always be in this position; very often you have to design the diary, distribute it and hope that when the time comes to have the diary returned you have harvested the type of data you need in a way that can be analysed.

Corti (1993) offers some very useful guidelines on constructing participant diaries.

1   An A4 booklet of about 5 to 20 pages is desirable, depending on the nature of the diary. Disappointing as it might seem, most respondents do not carry their diaries around with them.

2   The inside cover page should contain a clear set of instructions on how to complete the diary. This should stress the importance of recording events as soon as possible after they occur and how the respondent should try not to let the diary keeping influence their behaviour.

3   A model example of a correctly completed diary should feature on the second page.

4   Depending on how long a period the diary will cover, each page denoting either a week, a day of the week or a 24 hour period or less. Pages should be clearly ruled up as a calendar with prominent headings and enough space to enter all the desired information (such as what the respondent was doing, at what time, where, who with and how they felt at the time, and so on).

5   Checklists of the items, events or behaviour to help jog the diary keeper's memory should be printed somewhere fairly prominent. Very long lists should be avoided since they may be off-putting and confusing to respondents. For a structured time budget diary, an exhaustive list of all possible relevant activities should be listed together with the appropriate codes. Where more than one type of activity is to be

entered, that is, primary and secondary (or background) activities, guidance should
be given on how to deal with 'competing' or multiple activities.

6   There should be an explanation of what is meant by the unit of observation, such as a
'session', an 'event' or a 'fixed time block'. Where respondents are given more freedom
in naming their activities and the activities are to be coded later, it is important to give
strict guidelines on what type of behaviour to include, what definitely to exclude and
the level of detail required. Time budget diaries without fixed time blocks should
include columns for start and finish times for activities.

7   Appropriate terminology or lists of activities should be designed to meet the needs of
the sample under study, and if necessary, different versions of the diary should be
used for different groups.

8   Following the diary pages it is useful to include a simple set of questions for the
respondent to complete, asking, among other things, whether the diary keeping
period was atypical in any way compared to usual daily life. It is also good practice to
include a page at the end asking for the respondents' own comments and
clarifications of any peculiarities relating to their entries. Even if these remarks will
not be systematically analysed, they may prove helpful at the editing or coding stage.

(Corti, 1993)

These guidelines are as comprehensive as any I have found but, like me, you may
discover that there is no such thing as a 'best-fit' design. Consider the nature of your
participants, their daily routine and the time they are likely to have to devote to this
activity.

The researcher's log

The use of diaries or logs by researchers is nothing new. Keeping a journal of some
form has been standard practice in research for many years. Although many could
claim these diaries are nothing more than a log of activity, they are actually far more
valuable than that. Faraday is well renowned for the detailed and meticulous diaries
he left behind. Emphasis is usually placed on his detailed descriptions of outcome,
but as Bragg points out, the value of Faraday's diaries extends beyond the outcomes
of experiments: 'The main interest of the Diary lies quite outside the range of
propositions and experimental proofs. It centres round the methods of Faraday's
attack, both in thought and in experiment: it depends on the records of the workings
of his mind as he mastered each research in turn, and on his attitude not only to his
own researches but also to scientific advance in general' (Bragg, 1932, v). Diaries
create a lasting account of process as well as outcome. This is a valuable source of
information that is unlikely to be available through any other medium.

Many researchers advise the use of a log or reflexive journal. Ely goes further than
this and gives the log a central role in both data collection and analysis as they
'contain the data upon which the analysis is begun and carried forward. It is the
home for the substance that we use to tease out meaning and reflect upon them as
they evolve' (Ely, 1991, 65). Schatzman and Strauss (1973) suggest that a log can be

maintained in three parts: observational notes, theoretical notes and methodological notes. They describe *observational notes* as 'statements bearing upon events experienced principally through watching and listening. They contain as little interpretation as possible, and are as reliable as the observer can construct them. Each ON represents an event deemed important enough to include in the fund of recorded experience, as a piece of evidence for some proposition yet unborn or as a property of a context or situation. An ON is the Who, What, When, Where and How of human activity' (100). They go on to explain *theoretical notes* as 'self-conscious, controlled attempts to derive meaning from any one or several observation notes. The observer as recorder thinks about what he has experienced, and makes whatever private declaration of meaning he feels will bear conceptual fruit' (101). These notes provide the arena for ideas to be tested and assessed. Schatzman and Strauss describe *methodological notes* as statements 'that reflect an operational act completed or planned: an instruction to oneself, a reminder, a critique of one's own tactics. It notes timing, sequencing, stationing, stage setting, or manoeuvring. Methodological notes might be thought of as observational notes on the researcher himself and upon the methodological process itself' (101).

Methodological notes can also be referred to as the research log but it is more than a daily timetable of the fieldwork, a place to organize the logistics of the study; it is a place of reflexive learning. Methodological notes form the basis of the final audit trail in qualitative research. The researcher diary is an invaluable tool; it also acts as a place of retreat to reformulate plans and it provided an accurate and up-to-date account of the fieldwork that could not have been achieved through any other means. The discipline involved in keeping entries consistent, in many cases writing notes each day, focuses the research and brings order to a process that could easily become fragmented. These ideas and observations could get lost in the ever-growing mountain of field notes, literature searches and notes on methodological decisions. The log allows you to produce a record of every event in the study to which reference can be made as well as playing a part in the development of any theory that emerges.

Structure and recording

Although many researchers 'indicate that part of their research activities involves writing notes and keeping diaries, they do not tell us, in any detail, about how these diaries may be established and maintained' (Burgess, 1981, 75). Maintaining a research diary requires a huge commitment in time, energy and thought; it requires establishing a routine and sticking to that routine regardless of other events impinging on your time and energy. There is no prescribed formula for what goes into a diary but areas that could be included are:

- an ongoing bibliography of reading
- initial research design
- detail of all fieldwork
- any changes in fieldwork

- minutes of meeting
- individual observation notes
- reflection on emerging theory
- new research questions that arise but cannot be considered in this particular investigation.

I personally maintain my researcher's journal in a Word document with line numbers included so if I do need to use some of the content as evidence in my final analysis it is easier to refer to the text by line.

Summary

There are two types of research diary: participants' diaries and researchers' diaries (see Example 18.1). The researcher's diary has a long and successful tradition in positivist and interpretivist research as a recording mechanism and a place for interpretation and theory formulation. This is a standard technique and I recommend every researcher should maintain a diary, including as much depth and detail as is required by the research and the purpose of the diary. It should always be there in some form or another as a record of the research and an account of the researcher's activity.

Example 18.1 Structure of a participant diary

INSTRUCTION: Please keep a record of your information seeking using the framework provided on each of the following pages. Use one page per search and feel free to use the blank reverse side to add any other information.

PAGE 1

DATE	
LOCATION	
REASON FOR NEEDING INFORMATION	
RESOURCE USED	
SEARCH TERMS USED	
RESULTS	
How do you feel about these results and the resource you have used?	

Participants' diaries are a little more complex and can be extremely difficult as a data-collection technique; maintaining diaries takes commitment and can be time consuming and sometimes intrusive. Participants will need to be clear about the purpose and value of the diaries as well as how they will be used. There is also the subject of analysis to consider; the more 'free-form' the diary is the more complex the analysis. There are many reasons for dismissing participants' diaries because of the difficulties associated with them but there are times, depending on the research topic, when there is no other way of gathering the data you need. Think carefully about the purpose, design and value of the diary to maximize the chances of harvesting useful data; when they work they offer a fascinating and insightful glimpse of the behaviour and thoughts of research participants.

 PRACTICAL EXERCISE

Using the diary format in the example above keep your own diary of information-seeking over a period of two weeks. This exercise should demonstrate the level of demand placed on a research participant when we ask them to engage in this technique.

Reflection on the process (please answer these questions as honestly as possible):

1 How rigorously did you maintain your diary?
2 How easy was it to provide useful information in the framework?
3 How much time did you spend filling in the diary?
4 How would you go about analysing the data in the diary?

Suggested further reading

Burgess, R. G. (1981) Keeping a Research Diary, *Cambridge Journal of Education*, **11** (1), 75–83.

Corti, L. (1993) Using Diaries in Social Research, *Social Research Update*, **2**, www.soc.surrey.ac.uk/sru/SRU2.html.

Ely, M. and Anzul, M. (1994) *Doing Qualitative Research: circles within circles*, London, Falmer Press.

Marshall, C. and Rossman, G. (1995) *Designing Qualitative Research*, 2nd edn, London, Sage.

Schatzman, L. and Strauss, A. (1973) *Field Research: strategies for a natural sociology*, Englewood Cliffs, Prentice Hall.

Chapter 19

Focus groups

Introduction

Powell, Single and Lloyd define a focus group as, 'a group of individuals selected and assembled by researchers to discuss and comment on, from personal experience, the topic that is the subject of the research' (1996, 499). The focus group technique has been used in social research since the late 1930s (Kreuger, 1988), but possibly the most obvious use of the technique has been in market research where it is applied to investigate consumer preferences and habits. This technique is not usually recommended to new, inexperienced researchers as it demands a relatively high level of understanding.

In focus group research the researcher acts as a mediator between the question and the group and between the individual members of the group. Depending on their level of involvement in the topic this can be a rather difficult role, however, focus groups are becoming increasingly popular in qualitative research as a means of gathering data from a number of sources at the same time. A focus group allows 'a variety of perspectives and explanations [to] be obtained from a single data-gathering session' (Gorman and Clayton, 2005, 143).

Every researcher has to start somewhere and a number of my former students have conducted focus groups very successfully even though it was the first time they had attempted the technique and they were sometimes very nervous. As with every data collection technique, if it fits the purpose then I would recommend you go for it but not without testing your ability as a moderator first, and not without immersing yourself in the topic and being very clear about why you are there. You must remain in control of the situation and ensure that your research goals are achieved; you may be confronted with some strong characters and you must stay focused and keep the session on track.

Purpose of a focus group

There are many reasons for selecting focus groups as a data collection technique in qualitative research. Stewart and Shamdasani provide the following list of occasions when it is appropriate to apply this technique in your research:

1   obtaining general background information about a topic of interest;
2   generating research hypotheses that can be submitted to further research and testing using more quantitative approaches;
3   stimulating new ideas and creative concepts;
4   diagnosing the potential for problems with a new program, service or product;
5   generating impressions of products, programs, services, institutions, or other objects of interest;
6   learning how respondents talk about the phenomenon of interest which may facilitate quantitative research tools;
7   interpreting previously obtained qualitative results (1990, 15).

Essentially focus groups can be used at any point in the research design. During the early stages of an investigation focus groups can allow you to explore a topic, to establish just what the salient issues surrounding the topic are and what requires further investigation. Using 'open' focus groups allows your research participants to talk about the things that they feel are significant. This type of group can be rather difficult to moderate as there is less likely to be any formal structure to it but it is a very useful way of identifying the real areas of concern or interest. In this way the focus group could provide a useful guide to further data collection. If you are using an emergent design then the focus group results may suggest the next step. For example do you need to follow up the focus group meeting with individual interviews? Is there a need to prepare and distribute a questionnaire to a wider population? Not only do you have an indication of the potential salient issues but you also have an indication of what else you need to find out and possibly an indication of how you can best discover it. Ritchie and Lewis believe that 'the interaction between participants, will itself illuminate the research issue' (2003, 58).

As the data collection progresses focus groups can be used to explore issues in more depth. Interviews may have been carried out but you need to examine the data you have so far based on conflicting views. Focus groups can be conducted after observations in order to seek explanations for behaviour. They provide a very different forum; it is essentially a moderated discussion and as with any discussion individuals are allowed to reconsider their views based on something they hear. 'In a group situation many people are prompted to say or suggest ideas which may not occur to them on their own' (Gorman and Clayton, 1997, 142). Focus groups can also be used as the last element of data collection in order to confirm emerging findings: 'Focus group interviews also provide some quality controls on data collection in that participants tend to provide checks and balances on each other which weed out false or extreme views' (Patton, 1987, 135).

The purpose of focus groups is to enable a range of perceptions, feelings and attitudes from participants across a range of issues to be explored. It is possible to conduct relatively in-depth discussions with a small group of participants who may be only a small proportion of the target population or the entire target population. They have the potential to allow for a wide range of views, beliefs and perceptions to be generated in a single data collection exercise. Focus groups are useful as a data collection technique in their own right, to be used at any point during the research study, but they can also be used as a planning device in the early stages of the research or as an evaluation device towards the end of the data collection.

Organizing a focus group

Much of the literature will tell you that conducting a focus group is an art or skill that requires considerable experience and training. Many argue that the quality of the data obtained from a focus group discussion is the direct result of how well the moderator carries out the process. I would agree with this but would stress that it is a skill that can be learned; there is an art to focus group moderating that not all will be suited to but organization and knowing your topic can go a long way towards improving the quality of the data you harvest.

The process of organizing and running a focus group should follow a basic design:

- Identify your participants (usually six to ten people but make sure you have a backup for those unable to attend).
- Select and book a location.
- Prepare and send out an invitation which includes:
  - a description of the purpose of the focus group and who you are
  - a brief synopsis of the topic for discussion
  - logistics such as date, time, expected duration and location
  - any ethical considerations.
- Prepare the room in such a way that participants can see and hear each other and you have an appropriate place in the setting.
- Consider what equipment you will need:
  - a tape recorder if you are planning on taping the discussion although this is not usually the most successful way to record events as it becomes very difficult to analyse a group discussion on audio tape
  - a flipchart and pens
  - a briefing sheet
  - a disclaimer.
- Prepare a briefing sheet for yourself, this may not necessarily be a list of questions, it may be the issues you would like to cover but what it must be is a document that clearly sets out your own research goals.
- Open the discussion with a brief introduction; you may want the participants to introduce themselves at this point.
- Open up the discussion then begin the moderating process; Stewart and Shamdasani suggest that using questions 'that include words such as how, why, under what conditions, and similar probes suggest to respondents that the researcher is interested in complexity and facilitating discussion' (1990, 65).
- Keep the discussion on track.

- Probe for more detail when appropriate.
- Do not be tempted to 'jump into the silence' – try to say as little as possible.
- Thank everyone when the discussion is over and if they are involved in another element of the research take this opportunity to remind them of the next stage.

Although all of the theory in the world cannot prepare you completely for 'being there' my own experience and the experience of others allows me to offer a few points on the moderating process. Gorman and Clayton warn that a 'group can be dominated by a strong individual . . . with the result that its members acquiesce to a single viewpoint and perhaps do not even bother to mention their own convictions (2005, 142). It is your job as moderator to try and prevent this from happening. One way to do this is to invite each person to speak on a particular topic in turn; this ensures everyone has an opportunity to speak. You must be careful that this does not become too daunting, implying that everyone must say something. Impress on the group that they are being invited to speak, not ordered to speak. You must respect everyone's right to be quiet if they genuinely do not want to make a contribution on a particular point. If it becomes clear that there is a clique forming, or is already formed, you may want to suggest a break and you can take this opportunity to rearrange the seating.

You must always avoid personal confrontation; there is no room for your emotions when you are the moderator. You could always turn a difference of opinion into a topic for discussion; never appear to be taking sides in the discussion. There are a number of approaches you can take to encourage a free-flowing discussion but sometimes things will stall and you will have to get them moving again. There are a few things you could do here:

- Ask the group to write down their ideas on an issue.
- When they have been given time to do this ask them to read out what they have written; it would help if you could note this down on a chart or board for everyone to see.
- Once all responses have been given you could then ask your participants to write down any other ideas they have based on the other contributions they have heard.
- Use these responses to open the discussion.

It is impossible to say here what questions you should be asking but it is important that you make sure everyone is aware that you are here to discover their feeling and beliefs. There are no right or wrong answers; the discussion is concerned with how participants feel or think about issues.

Online focus groups

'The internet constitutes an important new domain in which the focus group method may be adapted and even transformed' (Mann and Stewart, 2000, 101). The principles and purpose of the focus group should remain the same regardless of the form but this is not necessarily the case in virtual environments as more options are available. I would like to concentrate here on the differing logistics of face-to-face and online focus groups and suggest that anyone intending to engage in online focus groups reads Mann and Stewart *Internet Communication and Qualitative Research* (2000).

Online focus groups are still a relatively new technique for data collection and although there are many perceived advantages there remains a great deal of debate as to the usefulness of this form of focus group. The first most distinct difference with online focus groups is the choice between synchronous or asynchronous interaction. Many researchers argue that the asynchronous option turns the technique into something other than a focus group, as one of the major reasons for holding a focus group is immediate interaction. If the 'conversation' is not happening in real time then it could be argued that the stimulus provided by interaction is lost. As this approach is still so new there is very little evidence to support or reject this claim.

A second issue to consider with online focus groups is the nature of your research population. If there is sufficient evidence to suggest that participants would feel confident and comfortable in a virtual environment then this could be a viable option. You would have to be very sure that members of your population were not disadvantaged because they were uncomfortable communicating in a virtual space or they lacked the skills necessary to take an active part in the 'conversation'.

The technology can be a barrier in more ways than one; access to robust and reliable conferencing software is a prerequisite for online group discussion. All of your participants must have access to the same software and be comfortable using it. There are occasions when this may be the most obvious approach to holding a focus group, for example if your research population already inhabits a virtual community and regularly takes part in synchronous discussions.

Where there is real debate about the nature of the focus group lies in the purpose of the technique:

- Interaction is essential; is it possible to encourage the same level of interaction online? There is a lack of visual clues online and a great deal of interaction depends on the use of visual clues.
- It is much easier to talk (or type) in parallel online than it is face to face. This makes it difficult for the moderator to follow the flow of the discussion.
- People are less likely to be intimidated by other focus group members online than if they meet in person, so the need to ensure everyone has their say may be less of a burden to the moderator.
- Transcripts of the focus group are available immediately online without the need for the moderator or participants to take notes.
- Online focus groups potentially offer access to a more geographically dispersed community but this is still restricted to those able and willing to use the required software.

These are a few of the issues surrounding the use of online focus groups but this list is by no means exhaustive; they are drawn from my experience and that of researchers I have worked with, who have highlighted these issues. There is no doubt that this is an exciting option for all researchers when it is appropriate. I would say again that your decision to use the focus group technique should depend on its fitness for purpose, the topic of the research, the nature of the research population and your experience. It would be wrong to engage in online focus groups just because it is an available option; it has to be the best possible available option before you decide to do it.

Summary

Much of the research methods literature highlights the need for experience when conducting a focus group. I agree with this completely, it is a situation which demands a great deal of confidence, concentration and understanding. But do not allow this to become a valid reason for not using this technique; everyone has to start somewhere. It is often recommended that to gain experience a new researcher should accompany a more experienced researcher and act as 'note taker' during focus groups to become familiar with the process. If there is an opportunity to do this then all the better; if there is not (which is more likely), then practise, but do not allow the fact that you've read somewhere that this technique requires experience to be an excuse for not attempting it. The important point is to be prepared, to know your topic, know why you are there and know what you hope to take away from the group. Your ability as a moderator will improve with practice and experience but if there is a role for focus group data collection in your research then prepare yourself well and go for it. Consider the benefits to the research and if they are substantial then you have little to lose and a lot to gain. The focus group technique has been used very successfully for a number of decades now; it is a more useful method of harvesting in-depth data from a wide range of participants than any other technique available.

 PRACTICAL EXERCISE

Identify a recent event; it could be something that has happened locally or a national or international event that has received wide publicity. Select a small group of acquaintances (no more than five) and arrange a group meeting with them. Schedule the meeting to last no more than one hour. Once this is arranged you are ready to conduct the exercise.

1 Write a brief synopsis of the topic including only known facts.
2 Prepare an invitation to the focus group which provides details of the date, time and location of the meeting along with the brief synopsis of the topic to be discussed.
3 Make a brief checklist of what you hope to achieve during the focus group, which could include:

- identifying what individuals think about the event
- whether there is a particular consensus about the cause or result of the event
- what facts participants feel are the most significant.

4 Conduct the focus group meeting remembering that your role here is as moderator; your opinions on the topic are not to be shared or included. You are here to gather the views of others.

5 After the focus group meeting analyse the data you have in relation to the checklist you made. Did you achieve your research goals?

6 Reflect on the experience in terms of your own behaviour during the session, how well you controlled the discussion, how comfortable you felt with the process, and how well you managed to maintain your neutral position.

Suggested further reading

Kreuger, R. A. (1988) *Focus Groups: a practical guide for applied research*, London, Sage.

Mann, C. and Stewart, F. (2000) *Internet Communication and Qualitative Research: a handbook for researching online*, London, Sage, Chapter 5.

Morgan, D. (1993) *Successful Focus Groups: advancing the state of the art*, London, Sage.

Morgan, D. L. and Kreuger, R. A. (1998) *The Focus Group Kit*, London, Sage.

Punch, K. (1998) *Introduction to Social Research: quantitative and qualitative approaches*, London, Sage.

Ritchie, J. and Lewis, J. (2003) *Qualitative Research Practice: a guide for social science students and researchers*, London, Sage.

Stewart D. W. and Shamdasani, P. N. (1990) *Focus Groups: theory and practice*, London, Sage.

Chapter 20

Usability testing

Introduction

Usability testing and systems evaluations can form part or all of the data collection in case study research, surveys, experimental research or action research; in fact I have recently advised on a records management project that included this type of data collection within a modified Delphi study. Again, choice of data collection is based on 'best fit for purpose' not some predetermined law that associates a data collection technique with a research method just because that's the way it has always been done. The most obvious restriction on these particular techniques is that they are all designed to evaluate or test systems; that is the sole purpose of this type of data collection so in that sense there is an obvious 'best fit'.

The major difference between user testing and expert reviews (heuristic evaluations or cognitive walkthroughs) is the role of the individual doing the evaluation. In usability testing the people asked to perform the test will be actual users of the system – either proposed users if it is a prototype test or actual users if it is a system evaluation – who are observed by researchers as they carry out the test. Heuristic evaluations and cognitive walkthroughs are performed by evaluators (researchers), who interpret their findings as they perform the evaluation and again this can be done at the prototype stage or after the system has been implemented. In terms of your own research there are two choices: you use a sample of users to perform usability tests on the system they are familiar with or will be expected to use, or you collect a group of 'evaluators' to perform cognitive walkthroughs or heuristic reviews of a system.

User tests

User testing is probably one of the most common ways of approaching user-centred design and is certainly the most widely used technique in LIS. The purpose of user testing is to gather data on how users interact with a system and how well the system responds to user behaviour. 'User testing' in the sense it is used in this chapter is concerned with the more formal, predesigned test, not the natural observation of users more usually associated with case study or ethnographic research. User testing in this more formal sense can be more easily associated with the quasi-experiment, where behaviour is watched, recorded and analysed in a structured context. This context can vary from a sample group of users being asked to perform a set of predetermined tasks on a system in their natural setting to a sample group being invited into a laboratory to be watched and often recorded performing the tasks set by the evaluator. These tests usually involve the following stages although not all will be used in every user test.

- Draw up a list of tasks to be tested by the user. These will usually be determined by the system requirements: what is it meant to do?
- Identify a test sample from existing users; it is vital that your sample is made up of actual systems users who have a reason to use the system. This could be a sample of staff who are working on a particular system daily such as the staff on an enquiry desk using a knowledge database to respond to customer requests, or a sample of casual users who have access to the system as one way of satisfying their information needs.
- Determine the location for user tests. You may not have access to a laboratory but you could simulate this environment if you have access to an area that could be dedicated to your sample for the duration of the test.
- Ensure that the location is suitably arranged to accommodate the sample.
- Decide in advance how you are going to record the test. There are a number of options here; it may be possible to set up the system to record the behaviour of the user, providing you with a map of their movements through the system during the test. Another option is to use 'think aloud protocol', where the user is asked to talk the researcher through what they are doing: why they select certain choices on the screen or why they type in certain keywords, for example. You could also prepare a 'questionnaire' that the user is asked to fill out as they perform the required tasks. If you choose this option you will need to keep the 'questionnaire' as simple as possible; be wary of asking too much of the users, it is your responsibility to record your data.
- Before the test begins it is important to establish rapport with your sample. They must be very clear that it is the system being tested, not them. It is difficult for anyone to perform well when they are being watched; you must be aware of this and do your best to remove any additional pressure from the members of your test sample.
- Once the test begins it is important that you remember that it is the system that is being tested, so avoid the temptation to help the user when a problem is encountered; this defeats the purpose of the test.
- During the test you must remain highly alert; your role is to take in all that you are seeing and hearing. That is the reason many commercial system evaluators use a laboratory with video cameras set up to monitor behaviour. It is unlikely that you will have the benefit of a purpose-designed room, so make the most of what you have. Alternatively conduct user tests one at a time; this may be time consuming but it will allow you to pay attention to what is going on.

- It is also possible to engage in dialogue with the user (if you are doing single tests); this will allow you to clarify your own understanding of what is happening and provide you with additional data. For example you may wish to know why a user selected a particular option; although you have asked them to engage in 'think aloud protocol' they may not always verbalize their feelings.
- Analyse your data from all users to identify common themes that emerge from the tests.
- Present your findings; it may be that you are in a position to implement system changes based on your data or offer advice to those that can.

User testing is usually concerned with implementing actual change, either at the design stage or to assist in creating systems specifications for a new design; it is not usually concerned with theory development but actual change. That is not to say that user tests cannot contribute to theory development, that is the purpose of publishing results, so we can all learn and move on, based on empirical knowledge.

Cognitive walkthroughs

> Cognitive walkthroughs involve simulating a user's problem-solving process at each step in the human-computer dialogue, checking to see if the user's goals and memory for actions can be assumed to lead to the correct action.
>
> (Neilsen and Mack, cited in Preece, Rogers and Sharpe, 2002, 420)

Cognitive walkthroughs (see Example 20.1 overleaf) are used by systems developers during the design of a new system but can also be used on an existing system as a means of evaluation. This is the most common application in student research unless that research involves designing and building a system; in that case cognitive walkthroughs can be applied in the usual way, at the prototyping stage. Cognitive walkthroughs are carried out by evaluators who do not use the system in question. They are given a set of predetermined tasks; they then 'walk through' those tasks and record the problems encountered.

The process of cognitive walkthroughs involves the following steps:

- identifying and documenting typical user characteristics and the tasks associated with system use
- developing a set of 'typical' tasks to focus on the aspect of the system being tested
- writing clear instructions for evaluators
- asking the evaluators as they work through the tasks to comment on the following questions for each stage in the task: Will users know what to do? Will they understand from the response of the system whether the action was correct or not?
- the evaluator responding in written notes to these two questions at each stage in the task

Example 20.1 Cognitive walkthrough

Cognitive walkthrough is based on the information-processing model of human cognition:

- A goal is set.
- The system is searched for available action to meet that goal.
- The action is selected.
- The action is performed.
- The user evaluates performance and remembers success or failure.
- The purpose is to evaluate the system not the user.

Description of user characteristics

Role...

Background...
....
....

Level of experience..
....

Degree of urgency of the task...
....

Description of the tasks to be performed:
....

List of all actions taken to complete the task

Please list every action taken during the process no matter how insignificant it appears. Evaluate systems performance after every task:

Action...
Response..
....

Action...
Response..
....

Action...
Response..

- the evaluator interpreting the cause of the problem, why it might occur and any possible solutions to it
- analysing evaluators' reports
- presenting findings
- recommending system revisions.

The major reason cognitive walkthroughs are not performed by users is the level of systems knowledge necessary to interpret what is happening during the walkthrough. Unless the user has knowledge and understanding of systems design they would be unlikely to be in a position to offer explanations and possible solutions: 'The assumptions about what would cause the problems and why are recorded. This involves explaining why users would face difficulties. Notes about side issues and design changes are made. A summary of these results is compiled' (Preece, Rogers and Sharpe, 2002, 421).

Cognitive walkthroughs have been used to evaluate anti-terrorist support systems (Garg et al., 2005), multimedia applications (Huart, Kolski and Sagar, 2004) and the use of ticket vending machines (Blandford, Connell and Green, 2004). This demonstrates the breadth of application of this data collection technique in terms of information and communication services and functions; it is not restricted to web technologies.

Heuristic evaluation

Heuristic evaluation is the most popular of the usability inspection methods. Heuristic evaluation is done as a systematic inspection of a user interface design for usability. The goal of heuristic evaluation is to find the usability problems in the design so that they can be attended to as part of an iterative design process. Heuristic evaluation involves having a small set of evaluators examine the interface and judge its compliance with recognized usability principles (the 'heuristics').   (Neilsen, 1994, online)

Although Neilsen highlights evaluation at the design stage, again it is also possible to conduct heuristic reviews on existing systems, which is how they are applied in many student projects where the student has no real say in the system design but wishes to evaluate the system as part of their research study. Heuristic evaluations (see Example 20.2) are concerned with testing an entire system based on predetermined guidelines. The evaluators are given a set of principles (the heuristics) and the system is evaluated based on those principles. Neilsen (1994) suggests that the heuristics are usually a set of usability principles. An example of such principles could be the Web Content Accessibility Guidelines (World Wide Web Consortium, 1999), where a set of principles have been established and adopted as an acceptable standard. Heuristic evaluations are essentially a 'free-flow' evaluation as opposed to the 'task-based' evaluation of cognitive walkthroughs.

Example 20.2 Heuristic evaluation
This feedback represents a brief heuristic review used by one usability specialist.

Screen information
System name: _____
Screen description:_____

_____

Compliance checklist (a tick indicates degree of compliance)

Predetermined heuristics (these would be selected using principles appropriate to the system)

Language and phrases familiar to user	___ Low	___ Medium	___ High
Screen information in a natural and logical order	___ Low	___ Medium	___ High
Facilitates user's decision making and task processing	___ Low	___ Medium	___ High
Provides an easy exit for the user	___ Low	___ Medium	___ High
Supports undo and redo functionality	___ Low	___ Medium	___ High
Prevents user error	___ Low	___ Medium	___ High
Provides visual cues for easy task processing	___ Low	___ Medium	___ High
Is quick and easy to use	___ Low	___ Medium	___ High
Provides user feedback and system status when needed	___ Low	___ Medium	___ High
Is designed to be visually pleasing to the user	___ Low	___ Medium	___ High

Summary comments and enhancement suggestions:

_____
_____
_____
_____
_____

Heuristic evaluations are carried out by a number of evaluators, usually up to five as this is the point at which it is commonly accepted that information saturation will be attained, any more than this and the overlap of identified issues outweighs the benefits of additional evaluators. The evaluators then examine an interface using the identified heuristics, judging the level of systems compliance. Similarly to the Delphi research method, the evaluators should be experts as this allows for deeper scrutiny of levels of compliance as well as the knowledge to suggest improvements. The evaluation process consists of the evaluators moving through the system once to familiarize themselves with the navigation structure used and the general scope of the system. On the second pass through the system the evaluator focuses on the specific elements of the system related to the heuristics identified as the standard. A 'heuristic evaluation aims at explaining each observed usability problem with reference to established usability principles' (Neilsen, 1994). This technique is referred to as 'discount usability engineering' as there are fewer ethical and practical issues when actual users are not involved.

Stages in heuristic evaluation are:

- identifing the set of principles to be used as the accepted standard (the heuristics of the evaluation)
- identifying between three and five 'experts' to carry out the evaluation
- evaluators carrying out the evaluation independently based on two 'passes' through the system
- identifying problems and issues as they are encountered, and noting possible solutions
- de-briefing evaluators to share their experience and discuss potential solutions
- analysing all evaluators' reports
- presenting findings
- recommending system revisions.

Heuristic evaluations are usually carried out by individuals who have the ability either to change a system or propose changes to those who do.

Summary

Usability testing is commonly associated with systems design, development and evaluation. Although by 'system' we usually assume some form of electronic or digital systems this does not always have to be the case; there are many manual systems that could be evaluated using the approaches mentioned in this chapter. The major difference between user testing and evaluator testing is the level of systems knowledge and the form of analysis required. User testing relies on users carrying out common tasks and being able to 'talk' the researcher through their behaviour; it is up to the researcher to interpret this behaviour. Evaluator testing allows the test and interpretation to go on simultaneously, again it is the purpose of the study that determines the choice of test.

The most common purpose of usability testing is during the iterative design phase to inform developments but they can also be carried out on current systems to inform new develops and future change. It is possible to use various combinations of tests and evaluations within the same study; it is not uncommon for a system to be evaluated using both user tests and expert reviews as did Shen and Liang (2000) in their evaluation of a web-based virtual-reality museum. As with all data collection techniques, the choice to use it depends on whether it is the 'best fit for purpose'; as the researcher you must decide on the technique which best fits your research objectives.

 PRACTICAL EXERCISE

Cognitive walkthrough

Using the example feedback sheet (Example 20.1, page 230), carry out a cognitive walkthrough of a system you are particularly familiar with. Rather than simply following your usual process, attempt to record each action and the system response to that action.

Heuristic review

Using a system you are familiar with, and using the set of heuristics given in Example 20.2 (page 232) as a guide, design the heuristics for an evaluation of that system. You may wish to use recognized usability standards as your principles or design a set of your own.

Suggested further reading

Nielsen, J. (1993) *Usability Engineering*, Boston, MA, Academic Press, Chapter 5.

Nielsen, J. (1994) *How to Conduct a Heuristic Evaluation*,
    www.useit.com/papers/heuristic/heuristic_evaluation.html.

Paterno, F. (2000) *Model-based Design and Evaluation of Interface Applications*, London,
    Springer Verlag.

Preece, J., Rodgers, Y. and Sharpe, H. (2002) *Interaction Design: beyond human-computer
    interaction*, New York, John Wiley & Sons.

Wharton, C., Rieman, J., Lewis, C. and Polson, P. (1994) *The Cognitive Walkthrough: a
    practitioner's guide.* In Nielsen, J. and Mack, R. L. (eds), *Usability Inspection Methods*, New
    York, John Wiley and Sons.

Data analysis and research presentation

PART 4

Data analysis and research presentation

In this section the aim is to discuss quantitative and qualitative analysis and how to present research. You have already been advised to read widely on the method and techniques of your choice, and this is emphasized even more in this section. It is out with the scope of this text to provide the detail and depth necessary for you to master any of the methods of analysis covered here. My aim is to introduce you to these procedures and provide you with enough detail to identify appropriateness, making sure you understand the nature of your data and how you can use that data. There are entire texts dedicated to statistical and narrative analysis procedures, and now a great deal of free software on the internet that performs particular tests on your data. I do not repeat these procedures here but rather discuss how they can be applied in terms of their appropriateness to the data gathered.

Chapter 21

Qualitative analysis

> By the term 'qualitative research,' we mean any type of research that produces findings not arrived at by statistical procedures or other means of quantification.
>
> (Strauss and Corbin, 1998, 10)

Introduction

Qualitative analysis is applied in any study that focuses on emerging theory, using the inductive analysis process to arrive at an understanding of the phenomenon under investigation. When applying qualitative analysis the purpose is to generate a hypothesis based on the data gathered and interpretation of that data. This chapter is concerned with the analysis of rich, detailed, qualitative data. In my opinion this does not include answers to open-ended questions in a questionnaire; this is rarely, if ever, qualitative data. We are talking here about the analysis of detailed responses to in-depth interviewing, observation and focus group discussion. In qualitative research the gathering and analysis of data occurs concurrently; it is a constant interplay of data and analysis, data informing analysis, and analysis informing new data collection. Morse (1997) believes that the process of qualitative analysis involves:

- *comprehending* the phenomenon under study
- *synthesizing* a portrait of the phenomenon that accounts for relations and links within its aspects
- *theorizing* about how and why these relations appear as they do
- *recontextualizing*, or putting the new knowledge about phenomena and relations back into the context of how others have articulated the evolving knowledge (26).

There are four recognized strategies for qualitative data analysis. By far the most often cited is the 'constant comparative analysis' developed by Strauss (1987). Because of the popular use of this strategy we will examine the process in more detail in this chapter. This strategy can also be applied in other contexts; a study may be a grounded theory study but a constant comparative analysis can still be applied. An ethnographic study can also apply some of the characteristics of this strategy although the focus will be slightly different. This is not to say this is the only option available to the qualitative researcher, but in my opinion this strategy provides the soundest framework for working with large amounts of descriptive data. It is also applied by some researchers in a modified form to assist with analysis in the three other strategies mentioned here, although clearly the focus is slightly different. Before we look at the constant comparative strategy in more detail, it is necessary to take a brief look at the other three options.

Phenomenological strategies

Phenomenological analysis is concerned with discovering the underlying structure of experiences; there is no attempt made to look for comparisons within the data from multiple sources, only to seek out detailed understanding of the phenomena under investigation as it is experienced by the individual. The form of analysis used in this type of study explicitly avoids comparisons and makes no attempt to identify themes; the purpose is to analyse the experience in depth and detail as a 'one-off' account of an event. It thus allows anyone reading the analysis to form a deeper understanding of that experience without having gone through it themselves. The end result of this approach is a detailed, systematic and exhaustive account of an event presented as descriptive narrative.

Colaizzi (1978) and Giorgi (1985) are phenomenologists who have structured the phenomenological viewpoint into a set of manageable steps and processes for working with rich, detailed data and are recommended reading for anyone wishing to take this approach. The use of this form of qualitative analysis is rare in LIS study as it is the most extreme form of 'individual experience' analysis and not often used to handle data that is often from multiple sources. Phenomenological analysis focuses on individual subjects in extreme depth rarely allowing the time to examine more than one case in the majority of research projects.

Ethnographic methods

In Part 2 we looked at ethnography as a research method. The form of analysis that usually accompanies this method may use some characteristics of the constant comparative strategy but the focus is different. Ethnographers document human experience as it happens from within the context in which it occurs. The focus of ethnographic analysis is the human experience as a whole, beliefs, ways of living and relationships. The purpose is to uncover and record variations in social and cultural enactments.

When we read an ethnographic study we assume the researcher has arrived at the narrative by immersion in the culture under investigation, including in the analysis all aspects of their 'living'. Analysing ethnographic data is iterative in the extreme, a constant cycle of watching, interpreting, sifting, sorting and linking data from every source available. Active involvement in the field is transformed and represented in the final written document. The anthropological tradition from which this method grew has traditionally focused on 'telling a story', not presenting an analysis of a particular theme but demonstrating how multiple themes join together to create the 'whole'. Analysis of ethnographic data still involves sifting and sorting and establishing themes but there is no attempt made to remove those themes from the specific context.

Narrative and discourse analysis

This approach to analysing qualitative data relies on the assumption that human experience is shaped, transformed and understood through linguistic representation. Our life experiences take on a different meaning from the cognitively unstructured experiences themselves once we attempt to articulate them in oral or written form. The actual experience is transformed into a communicable representation only when we represent that experience in a form others can understand. Speech and narrative forms are not experiences in themselves but a cultural construct for creating shared understanding about experience.

Discourse analysis is a way of recognizing speech as a tool shaped by cultural and social influences; speech itself has meaning beyond the actual word that is spoken. The major concern with discourse and narrative analysis is to understand how individuals represent experiences in a shared form. Meanings and underlying assumptions define our use and understanding of language; the purpose of this strategy is to present an explanation of those shared meanings and assumptions. This form of analysis is usually engaged in by socio-linguistic specialists who have a recognized framework and point of reference for narrative and discourse form; it is far more than merely analysing the words, it is analysing the words based on a shared understanding of form, structure and meaning.

Constant comparative analysis

Constant comparative analysis was originally developed by Strauss (1987), for use in the grounded theory methodology of Glaser and Strauss (1967), which itself evolved out of the sociological theory of symbolic interactionism. This strategy involves taking one piece of data and comparing it with all others that may be similar or different in order to develop conceptualizations of the possible relations between various pieces of data. Although I have presented a brief description of three alternative ways of analysing qualitative data, this particular strategy can be applied in all but phenomenology, although it will not be the only approach to the data. Constant comparative analysis demands that the creation of categories is driven by the raw data and not established a priori, although it is inevitable that prior research will have identified some of the salient issues: 'The original version of grounded theory stressed the idea that theory emerged from, and was grounded in, data. Careful analysis of data items using the constant comparative method would lead to the emergence of conceptual categories that would describe and explain the phenomenon under study' (Melia, 1997, 31).

In 1992 Barney Glaser claimed that Strauss was beginning to move away from the original intentions of grounded theory: 'Anselm's [Strauss] methodology is one full of conceptual description and mine is grounded theory. They are very different, the first focusing on forcing and the second on emergence. The first keeping all of the problems of forcing data, the second giving them up in favor of emergence, discovery, and inductive theory generation' (1992, 122).

This has left us with two fundamental approaches to grounded theory research, Strauss offering the structured approach to analysis through the constant comparative technique and Glaser encouraging the less structured approach of 'theoretical sensitivity' (1978). Choosing between these two approaches is up to the individual researcher. I am not claiming here that one is superior to the other but I would say that for the neophyte qualitative researcher Strauss offers something to hang on to in what can often be a turbulent sea of excessive amounts of unbounded, descriptive data.

Strauss more recently revised his original analytical model to ensure that the data did in fact drive the coding and was not forced into categories that represented a distortion of the empirical evidence. This process of 'microanalysis' involves a line-by-line examination of the data and begins with 'open coding' to identify categories from the data. This is then followed by 'axial coding' to determine links between categories and sub-categories and finally 'selective coding' may be used to refine the theory generated by the data (Strauss and Corbin, 1998). This is still referred to as the constant comparative method of analysis and retains the basic principles of ongoing inductive analysis established by Glaser and Strauss in 1967.

The purpose of coding in the constant comparative technique is to:

- build rather than test theory
- provide researchers with analytic tools for handling masses of raw data
- help analysts to consider alternative meanings of phenomena
- be systematic and creative simultaneously
- identify, develop, and relate the concepts that are the building blocks of theory.

(Strauss and Corbin, 1998, 13)

There is more to the constant comparative strategy than I have room to discuss here. If this is your intended approach to analysis then I strongly suggest you read the recommend texts at the end of this chapter. For now I would like to outline the major elements of this strategy and present you with the basic process involved. In the constant comparative process coding is broken down into a series of activities: *open coding*, *axial coding* and *selective coding*. Microanalysis also forms part of this approach, although it is relevant to the whole process of coding, not a specific phase in itself. It is concerned with the level to which we examine the data we harvest and the level of attention we pay to that data. Qualitative analysis demands a deep and focused interaction with the raw data, analysing line by line and, in some cases, word by word, and taking nothing at face value.

Open coding

'The analytic process through which concepts are identified and their properties and dimensions are discovered in data' (Strauss and Corbin, 1998, 101). This is the initial phase of the analytic process and involves 'de-constructing' the data, taking it apart and examining the discrete parts for differences and similarities. 'Data' is used to describe any unit of analysis you find – a word, a sentence, a paragraph – and these can come from any of your sources: an interview transcript, an observation note, a video recording, a journal article or your own researcher's diary. De-constructing the data also requires questioning of the data. You will be asking questions like 'What is the basis for this point of view?' 'Do other participants hold similar beliefs?' 'Is there a specific theme or concept to which this issue relates?' You are actively engaging with the data, challenging what you read and attempting to interpret what you find. The purpose of this stage of analysis is to identify discrete concepts, which are the basic units of analysis in your emerging theory (Strauss and Corbin, 1998).

Asking questions and keeping a sharp eye out for similarities will lead eventually to concepts that are in essence very similar, being labelled with the same name thereby creating a category. Each category can then be defined in terms of a set of discrete properties and dimensions to add clarity and understanding. As your analysis continues, the list of categories generated will need to be sorted into groups of similar or related phenomena, which in turn become the basis of your emerging theory. Categories have conceptual power because they can pull together groups of concepts or sub-categories. It is this feature that moves open coding on to axial coding.

I ask my students to imagine they have a row of shoe boxes. On the side of each shoebox they write the name and definition (discrete properties and dimensions) of a category; they create each new shoebox in response to an actual item of data, not from an abstract concept. That means every shoebox contains at least one item of data; each time a new item of data is located in the evidence it is cut out and dropped in that box or photocopied if it can fit into more than one box.

Axial coding

'The process of relating categories to their subcategories, termed "axial" because coding occurs around an axis of a category, linking categories at the level of properties and dimensions' (Strauss and Corbin, 1998, 123). At this stage we have moved away from the raw data in its original form; we are now handling the categories that have been formed through the first stage of data analysis (although we constantly refer back to the original units of data that led us to create that category in the first place). The major difference at this stage of the analysis is the identification of the conditions that give rise to a particular phenomenon and the context in which it occurs. At this stage you are guided to think about a number of things: what caused the phenomenon to occur, the context in which the phenomenon occurred, what intervening conditions were present, and what actions and consequences arose as a result. As we move through this stage patterns in the data begin to emerge; links between categories suggest relationships and a working hypothesis begins to emerge. Once we start to develop those links it is vital that they are checked for relevance to all units of data in the category; not only does this contribute to developing theory but it may also suggest further data collection. Remember with this type of analysis we are analysing as we collect our data, not waiting until the end of the data collection. Analysis and data collection work in tandem in qualitative research. So we are now looking for verification of our categories and variations and contradictions in the data.

We are checking, sorting and linking the category name and list of properties we have on the outside of our shoeboxes, looking for links between the shoeboxes (maybe even deciding that one or more of the shoeboxes is now redundant). At the same time we are checking the contents of the shoebox to ensure it still relates to the category and the connection we have identified.

Selective coding

'The process of integrating and refining the theory' (Strauss and Corbin, 1998, 143). This is the final stage in the process, the point at which we have reached *theoretical saturation* and no new properties, relationships or dimensions are emerging from the analysis; our category is established. Usually this will involve identifying one or two core categories to which all other categories are linked as subcategories. This is our conceptual framework, which forms the basis of our emergent theory, our working hypothesis generated from the data, by the data. There is little question among researchers that this is the most difficult stage in the process, not least because it involves 'throwing away' a lot of hard work, or at least it appears to. You have to formulate a coherent theory that integrates your data and presents your interpretation to your audience. Because of the vast amount of data you are likely to have been working with it is inevitable that it cannot all be included. But remember that there is always another question to be asked, another path to explore; you will be expected to suggest further research and this is maybe where your 'redundant' categories fit. At this stage the true *grounded theory* is developed. In many research studies you will find that researchers stop short of this and choose to present all of their findings grouped in thematic units. There is nothing wrong with this but it is wrong to claim you have taken a grounded theory approach if this final stage is not present.

There is a framework for choosing a central category provided by Strauss and Corbin (1998); the category is only central if all other categories are related to it in some way. It must appear in all or almost all cases and evolves logically without forcing your data to fit. If you have followed the first stages of analysis and allowed the data to drive the development of categories then this should occur naturally. Do not be tempted to force and manipulate your data to make it fit. The difficulty of course is that there is usually more than one possible central category; it's you, the researcher, who has to decide and interpret what you have discovered.

At this stage it's time to throw away the shoeboxes; if they are not linked to that central shoebox then they fit into the category of 'suggestions for further research'. Do not be tempted to include everything, tempting as it is after all your hard work;

it will only succeed in masking your theory and preventing your reader from seeing the true theory you have developed from the data.

Memo writing

Memo writing is a formal process of commenting on the data. It is essential that any qualitative researcher maintains a running commentary on themes emerging from the data and we do this in the form of memos attached to the data. Memos could be concerned with how a new piece of data contributes to our understanding, or creates a contradiction to a growing theme; or they may deal with anything that needs an aide memoir to help us to define and refine our theory. It is important that memos stand out from the data in such a way that there is no likelihood that they could be mistaken for data at a later stage. Memos are your interaction with your data; they are a private dialogue you maintain with yourself and the data, never to be confused with actual evidence.

Presenting qualitative findings

One of the most difficult aspect of qualitative analysis always appears to be presentation. This is usually because researchers are faced with vast amounts of evidence and it seems to be a momentous task to decide what to represent and how to represent it. Whatever you do, never be tempted to try and quantify your data; there is no point in telling your reader how many people said this or that. We are concerned with the specific not with reducing the data. One of the most common errors I come across in the analysis of qualitative data is the treatment of that data. In an attempt to reduce uncertainty many new qualitative researchers will attempt to create a sense of certainty by quantification; resist this temptation at all costs. This is not why you chose to engage in qualitative data in the first place. We no longer have the comfort of a single, recognized graph or chart; a table is not going to be particularly useful, so what are we left with? Words! And lots of them. Many times a student has burst into my office and asked, in a despairing voice, 'What am I going to do with all of this?'

There are a number of options open to you for presenting qualitative data:

- Without doubt the most common way of presenting qualitative analysis is the *story* (see Example 21.1 overleaf), descriptive narrative used to tell our audience what we have found. This is a perfectly acceptable form of data presentation, your written theory and all of the evidence that contributed to the emergence of that theory.
- A *concept map* (see Example 21.2, page 248) details the links and connection in your theory.
- A *rich picture* (see Example 21.3, page 248) provides your reader with a very clear visual demonstration of your theory.

Example 21.1 Extract from a narrative case study used to provide context. Each case in the study was presented in this way but appended to the main text. The main text focused on the theory and the relationship between categories within that theory (see Example 21.2, page 248).

EDDIE

Eddie lived in a large house in the centre of the city, he shared his home with his mother and father and one younger sister. Both parents were in full time employment and both had a degree. His parents placed a great deal of importance on academic achievement and provided Eddie with as much guidance as he needed. Eddie had lived in the same area all of his life and had a small circle of close friends, all of whom were very interested in new technologies. He was a keen sportsman, he was on the school football team, rugby team and swimming team. Eddie was a very private person and did not like to talk too much about anything he did not see as significant to the research. He did not give any details of his personal life without being specifically asked about them and even then the information was limited.

At home Eddie divided his time between sports and computer activity, although he did say that it was more important to increase his knowledge of new technologies. He had no particular interests other than football and new technologies outside of school. Although he was a high achiever in school, he preferred to keep a very low profile, initially he was rather reluctant to let any of his friends know that he was taking part in this research. This changed as the fieldwork progressed and he became more interested in the subject of study. Eddie asked more questions about the progress of the research than any other participant and maintained regular contact with the researcher using email throughout the study. Contacted ended as soon as the researcher exited the field.

Eddie had access to the internet, CD ROMs and other software from home. There was one family computer available in the home and his father had an additional machine from which Eddie could access the Internet if another family member was using the shared machine. His parents encouraged both Eddie and his younger sister to make use of all the electronic resources available, although they did outline strict guidelines, Eddie was allowed to access the internet for a maximum of one hour each day. He knew that he could only use certain sites and although there was nothing definite about what he could not access, he appeared to have a very clear understanding of what would be allowed and what would not. His father had spent considerable time explaining the Internet and how it worked, he also gave clear guidelines as to how the information should be used. Both children were encouraged to use the Britannica CD ROM for a lot of factual information seeking in relation to schoolwork.

At school Eddie had no access to the internet, he thought this was wrong but said that if they did have access it should only be through a school intranet which could be controlled centrally otherwise people would *'do really stupid things and get the school into trouble'*. School did provide access to CD ROMs and a school database but this was limited, it was only available with special permission for specific projects. As a result of this Eddie relied heavily on home access. Although his Public Library Authority did provide access to electronic resources these were only available at the central library and Eddie only used the local branch. He was a regular user of the local branch library but this was mainly for recreational reading material. He had a very clear understanding of the benefits and shortcomings of electronic information. He understood the need to clarify information from more than one source and was reluctant to place too much trust in information found on the Internet unless he was able to verify the source.

Eddie had his own website which he worked on with his friends, they each had their own site and they worked together to try out new ideas. They had each created a discussion group within their own web sites and they used this to communicate with each other and discuss their ideas about designing the pages. The researcher was invited to join the discussion group and the other members would frequently enquire about the research and make contributions concerning their own thoughts and ideas.

Eddie was a very high academic achiever, he was in the top set for all subjects but he did not enjoy school, he saw it as a means to an end. He wanted to work in information technology and was aware that competition was high, he wanted to do really well now in order to increase his chances of following the career of his choice. Eddie had received information skills training at school and frequently received help from his father. He preferred to learn by doing. He was aware that it was possible to use electronic resources to carry out surface learning, in terms of fact gathering, but was also aware that he did not always learn this way. He was prepared to take whichever approach to learning suited the purpose. Usually this purpose was to attain the highest marks possible but in areas of particular interest to him, usually Information Technology, he would often carry out extensive research that went well beyond the remit of the assignment. Eddie was very conscious of *'remembering things for tests, because that's where it counts'*. Eddie usually took a very pragmatic approach to searching for information, he did use the Internet a lot but pointed out that he usually used links from his Encarta or Britannica CD ROMs to be sure that the site would be useful.

Pickard, A. J. (2002) *Access to Electronic Information Resources: their role in the provision of learning opportunities to young people. A constructivist inquiry,* PhD thesis, Northumbria University.

Example 21.2 A concept map

Variables impacting on user interaction with electronic information (Pickard, 2002).

Negative or positive barriers

Technical and organizational variables	Cognitive variables	Affective variables	Social variables
Hardware and software availability Technical support	Information skills Practical purpose Location Use Self-evaluation Hypertext navigation	Motivation Personal purpose Physical location User expectations Self-concepts	Economic factors Peer interaction Gender

Example 21.3 A rich picture

A 'rich picture' can be used to present qualitative research findings.

Case study: Access to R&D support and information for the GP

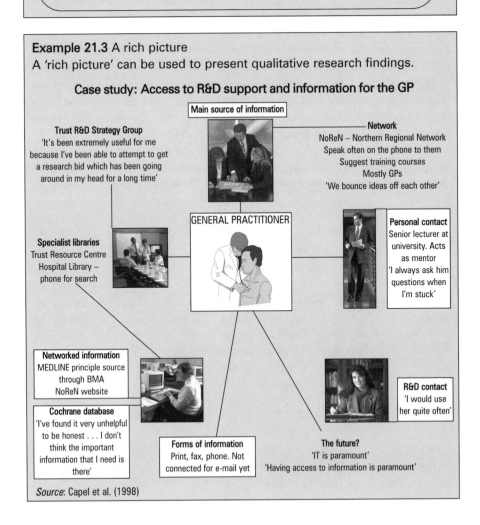

Main source of information

Trust R&D Strategy Group
'It's been extremely useful for me because I've been able to attempt to get a research bid which has been going around in my head for a long time'

Network
NoReN – Northern Regional Network
Speak often on the phone to them
Suggest training courses
Mostly GPs
'We bounce ideas off each other'

GENERAL PRACTITIONER

Specialist libraries
Trust Resource Centre
Hospital Library – phone for search

Personal contact
Senior lecturer at university. Acts as mentor
'I always ask him questions when I'm stuck'

Networked information
MEDLINE principle source through BMA
NoReN website

Cochrane database
'I've found it very unhelpful to be honest . . . I don't think the important information that I need is there'

Forms of information
Print, fax, phone. Not connected for e-mail yet

The future?
'IT is paramount'
'Having access to information is paramount'

R&D contact
'I would use her quite often'

Source: Capel et al. (1998)

Summary

This chapter has presented a particular approach to the analysis and presentation of rich, detailed, in-depth data produced by in-depth interviews, observation, diaries and focus group discussion. One point I would like to emphasize before we move on is the iterative nature of this type of analysis. We do not leave our analysis until the last element of data has been gathered; we begin with the very first item of data we collect and we continue until the last element has been added. The analysis grows throughout the data collection process: do not wait until all your data is in before you begin your analysis. Unless you do this you are missing the point true qualitative analysis. Do not be tempted to waste your rich data by engaging in some quantification exercise which reduces the detail and depth that was your purpose in the first place. Organize your data analysis the minute you have your first element of data (if you haven't done so already) and continue through the stages of constant comparison throughout your data collect. You must maintain the depth and detail in order to present a rich picture of the phenomenon under investigation and the only way to do this is to engage in time consuming and meticulous attention to detail. On a final note, do not be tempted to lose that detail in the process of presentation; select the form or forms of presentation that truly 'tell your story'.

 PRACTICAL EXERCISE

You may find it useful to go back to Chapter 2. Analysing descriptive narrative has a lot in common with literature reviewing.

1 Read Example 21.1 (page 246), Eddie's story. Taking that story line-by-line or word-by-word, form your own categories. As this is the presentation of a case, finding themes here should not be too difficult.
2 Select a newspaper article of a recent event, cut out the article and begin to look for categories in the data. Sort out these categories and then examine the content of each category to see how they relate to each other. Locate another article covering the same event from a different newspaper. Analyse the content of this article in the same way but this time attempt to integrate the data with the data from the initial article. Use existing categories where appropriate but create new ones where necessary.
3 Using this data continue through the constant comparative process until you are left with your theory as it has emerged from the data. You can do this with as many articles as you wish to see what happens to your theory as you engage in iterative analysis.

Suggested further reading

Charmaz, K. (2006) *Constructing Grounded Theory: a practical guide through qualitative analysis*, London, Sage.

Dey, I. (1993) *Qualitative Data Analysis: a user-friendly guide for social scientists*, London, Routledge.

Glaser, B. (1998) *Doing Grounded Theory: issues and discussion*, Mill Valley, CA, Sociology Press.

Strauss, A. and Corbin, J. (1998) *Basics of Qualitative Research: techniques and procedures for developing grounded theory*, London, Sage.

Chapter 22

Quantitative analysis

Introduction

As I said in the introduction to Part 4, there is neither the space nor the necessity for me to provide a guide to each statistical process and test discussed in this chapter. There is a plethora of information available on these procedures, explaining how to perform then and indeed even explaining the software to perform them. Some internet sites will even perform certain tests on datasets without the need to purchase specific software. The purpose of this chapter is to present a discussion on the nature of numerical datasets, the appropriateness of statistical analysis and the fundamental principles involved in the procedures for this analysis. This chapter is concerned with techniques for processing and displaying data, ways of exploring datasets and analysis of relationships between datasets; it is not about how to do it. The discussion is concerned with when to do what to your data and why you do it. I would strongly urge that you use one or more of the recommended texts listed at the end of this chapter to become familiar with the processes involved.

It has become relatively simple to apply complicated tests to datasets using particular software; we discuss SPSS in more detail in the following chapter, and my concern is that you understand why you are performing these tests and what is actually happening to the data when you do it. I still teach statistical analysis in a 'classroom' setting with students calculating many tests by hand before going on to use software for larger datasets, rather than in a computer laboratory using dedicated software; that comes later. I do this because I feel it is essential to understand what is being done if you are to provide a real description of what the results are showing us, so you understand what has happened to your data and what your findings actually say about that data. You may now be pleased that I do not have the space here to go over these procedures but please take the time to understand the statistical procedures you apply to your data; even something as simple as a manual exercise using a very small dataset can clarify what is going on when you run a particular operation on your data in SPSS or some other dedicated software package. If you don't understand, believe me it will be very obvious when you come to write up your findings. Be sure you understand why and how your results contribute to the discussion on the phenomena you are investigating.

In any quantitative research design you should have thought about your analysis in the very early planning stages. As you designed your data-collection instrument considering your eventual analysis, it should already have contributed to the design of your questions. You would have identified your variables, considered potential ways of looking at these variables and considered your approach to analysis. Doing this ensures that you collect data relevant to your question and data that will allow you to investigate the issues you are concerned with. In all research it is inevitable that something will come along that you were not expecting; this is the nature of asking questions. You may have to shift your plan slightly to accommodate any new and interesting developments, perhaps looking at variables in more detail or in different ways, but essentially you will have a firm basis to begin your analysis because you knew why you were asking the questions you were asking.

It is important to 'live with your data' as you carry out your investigation. Pilot your research instrument to ensure that responses match what it was you were hoping to get. This is *not* an attempt to predict actual responses to the questions but to ensure that the question allows the respondent to give you an answer in a meaningful way. What that answer is will obviously differ from respondent to respondent, but you must be sure that the question performs as you intended it to perform. Once you have seen the results of your pilot study you will have a real sense of what your raw data will look like. We will look first at levels of measurement, distinguishing between the types of responses you will have and how you can actually deal with them.

Levels of measurement

In Chapter 3 we briefly discussed the nature of variables in research, and provided a broad description of the type of variable you may wish to include in your research question or hypothesis. In Chapter 3 a *nominal* variable was defined as one that can be classified by categories which cannot be ordered and will have names, for example gender and colour. An *ordinal* variable is one in which the order of data points can be determined but not the distance between data points, for example letter grades such as 'A' and 'B'. The variable value will be numbers but only ordinal numbers. An *interval* variable is one in which both order of data points and distance between data points can be determined, for example percentage scores and distances. There are two forms of interval variable: *discrete* variables, which have a definite value and can be counted, and *continuous* variables, which can occur on an infinite number of points on a continuum such as a tape measure. Now let us look at these levels of measure in more detail to help us decide what methods of analysis are appropriate for each measure; incorrect choices at this stage can lead to meaningless or incorrect results (see Table 22.1).

Nominal level of measurement

Nominal data (named data) is also referred to as *categorical*, *qualitative* or *discrete* data. What this means is that this variable has different categories but no obvious rank order; there is no rank order for eye colour, religion or fiction genre. They are categories that individuals may choose from in response to a question but there is no way of *quantifying* the response in a meaningful way. The data can be coded for entry into software such as SPSS but the code is nothing more than a numerical label given for identification purposes, not a meaningful numerical quantity. These variables cannot be subjected to any arithmetic operations; the major analytical process applied to nominal data is frequency distribution and chi square (χ^2).

Ordinal level of measurement

Ordinal measurement has an inherent logical order or rank in so much as their relative magnitude has meaning in relation to the other choices available for response. There is no way of ranking a person's choice of favourite fiction genre in relation to the other choices available, this is arbitrary; however, there is an inherent logical order to a person's choice of their top four favourite fiction genres. Analytical procedures available for ordinal data are those available for nominal data plus; the Mann-Whitney U-test for when you are looking for differences are similarities between two independent groups, and the Wilcoxon sign ranked test for when you are looking for comparisons between performance of the same subjects under two conditions.

Interval level of measurement

Interval data are by far the strongest level of measurement in statistical analysis because the interval variable has 'different categories; the categories can be rank-ordered; the differences or intervals between each category can be specified in a meaningful numerical sense' (De Vaus, 2002a, 40). What this means is that interval data has all the characteristics of the other two levels of measure plus the property of specific numerical value, so they are quantifiable and open to arithmetic manipulation. Example interval measures are age, population size, number of years spent in an occupation, and distance between one location and another.

Table 22.1 Levels of measure and choice of analytical procedures

Level of measure	Analytical procedure
Nominal	Frequency distribution
	Chi square (χ^2)
Ordinal	Frequency distribution
	Chi square (χ^2)
	Wilcoxon
	Mann-Whitney U test
	Rank order correlation
Interval	Whole range of parametric statistics

Frequency distribution

One of the first stages in analysing your data is to calculate and present the frequency distribution of your dataset. Some say that frequency distributions are the 'bedrock' of subsequent analysis of your data, as the distributions relate to the number of responses you get to each of the options available to your respondents in each question you ask. It is easy to assume that this is too boring; you may be eager to perform more complex calculations on your data and start to look for deeper meaning behind your evidence. This is all well and good but remember that before you do anything you should give your reader an overview of the data you are working with. Provide them with the information they need to make sense of the results you present from the analytical procedures that follow. Frequency distributions are often seen as data processing, sorting your data and saying very little about any relationship between the variables. This is true but presenting your frequency distributions provides your reader with the basic facts. You need to understand what they mean for your data and how they could influence any subsequent analysis.

The elements of a frequency distribution table differ depending on the level of measurement used. See Table 22.2 for all possible elements of a frequency table but remember they will not all be used, depending on your level of measurement. The columns are:

- column 1 - a value or category of variable
- column 2 - a frequency of response to column 1 (number of respondents choosing that option)
- column 3 - the percentage of respondents from the *entire* sample that belong to that category
- column 4 - the *valid* percentage of respondents that belong to that category
- column 5 - a cumulative percentage giving a rolling addition of the valid percentages of responses. This column can only be used with ordinal and interval levels of measurement.

Table 22.2 Frequency distribution table

'Book reviews influence people's choice of fiction titles'	Frequency	%	Valid %	Cumulative %
Strongly agree	701	37.0	38.2	38.2
Agree	701	37.0	38.2	76.3
Neither	251	13.2	13.7	90.0
Disagree	163	8.6	8.9	98.9
Strongly disagree	21	1.1	1.1	100.0
Total	1837	96.8	100.0	
Missing	60	3.2		
Total	1897	100.0		

Cross-tabulation

Frequency distribution provides a picture of individual variables but you may want to learn more about any links between variables; cross-tabulation allows you to look at any links there may be between two variables. Just as a frequency table can show the pattern of data from one variable, a cross-tabulation can show any links between two variables. For example we may be interested to see if the use of book reviews to guide choice of fiction titles is related to gender – are females more likely to be influenced by a book review than males? To explore this question we would have prepared a frequency distribution table for the question 'Do book reviews influence your choice of fiction title?' (see Table 22.3). We would then go on to determine responses in relation to gender (see Tables 22.4a and b). In the cross-tabulation (Table 22.5) we provide the following information:

- column 1 – the variable (influence of book reviews on choice)
- column 2 – response category
- column 3 – number and percentage of females in that response category (percentage of female sample, not entire sample)
- column 4 – number and percentage of males in that response category (percentage of male sample, not entire sample)
- column 5 – total number and percentage of the entire sample in that response category.

Table 22.3 Frequency distribution for use of book reviews in the selection process

'Do book reviews influence your choice of fiction title?'	Frequency	%	Valid %	Cumulative %
Always	965	32.2	32.2	32.2
Sometimes	1399	46.7	46.7	78.9
Never	630	21.0	21.0	99.9
Total	2994			
Missing	0			
Total	2994	100.0		

Table 22.4a Frequency distribution for use of book reviews in the selection process by females

		Frequency	%
'Do book reviews influence	Always	577	39.7
your choice of fiction title?'	Sometimes	636	43.8
	Never	239	16.5
Total		1452	100.0

Table 22.4b Frequency distribution for use of book reviews in the selection process by males

		Frequency	%
'Do book reviews influence	Always	388	25.2
your choice of fiction title?'	Sometimes	763	49.5
	Never	391	25.4
Total		1542	100.0

Table 22.5 Cross-tabulation of use of book reviews in the selection process by gender

		Gender		Total
		Female	Male	
'Do book reviews influence your choice of fiction title?'	Always	(577) 39.75%	(388) 25.2%	(965) 32.2%
	Sometimes	(636) 43.8%	(763) 49.5%	(1399) 46.7%
	Never	(239) 16.5%	(391) 25.4%	(630) 21%
		(1452) 100%	(1542) 100%	(2994) 100%

After this process it would be usual to perform a significance test on these results. In this case it would be a chi-square test because of the level of measure used.

Measures of central tendency

Often it is useful to summarize an entire distribution by using a single score to show the grouping of figures around some *central* point in the data, the most common term for this is *the average*. There are three different ways of calculating the measure of central tendency (average) of a data set: the *mean*, the *median* and the *mode*.

The mean

The mean is the arithmetic mean and is calculated by using the formula:

$$\text{The mean} = \frac{\text{total of all values}}{\text{number of cases}} \quad \text{or} \quad M = \frac{\Sigma X}{N}$$

Advantages:
- easily understood and calculated
- responsive to each score in the distribution equally
- provides *typical* use, cost, incidence etc. of the variable
- is fundamental to further calculations of standard deviation
- most stable of measures of central tendency.

Disadvantages:
- can be misleading if the data set contain atypically high or low values, for example:

A set of ten people and their ages are:
11 10 12 13 10 11 90 13 11 10
This distribution of scores is said to be *skewed* because it has an extreme value (90).
Mean = 11 + 10 + 12 + 13 + 10 + 11 + 90 + 13 + 11 + 10 = 191 = 191/10
M = 19.1

This clearly says very little about the average age of this group; in this case the mean becomes untypical, unrealistic and unrepresentative.

- can only be calculated for interval data where a numerically meaningful interpretation exists.

The median

The median is the mid-point or the middle value of a set of data. In order to calculate the median of a set of data the values have to be ranked in order of size. The median is the value of the middle item of the distribution, for example:

You have a series of nine scores: 16 6 11 24 17 4 19 9 20
Order these scores in relation to size: 24 20 19 17 **16** 11 9 6 4

median value

This is simple when you have an odd number of scores. When you have an even number there is an additional step to include in the process:

16 11 24 17 4 19 9 20 8

Ranked order shows the following:

24 20 19 17 **16 11** 9 8 6 4

$$\text{Median} = \frac{16 + 11}{2} = 13.5$$

Advantages:
- insensitive to extreme scores when the distribution is skewed
- provides a dividing line between upper and lower values; an item chosen at random from the list has a 50/50 chance of being greater or less than the median score
- most useful average when dealing with skewed data.

Disadvantages:
- may not be characteristic of the data set
- gives only the value of one score in the set (the central score); the other values are used to determine the position of the median but the value of those scores does not influence the value of the median.

The mode

The mode: is the most frequently occurring score in a distribution. In order to work out the mode you are looking for the most common or fashionable (*à la mode*) score. To calculate the mode the frequency of each score in the set has to be established. For example, the favourite colour of a sample of pre-school children is shown in Table 22.6.

Table 22.6 The favourite colour of a sample of pre-school children

Colour	Frequency	Cumulative Frequency
Red	3	3
Blue	16	19
Purple	17	36
Pink	7	43
Orange	3	46
Yellow	2	48

Table 22.6 shows that in this data set Purple is the mode. The mode is the only measure of central tendency that can be applied to nominal data. There can be more than one modal value in a distribution.

Advantages:
- easy to obtain
- unaffected by extreme scores in a skewed distribution
- a good representation of a 'typical' item or value, but this should only be used when most values cluster around the mode.

Disadvantages:
- lacks the precision of other measures of central tendency
- distribution may contain more than one mode of differing values; in this case the median or mean would be used
- of little use in more advanced analysis techniques
- not representative if the majority of values cluster around a value that differs from the mode.

Each of these types of 'average' perform a different function; you need to understand which is appropriate for what data sets.

Comparing use of the mean, median and mode

One example of the differing ways in which *typical* or *average* scores can be applied is as follows.

A sample of ten homes is taken from a constituency. The yearly income (in thousands of pounds) of these households is

25 25 25 25 40 40 40 50 50 1000

The mean = $\dfrac{1320}{10}$ = 132 = £132,000

The median = £40,000
The mode = £25,000

A politician could use whichever of these averages supported the case being put forward, for example, the mode to argue for more resources for the area or the mean to demonstrate affluence. This is why it is important for you to know which average is being used and how representative it is. Generally speaking, where data is skewed the median or the mode is preferable to the mean; the typical occurrence in nominal data can only be calculated using the mode. For more sophisticated analysis the arithmetic mean is the only choice you have.

Measures of dispersion

As you have discovered with some of the examples used here, reducing large datasets to a single statistic can result in a serious loss of information. In order to provide a clearer picture of the data it is necessary to give some central point, or average, but it is also necessary to be able to say how the rest of the data appears around that central point. To do this we can use measures of dispersion. There are three common ways of calculating the dispersion of data around the average: the *range*, the *variance* and the *standard deviation*.

Look at the example of three sets of data below:

a.	8	9	10	11	12
b.	10	10	10	10	10
c.	1	5	10	15	19

The mean and the median for all three datasets are the same (10), but there is a marked difference in another of the characteristics of these datasets. What is it? It is clear that although we can arrive at the same measure of central tendency, that gives us no indication of the obvious differences in the pattern of the individual data components of the dataset. In order to provide a clear picture of the data we need to go a stage further.

The range

The simplest of measures of dispersion is the range, which calculates the difference between the highest and the lowest score in the dataset. For the three datasets above the range would be:

a.	12 – 8 = 4
b.	10 – 10 = 0
c.	19 – 1 = 18

The range is useful but it only uses two scores in the dataset so tells us very little about the set as a whole.

The variance

Calculating the variance allows us to consider how each score in the dataset varies from the mean (or average) score. In order to calculate the variance we need to know the mean of the dataset.

$$\text{Variance} = \frac{\text{sum of (score - mean score)}^2}{\text{total number of scores}}$$

Table 22.7 illustrates how this is done for dataset 'c' in the example given above, where

Dataset = 1 5 10 15 19
Mean = 10

Table 22.7 The variance for dataset c

Score	score - mean	(score - mean)^2
1	1 - 10 = -9	$(-9)^2 = 81$
5	5 - 10 = -5	$(-5)^2 = 25$
10	10 - 10 = 0	$0^2 = 0$
15	15 - 10 = 5	$5^2 = 25$
19	19 - 10 = 9	$9^2 = 81$

Sum of (score - mean)^2 = 212

Variance = $\dfrac{212}{5}$ = **42.4**

Standard deviation

This is the most important of all measures of dispersion. The standard deviation shows the dispersion of the scores around the mean in the same units as the original score. The variance has changed the unit of measurement so calculating the standard deviation returns us to the original unit. For example, if our scores were in centimetres the variance is expressed in square centimetres. In order to compare this to the mean we need to return to the original unit of measurement. Standard deviation is calculated by taking the square root of the variance.

Standard deviation is represented by the Greek lower case sigma = σ.

$$\sigma = \sqrt{\text{Variance}}$$

From the previous example we see that

$\sigma = \sqrt{42.4} = 6.511528238$; shown to three decimal places unless otherwise instructed = 6.512

Generally the larger the standard deviation the greater the dispersal of scores, but remember to use caution, as skewed data can produce an unrepresentative standard deviation, just as it could an unrepresentative mean. In describing a collection of data researchers will typically present two descriptive statistics, the mean and the standard deviation. When interpreting the standard deviation results, those which are assumed to be typical of a population are the ones that fall between two standard deviations below the mean and two above. Results outside this will usually be the result of skewed datasets.

Correlation

If we want to examine two sets of data to see if there is any relationship between them then we are looking for *correlation*. If one variable increases when another variable increases there is a positive correlation between them. If one variable increases as another decreases then there is a negative correlation. No relation between variables give us a zero correlation. What you must be aware of is the fact that correlation only shows us a general trend, it does not establish a fixed rule or law. There are a number of tests available for correlation depending on the type of data we have gathered. See the final section in this chapter for more details.

Displaying data
Bar charts

It is often useful to represent data visually to allow any patterns to be communicated to the reader. Bar charts are used to show frequencies or percentages and there are three forms: *simple bar charts*, *compound bar charts* and *component bar charts*. There are a number of rules that are common to all examples:

- The horizontal axis shows the type of data being displayed; this should be given a title and labelled where possible, otherwise a key should be included.
- The vertical axis shows the frequency or percentage, indicated as a title and should be scaled accordingly, always beginning at 0.
- Bars should be of equal widths as it is the area of the bar that indicates the size of the group.
- Gaps must be left between bars.

Simple bar charts

Table 22.8 shows the frequency distribution for the number of people who use a park and ride facility from Monday to Saturday. The largest frequency is 500, so the vertical axis of the barchart used to illustrate this (Figure 22.1) is scaled from 0 to 500.

Table 22.8 Frequency distribution for people using park and ride, Mon–Sat

Day	No. of people
Mon	240
Tues	300
Wed	350
Thurs	280
Fri	450
Sat	500

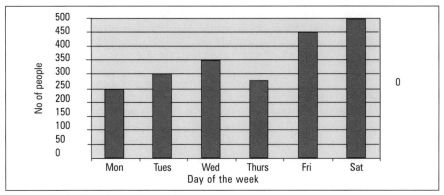

Figure 22.1 Number of people using park and ride, Mon–Sat

Compound bar charts

In order to compare data from more than one location it is useful to display that data in a form that encourages visual comparison. This can be done by showing data from different locations within appropriate groups. In Table 22.9 and Figure 22.2 the year was chosen as the group and figures from both locations were given in that year.

Table 22.9 Sales in Britain and Europe 2000–2005 (£ millions)

	Britain	Europe
2000	2.5	1.3
2001	3.0	2.6
2002	1.5	1.2
2003	4.0	2.9
2004	1.5	2.0
2005	2.8	2.1

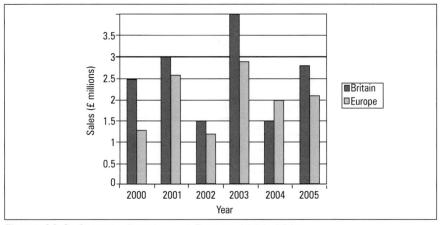

Figure 22.2 Sales in Britain and Europe 2000–2005

Component bar charts

We use component bar charts when we are displaying data that needs to demonstrate comparison, but instead of using multiple bars to represent each piece of data connected with each group, all data elements are included in a single bar. Table 22.10 shows the number of CDs owned by five families by musical category.

Table 22.10 Number of CDs owned by five families by musical category

	Burns	Edwards	French	Stephens	Travis
Blues	18	3	1	10	15
Classical	4	1	14	9	7
Rock	22	2	16	16	1
Techno	1	19	5	2	12

By displaying this data as a component bar chart we can show the total number of CDs owned by each family as well as the proportion of each collection by music type (see Figure 22.3).

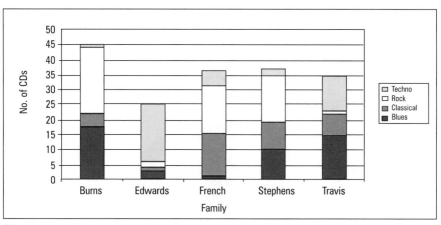

Figure 22.3 Number of CDs owned by five families by musical category

Pie charts

Pie charts are used to show figures in proportion to the whole and in proportion to other figures. To construct a pie chart it is necessary to calculate the angle represented by each set of figures being presented in the chart. Each group of data is calculated as a percentage of 360 degrees.

The first step is to find the total being represented by the pie chart. We do this using a table. An example is given in Table 22.11.

Table 22.11 Number of people who have golf, cinema, skiing or motor racing as hobbies

Hobby	No. of people
Golf	360
Cinema	540
Skiing	90
Motor racing	90
Total	1080

The total here is **1080** so 1080 is 360°:

$$\text{Golf} = 360 \times \frac{360}{1080} = 120°$$

$$\text{Cinema} = 540 \times \frac{360}{1080} = 180°$$

$$\text{Skiing} = 90 \times \frac{360}{1080} = 30°$$

$$\text{Motor racing} = 90 \times \frac{360}{1080} = 30°$$

You could always add up the angles to ensure your calculations are correct: 360°.
Figure 22.4 shows what the pie chart for this data would look like.

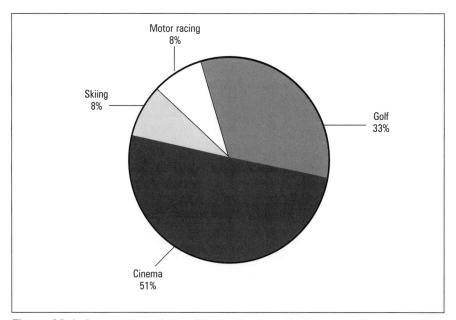

Figure 22.4 Percentage of people who have golf, cinema, skiing or motor racing as hobbies

Frequency polygons

Frequency polygons show the shape of the distribution of grouped data and are often used to compare two or more sets of data. Frequency polygons can be used for grouped nominal data, as demonstrated in this example.

The number of people visiting two branch libraries per hour was recorded for a 72-hour period, in equal groups of 1 to 5, 6 to 10, 11 to 15, 16 to 20, 21 to 25, and 26 to 30. The data was recorded in Table 22.12.

Table 22.12 Number of people using libraries A and B by group size

No. of people	1-5	6-10	11-15	16-20	21-25	26-30
Library A	6	10	21	18	13	4
Library B	3	7	10	14	24	14

In order to plot a frequency polygon we need to find the midpoint of each of the class intervals. We do this by finding the average of the upper and lower boundaries of the class group. For example:

The first class is 1-5; the midpoint is $\dfrac{1+5}{2} = 3$

We find the other midpoints in the same way, as shown in Table 22.13.

Table 22.13 Number of people using libraries A and B by group size, showing midpoint of each class

No. of people	1-5	6-10	11-15	16-20	21-25	26-30
Midpoint	3	8	13	18	23	28
Library A	6	10	21	18	13	4
Library B	3	7	10	14	24	14

We now need to calculate the midpoints for the class group before 1-5 and the class group after 26-30, which allows us to complete the start and end points of the polygon. The class before 1-5 is − 4-0, and the class after 26-30 is 31-35 so the midpoints are

$$\dfrac{-4+0}{2} = -2 \text{ and } \dfrac{31+35}{2} = 33$$

We can now produce Table 22.14:

Table 22.14 Midpoints for the number of people using libraries A and B

Midpoint	-2	3	8	13	18	23	28	33
Library A	6	10	10	21	18	13	4	
Library B	3	7	7	10	14	24	14	

Using this data we can plot the frequency polygon for the number of people visiting two branch libraries over a 72-hour period, as shown in Figure 22.5.

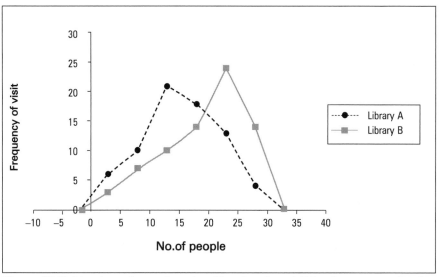

Figure 22.5 Number of people using libraries A and B by frequency of unit

Histograms

We use histograms to summarize and display the distribution of a data set graphically. They allow us to highlight the most common response and the pattern of data distribution, to identify any skewed element and to show up any outliers. In a traditional histogram the width of the bar is proportional to the class interval and the area of the bar is proportional to the frequency. The horizontal axis is a continuous scale including all the units of the grouped class interval. Software such as SPSS produces histograms relatively simply without the need for any such manual calculations.

We will now construct a histogram for the following data. Once again this is the number of people visiting a branch library per hour over a 72-hour period. We have grouped the data onto bins ('bin' is the term used to describe the disjointed categories used to group observed data) of 5, as shown in Table 22.15.

Table 22.15 Number of people visiting a branch library by group size and frequency of visit

No. of people	1–5	6–10	11–15	16–20	21–25	26–30
Frequency	6	10	21	18	13	4

The first thing we have to do is to establish the upper and lower class boundaries of each class group. We can assume that the class boundaries are at the halfway points between each class. That would give us class boundaries of 0.5, 5.5, 10.5, 15.5, 20.5, 25.5 and 30.5. All the classes have a width of 5. The area of the rectangle we draw will be equal to the frequency. To calculate the height of the rectangle for the first class group we must divide the area by the width:

$$\text{Height} = \frac{\text{frequency}}{\text{class width}} = \frac{6}{5} = 1.2 \text{ This is known as the } \textit{frequency density.}$$

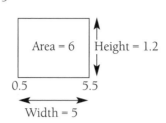

We can now add another row to the table that shows the frequency density for each class group, as shown in Table 22.16.

Table 22.16 Number of people visiting a branch library by group size, frequency and frequency density

No. of people	1-5	6-10	11-15	16-20	21-25	26-30
Frequency	6	10	21	18	13	4
Frequency density	1.2	2	4.2	3.6	2.6	0.8

Plotting histograms in SPSS and Excel is relatively straightforward once you understand the data you are inputting.

Testing for statistical significance

Before we look at statistical test for significance we must understand the concept of probability. The simplest way of defining probability is the likelihood of something to happen. Understanding probability can help you to consider how significant research results are and how confident you can be about them. There are two types of probability: *theoretical probability* and *practical probability*.

Theoretical probability

Theoretical probability can be calculated in advance and known exactly. There are a finite number of likely outcomes of an action or an experiment. Theoretical probability can be calculated using the formula:

$$\text{Probability} = \frac{\text{number of outcomes classified as A}}{\text{total number of possible outcomes}}$$

The theoretical probability of the two dice game can be calculated by taking the number of ways it is possible to achieve each score and divide by the total of possible outcomes, which is 36. Table 22.17 shows the number of ways it is possible to achieve each score.

Table 22.17 Ways of achieving a score in a two-dice game

Score =	2	3	4	5	6	7	8	9	10	11	12
Ways of achieving this score	1,1	1,2 2,1	1,3 2,2 3,1	1,4 2,3 3,2 4,1	1,5 2,4 3,3 4,2 5,1	1,6 2,5 3,4 4,3 5,2 6,1	2,6 3,5 4,5 5,3 6,2	3,6 4,5 5,4 6,3	4,6 5,5 6,4	5,6 6,5	6,6

Probability of throwing a 2 or a 12 $= \dfrac{1}{36} = 0.03$

Probability of throwing a 3 or an 11 $= \dfrac{2}{36} = 0.06$

Probability of throwing a 4 or a 10 $= \dfrac{3}{36} = 0.08$

Probability of throwing a 5 or a 9 $= \dfrac{4}{36} = 0.11$

Probability of throwing a 6 or an 8 $= \dfrac{5}{36} = 0.14$

Probability of throwing a 7 $= \dfrac{6}{36} = 0.17$

You will see that from the distribution of scores in Table 22.17 that the following is true:

The median   = 7
The mode   = 7

The mean $\dfrac{77}{11} = 7$

You will also see that the score of 7 has the highest probability of occurring.

Testing the theory

The theoretical probability is the expected outcome in the long run. You would expect that testing out this theory would produce a symmetrical model similar to that in the table above. However, it may be that this pattern would take some time to emerge. You would have to conduct a significant number of trials in order to achieve the desired result. To calculate the practical probability we carry out the following experiment.

Three groups roll two dice 20 times. Each time they tally the score to see how many times they achieved each of the possible scores. We then calculate the cumulating proportions from each group, for example:

Group 1 throws a 2 once, Group 2 throws a 2 twice and Group 3 throws a 2 once.

We calculate the proportions as they grow. A 2 was thrown:

$$\frac{1}{20} = 0.05$$

$$\frac{3}{40} = 0.075$$

$$\frac{4}{60} = 0.066$$

Reaching the theoretical probability becomes more likely as the number of throws increases, thereby increasing the statistical significance of the sample of throws taken.

The law of large numbers

We have established that increasing the number of trials brings us closer to the theoretical probability of an event taking place. In that case we knew what the total number of possible outcomes was, but this is not always the case. When trying to understand a phenomenon we take a sample of the population and take measures in order to reach an estimate of that phenomenon in the whole, or parent, population. A small sample is unlikely to provide an accurate estimate and this accuracy increases as we increase the number of trials or the sample size. The *law of large numbers* simply means that the larger the sample the closer we will get to an accurate representation of the population as a whole.

Mutually exclusive events

A mutually exclusive event is one in which one event happens and the others cannot; when we toss a coin and get a head, we cannot, at the same trial, get a tail. The success of the head is complemented by the failure of the tail. In some statistical processes we need to know the probability of both an event occurring or not occurring.

p = the probability of an event which is desired.

For example if the desired event of throwing two dice is a score of 8, the probability of that success is $\frac{5}{36}$ or 0.14, so **p = 0.14**

q = the probability of an event **not** occurring.

For example the probability of the failure to score 8 when throwing two dice is $\frac{31}{36}$ or 0.86, so **q = 0.86**

p and **q** refer to the probability of an event at *each* trial; for each of those trials **p + q = 1**

Joint probability

Sometimes there is a need to find out the probability of two or more events happening together. These are *non-mutually-exclusive events*. When tossing a coin twice you could throw a head and then also throw a head at the next turn as one does not exclude the other. If you had a bag containing two marbles, 1 red, 1 black, and you replaced the marble after each turn, you could pick out a red each time because one event does not exclude the other.

The probability of picking a red would be $\frac{1}{2}$ or 0.5

The probability of picking a black would be $\frac{1}{2}$ or 0.5

A tree diagram can determine the possible outcomes of a trial. The tree diagram for the joint probability of picking the red marble from the bag are shown below:

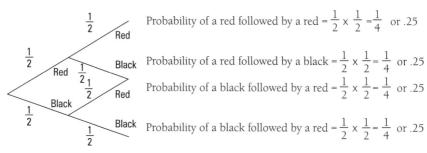

$$\text{Probability of a red followed by a red} = \frac{1}{2} \times \frac{1}{2} = \frac{1}{4} \text{ or .25}$$

$$\text{Probability of a red followed by a black} = \frac{1}{2} \times \frac{1}{2} = \frac{1}{4} \text{ or .25}$$

$$\text{Probability of a black followed by a red} = \frac{1}{2} \times \frac{1}{2} = \frac{1}{4} \text{ or .25}$$

$$\text{Probability of a black followed by a red} = \frac{1}{2} \times \frac{1}{2} = \frac{1}{4} \text{ or .25}$$

Which statistical significance test to apply

In order to determine the statistical significance of our results we need to consider a number of options before we select the most appropriate test. There is no need to go over the detail of every available test in this text as there are numerous sources of that data available, both in the recommended texts at the end of this chapter and through resources such as SPSS. The purpose of this chapter has been to provide you with guidelines for making choices, giving you an overview of the potential tools available to you and helping you to choose between those options. So let us look at the options available and, more importantly, what should influence your choice of option. Table 22.18 shows the factors that need to be considered when selecting a particular test.

Summary

Always remember the saying 'garbage in, garbage out'. No amount of sophisticated statistical testing or graphical representation can 'create' good analysis, this only comes as a consequence of the data you have collected. It is important to think about your data. Understand the nature and type of data you are working with before you decide how best to analyse it, although you can think about this long before you

Table 22.18 Choosing a statistical significance test

Test	Variable(s)	Sample	When to use it	Type
The chi-square test χ²	Nominal	Independent groups, no pairing needed	Cross-tabulation	Non-parametric
Mann-Whitney U-test	Nominal	Independent groups, no pairing needed	To establish the level at which overlap between two samples could occur by chance	Non-parametric
T-test	Interval	Dependent or independent	To establish if the means of two normally distributed populations are equal	Parametric
Wilcoxon sign rank test	Interval	Paired or matched sample group or repeated measure of single sample	When comparisons of measurement are required	Non-parametric
Spearman's rank order correlation	Nominal Ordinal	Linked, matched or paired sample groups	To describe the relationship between two variables	Non-parametric
Pearson's product-moment correlation	Interval	Linked, matched or paired sample groups	To identify correlation	Parametric

collect the data. Handle your data realistically and meaningfully; this is not an exercise is demonstrating everything you know about statistics, it's about demonstrating that you understand your data and the purpose and process of statistical analysis. Plan your research as an integrated activity, not a group of separate, unconnected activities. This way you will ensure that you harvest the type of data you need to address the research question you began with in a way that is appropriate to the data.

 PRACTICAL EXERCISE

1a Calculate the mean, median and the mode for the following sets of data:

17 13 12 17 12 15 13 20 13 14 19
Mean...................... Median...................... Mode..........................

345 226 1032 234 65 132 78 35 22
Mean...................... Median................. Mode..........................

45 32 45 17 35 32 45 17 89 12 15
Mean...................... Median...................... Mode..........................

1b The table below lists the annual holiday entitlements of employees of a manufacturing firm.

Position held	Holiday entitlement	No. of people
Chairperson	9 weeks	1
Managing director	3 weeks	1
Accountant	2.5 weeks	1
Cleaner	2 weeks	4
Secretary	1.5 weeks	2
Cabinet makers	1 week	3
Production workers	0.5 weeks	10

Find the mean, median and mode for holiday entitlements among employees.

Mean.....................................

Median..................................

Mode....................................

1c The union representative is campaigning for extra holidays, but the managing director claims the holiday entitlement is fair. Which average will be chosen by:

the managing director?......................................

the union representative?..................................

Explain your answer.

2a Calculate the range for the following datasets:

a.	23	22	19	18	22	9	24	10	16	range =
b.	2	2	17	12	12	16	15	22	17	range =
c.	11	21	31	41	35	78	65	64	59	range =

2b Complete the following table, calculating the mean for each dataset then working out the variance and the standard deviation.

Mean = score	score – mean	(score – mean)²
35		
40		
48		Variance =
52		
54		Standard deviation =
59		
56		
65		
68		
70		

3   Construct bar charts for the following tabulated data:

Staffing

	Newtown	Midfield	Southward
Professional	8	10	6
Non-professional	16	18	19
Manual	32	29	42

Method of travel to work

	Bus	Car	Train
Mon	240	240	220
Tues	300	300	100
Wed	350	350	0
Thurs	280	220	200
Fri	475	0	225
Sat	300	225	175

Cinema attendance over one week

	No. of people
Mon	98
Tues	67
Wed	350
Thurs	120
Fri	475
Sat	600

4   Construct pie charts for the following data:

a Holiday destination	No. of people
Britain	254
America	265
Russia	110
Europe	345
Other	78

b Type of car	No. of people
Peugeot	98
Volvo	65
Saab	23
Ford	145
Other	32

5 Construct a bar chart for the following data:

The age of a sample of 200 children visiting two museums during one week.

Age	0–5	6–10	11–16
Museum A	65	84	51
Museum B	58	75	67

6 Construct histograms for the following data:

a The marks gained by 100 students in a test

Mark	1–10	11–15	16–20	21–25	26–30	31–50
Frequency	10	15	20	24	21	10

b The number of visits paid to the information centre by company employees during one week

No. of visits	1–5	6–10	11–15	16–20	21–25
Frequency	9	12	10	4	1

7a Construct a frequency polygon for the following data:

The masses of a sample of 100 parcels recorded at two sorting offices over a period of one week

Mass (kg)	1–2	3–4	5–8	9–12	13–16
Location A	28	22	18	20	12
Location B	26	20	20	18	16

7b Decide which type of chart you would use to display the following data and give your reasons for your choice:

- hair colour of a sample of 200 people
- the percentage of employees in each section of a company
- the annual profits of two sister companies over a ten-year period from 1985 to 1995.

8 Calculate the angles needed to construct pie charts for the following data:

Holiday destination	No. of people	Angle
Britain	254	
America	265	
Russia	110	
Europe	345	
Other	78	

9a When throwing a single dice, what is the probability of throwing:

- 5?
- a number less than 3?
- anything except a 6?

9b A bag contains some counters: 3 red, 4 green, 2 yellow, 1 black.
Find the probability of picking the following from the bag (the counter is returned after each pick):

- the black counter
- a red counter
- a green or yellow counter
- anything except a yellow counter.

9c When tossing two coins simultaneously, what is the probability of getting two heads?

9d Draw a tree diagram to show all the possible results of throwing a coin four times. Use this diagram to find the probability of throwing:

- No heads
- 1 head
- 2 heads
- 3 heads
- 4 heads.

Suggested further reading

De Vaus, D. (2002) *Analyzing Social Science Data: 50 key problems in data analysis*, London, Sage.

Diamond, I. and Jefferies, J. (2001) *Beginning Statistics: an introduction for social scientists*, London, Sage.

Stephen, P. and Hornby, S. (1997) *Simple Statistics for Library and Information Professionals*, 2nd edn, London, Library Association.

Chapter 23

An overview of software for analysis

Introduction

This chapter is not a user guide to specific software, it is a discussion of the advantages and disadvantages of specific software for data analysis and an overview of what is available. If you decide to make use of the software it is up to you to become familiar with that software and find and use an appropriate guide to the specific version of the software you are using. You must remember one thing: no matter how sophisticated the software may be it is not a substitute for understanding the process of analysis you are engaging in. There is little point in performing sophisticated statistical tests using available software if you don't understand why and how the test was performed. Without this understanding you will have little chance of presenting your findings to your reader in a logical and meaningful way.

Quantitative analysis

In the past the researcher has been required to spend large amounts of time undertaking statistical analysis on data and producing the data in a clear and concise format representing the results. The manual analysis of quantitative data can be particularly time consuming and subject to human error. The advent of powerful statistical computer packages has removed this time consuming task. Despite this, I still teach analysis using pencil, paper, calculators and a ruler, but only until students are really aware of what they are doing with the data; once they understand the purpose of the tests and calculations being performed then computer software really does come into its own.

There are a number of computer packages which assist the researcher in undertaking this process. Large amounts of data can be analysed quickly and easily using these statistical computer packages. However, this can have an adverse effect as the data can be subjected to the wrong kind of testing. Although the computer will undertake the analysis the researcher has to tell it what to perform. It is therefore important to understand the theory and application of various statistical methods in order to be aware of when and how to apply them (hence the discussion in Chapter 22). I will only discuss two packages here to provide you with an awareness of the capabilities and scope of such packages.

SPSS

Launched in 1989. SPSS Inc. (the Statistical Package for Social Sciences) has become a powerful statistical and data analysis software. Initially developed as a statistical package for the social sciences it offers researchers flexible and powerful tools for better, simpler research. It is a powerful, comprehensive and flexible general-purpose data analysis package. Originally written for social scientists, it is now used widely across the disciplines. It provides the opportunity to apply statistical rather than computer analysis. SPSS offers powerful and easy ways to extract meaningful information from data.

SPSS has now become the standard analytical tool for most quantitative researchers, but it is and will always be a tool; you are still the analyst, it is you who decides what SPSS will be asked to do and why. It covers a basic range of:

- various parametric and non-parametric tests, and regression techniques (including *general linear, non-linear, mixed-effects, logistic, ordinal* and *log-linear* methods)
- multivariate analyses (including *cluster, discriminant, principal components* and *scaling analyses*)
- survival analysis (including *Cox proportional hazards* with and without time dependent variables)
- high-resolution graphics (including *basic descriptive charts* and *scatter plots*).

Advantages of SPSS
SPSS will:

- reduce the time required to analyse data
- reduce the errors involved in coding data
- thoroughly analyse data with in-depth statistics and charts
- present results clearly with flexible reports and charts.

MINITAB

MINITAB was originally designed for teaching statistics and has become a highly respected and trusted statistical teaching tool on the market. It is an easy-to-use, general-purpose software package for statistical analysis. It is an interactive system for organizing and analysing data and reporting statistical results. It provides the opportunity to learn about statistics rather than about computer software.

The software covers a basic range of:

- statistical analyses (*descriptive statistics, hypothesis testing – t-tests* and *chi-square tests, analysis of variance, non-parametric methods – Wilcoxon signed rank tests*)
- high-resolution graphics (including *basic descriptive charts* and *scatter plots*).

Advantages
MINITAB provides:

- an intuitive user interface and simple tutorials
- a clear, concise output
- extensive statistical capabilities
- the opportunity to explore data more thoroughly
- the ability to organize and present findings clearly.

This outline of SPSS and MINITAB is only to provide you with an awareness of the capabilities of such statistical software packages. There is neither the space nor the need to proved a full guide; these are widely available and need to be specific to the version you are using. I strongly recommend that if you intend to use one of these packages you seek expert guidance in the form of a class or workshop or an individual with experience who has the time to act as a mentor and teacher.

Qualitative analysis

> QDA [qualitative data analysis] programs neither promise nor threaten to think. QDAs cannot theorize, nor do they automatically create complex data codes. What they can do is improve our relationship to data.   (Durkin, 1997, 92)

Many social researchers have argued that using computer software to analyse qualitative data divorces the researcher from that data; the common misconception is that the software does the thinking for the researcher. This has never and will never be the case with tools designed to manage qualitative data. The interaction needed between the researcher and the data remains pretty much as it always has been from the days of pencil-written notes, through the print-out and highlighter pen era that still reigns supreme today with many social researchers. The analysis of qualitative data has traditionally been a paper-based exercise involving a lot of lists and index cards with headings on them and referenced pieces of data and information. Countless photocopies of evidence were placed under different categories; extended maps of emerging theory have consumed vast amounts of wall and even floor space in many offices. There have always been dangers that this kind of analysis would not be comprehensive and therefore not totally reliable, and also it is extremely time consuming. The introduction of word-processing packages and the possibility of building databases of information began to introduce changes to the execution of such work. Larger amounts of data could be organized more quickly and more flexibly, which supported the more comprehensive analysis of such data and therefore increased its reliability. In turn, this raised the expectations of researchers working with qualitative data and they began to explore the possibilities for qualitative computing.

NUD.IST

In 1981 Lyn and Tom Richards designed the first version of what later became known as QSR NUD.IST, a software package to support social research, for QSR International. NUD.IST is a computer software analysis package developed by Qualitative Solutions and Research Pty Ltd, designed to aid users in handling Nonnumerical, Unstructured Data in qualitative research. It does this by supporting the processes of Indexing, Searching and Theorizing. It supports both the organization and the exploitation of qualitative research data. More recent developments have seen the growth and expansion of software tools available. QSR went on to develop Nvivo 7, launched in 2006, which offers even more detailed analysis and modelling capabilities, and XSIGHT, which is focused more on the interview process.

The data from qualitative research is complex and rich, encompassing interview transcripts and other documentary evidence of a variety of forms. Qualitative analysis packages enhance handling such material by:

- creating a document system to store documents without losing their complexity or context
- combining documents that are on the computer with text or other documents that are offline (such as photos, reports, letters and news cuttings)
- storing and retrieving text from any document
- recording factual information about documents, cases, people and so on
- writing and editing memos about documents
- searching for words or patterns of characters in the text of documents
- automatically indexing the finds from text searches.

These packages are also able to support the researcher in the investigation and exploitation of the research data. This is the process of categorization of themes contained in the data, followed by the linking of themes and ideas and exploring new ideas. They help the researcher to create such categories and manage them in an indexing system. This software allows you to:

- create categories or codes for thinking about the data and to manage the categories in a flexible index system
- index segments of text on screen
- bring together passages of text and related ideas as a category for interpretation and analysis
- search for combinations of indexing, explore patterns in the data and ask questions about it
- record, in notes and memos, emerging theories and explanations of the data
- record the answers to questions and use them as the basis for further exploration
- test emerging theories and hypotheses.

These are not intelligent packages; they will not do anything that you couldn't do by hand with cards, lists and bits of paper. But they do allow you to be much more comprehensive. This therefore may improve both the quality and the validity of your analysis and eventual conclusions if the scale of the project warrants it. These packages can be used for projects of any size, but really come into their own when used in large and complex projects. Once the indexing structure for the project has been established then economies of scale mean that the larger the amounts of data being handled, then the more effective the package will prove. You can seamlessly combine all the different kinds of written material that the project may consist of. On the other hand, the time taken to train with the software and understand the intricacies involved is often too demanding for a small scale project.

Qualitative computing is a rapidly developing area and new packages are being developed and marketed all the time. The promise of intelligent packages pervades the whole of computer science, and qualitative computing is no exception. Time will tell whether or not the promise is fulfilled and indeed whether or not social researchers would ever accept such a package were it to be possible. It is important to emphasize that the software does not do the analysis for you; to return to the shoeboxes we discussed in Chapter 21, it creates an electronic form of organizing your shoeboxes and memos but you are still responsible for all of the creativity, coding, sorting and indexing.

Summary

SPSS is by far the most popular tool for statistical analysis but you must remember that it is a tool. It will perform tests, provide charts and graphs assist with coding and many other things, but these are concerned with process. As with any analysis software, qualitative or quantitative, you must understand what you are asking the tool to do and why you are asking. Be confident in what is happening to your data when you request a function within the software, what is going on and what is being done. It is only with this knowledge that you will be in a position to talk about your findings in an intelligent and meaningful way. Producing charts, graphs and output from statistical tests is not enough, you need to explain what they mean and highlight what this is telling us about the data and the research questions. Avoid the temptation to do it just because you can, this holds very little weight in research; only do it if there is a jolly good reason to do it and make sure you know what that reason is.

Suggested further reading

These are given as examples; you will need to read and use the guide to the specific version of the software you are using.

Bryman, A. (2000) *Qualitative Data Analysis; explorations with Nvivo*, Maidenhead, Open University Press.
Coombs, H. (2001) *Research Using IT*, Basingstoke, Palgrave.
Kerlin, B. (2002) *NUD.IST4 Classic Guide*, http://kerlins.net/bobbi/research/nudist/.

Kinnear, P. R. and Gray, C. D. (2004) *SPSS Made Simple*, Hove, Psychology Press.
Pallant, J. (2005) *SPSS Survival Manual*, 2nd edn, Maidenhead, Open University Press.

Chapter 24

Presenting the research

Introduction

The way you present your research will depend on the nature of the research and the audience. My own experience is very much focused in two areas: preparing students for their academic dissertation and presenting my own research in the form of journal articles and conference papers. For the purposes of this chapter I am going to focus on the presentation of a research dissertation, as this is the research report that more often than not will be expected to cover every aspect of the research process. You will have to decide which elements to include and which to leave out depending on the form of presentation you are preparing. Having said that, even the shortest of research papers will usually include a section on each stage in the process depending at which stage in the research the paper is written.

Before I discuss the stages of presentation I would like to say something about the writing process itself. Very often neophyte researchers make the very peculiar and to me totally incomprehensible decision to leave all of their writing until the end. I am still amazed when a student arrives at a tutorial without having sent me something to read beforehand; in they walk and say they would like to talk about 'such and such'. They then tell me a lot about 'such and such' but it is very difficult for me to make any real contribution other than offer my verbal response to their ideas (it's also amazing that some of them have incredible memories and do not feel the need to take down any notes during the discussion!). I would strongly urge anyone engaged in research to write often and share what they have written. Identify a 'critical friend' early on; this may be a project supervisor or a line manager or a friend who understands something of what you are trying to do, someone to share your thoughts with in the form of written conversation.

For almost all new researchers the prospect of writing the report or dissertation is very daunting; instead of thinking of the whole, try arranging it in your mind as a series of essays on the stages of the research. You have engaged in a lot of hard work to reach the stage of presenting your research. Don't waste all of that hard work by leaving things until the last minute and end up with a weak representation of what was actually done. You can write up various parts of the whole as soon as they are finished and have these sections read by your critical friend; you will find your voice but only through practice and sharing.

Planning the final report

It pays to plan out the final document fairly early in the research process. With the tools available in word-processing packages it is possible to set up a template and add to that template as you go along. This will ensure continuity of form and presentation, while still allowing you to take this one essay at a time. Seeing the final report grow in this way gives you a sense of achievement; each section is a goal reached and a step closer to the final one. It pays to set staged deadlines. You may have already done this in your research proposal; unless you have received comments to the contrary, this should act as your deadline schedule for the report. Working out the research timetable will allow you to identify periods of intense activity and periods where you may be left waiting; don't wait, write! If you are waiting for questionnaires to be returned use that time to fine tune your literature review or draft out your methodology; there is no point during the research process when you will be unable to write something, so use your time well. Seeing a sketch of how the final document will look gives you a sense of control and focus; you can see how things are developing and see your final goal moving ever nearer.

Form and structure

Depending on the purpose of your research there is likely to be an expected form and structure for the presentation of your report. In a university context there are likely to be official guidelines for the presentation of a dissertation or thesis. Make sure you are very familiar with these from the outset so you know exactly what is expected of you and you work towards those guidelines from the very beginning, your template reflecting the specifications provided by the institution. If this is not the purpose of the research report then make sure you know what is expected by those commissioning the research or the standards used in the journal you are hoping will accept your paper. In this chapter I present an overview of the structure I expect from my students; it may not be the same as that expected by other dissertation supervisors but it should provide you with sufficient detail to structure your own research report.

Introduction

This chapter or section should include an overview of the research question, where the question came from and why you have chosen to investigate this particular issue. You are setting the scene, the fine detail will follow. For now you want to introduce your reader to the research question, the purpose of asking the question and the reasons why you believe the question matters. After you have set the scene you will provide the reader with your specific research aim and your objectives; if you are using a research hypothesis then this is where you present that hypothesis. Everything that follows was driven by this aim or hypothesis so spell it out from the beginning and make it as clear as you can; there is little point in attempting to dress it up, this will only lead to confusion and may even suggest that you were not quite sure what it was you were investigating.

Methodology

This is possibly the chapter or section where there could be some disagreement. In much of the literature on presenting research you will be advised to place your review of the literature before your methodology. I can understand this but I don't agree with it. Your literature review was an element of your data collection. Although it may have been the first thing you did, even before you had clearly defined research aims, it is data collection and for that reason I feel it should be placed immediately before your empirical findings to allow your reader to see how your findings relate to the findings from the review of the literature.

Your methodology should include a very clear picture of your research design, your methodological approach, and whether you use a qualitative, quantitative or a mixed methodology. You should be sure to use the research methods literature to defend every choice you have made in constructing your research design. You will then discuss your research method or methods followed by your chosen data collection techniques. Try not to get lost in a theoretical debate about available choices here; sometimes it can be difficult to see what has been done if you spend a lot of time arguing about possible alternatives. In any research there are always alternatives; you could write a book on the choices available to you, but you don't have the space in a dissertation. Describe what you have done and justify your choice; you must provide a very clear picture of what you have done, not describe what you could have done. Define and defend your methodology, your research method(s), your data collection technique and the research instrument(s) you have used. It helps to place a blank copy of your research instrument in the appendices so your reader is very clear about the design and content of it. Discuss your research population and your sampling; you are not attempting to hide anything, you are aiming to draw as clear a picture of the research activity as possible. Explain how and why your sample was selected and clearly define your final research sample.

Literature review

Chapter 2 covers this in detail but remember that you may have started work on the literature review very early in the process, before the research proposal was written. Make sure you present your final review in a form that is appropriate to the research question - this means ensuring that it still fits your research questions. Depending on the length of time spent on the study it may be necessary to carry out a final scan of the literature to make sure you have included all relevant material.

Research findings

Chapters 21 and 22 discuss analysis and presentation. In your final report make sure you begin your presentation of findings by giving your reader a true picture of your sources; refer back to your sample and be very explicit about your response rate, making it clear what your findings are based on. Depending on the nature of your research this chapter will vary greatly in appearance; you may be presenting a story, a narrative account of the phenomenon, or a set of charts and graphs. Remember that providing a string of charts and graphs or a list of respondent's quotations is not a presentation of your findings. You must provide some level of interpretation to accompany your findings; this includes referring back to the literature where appropriate. You have two choices here: to present all your results first, then present the analysis and discussion of those results, or to present the findings for each theme, followed by the analysis and discussion. Your decision will depend on the nature of the research and your expectations of your reader.

Conclusion

Your conclusions should be linked back to your research objectives, after all they describe what you set out to do so your findings should be directly associated with those objectives. It is important that your reader is not given any surprises in this chapter. You have already put forward your findings; what you are doing here is spelling them out very clearly but making sure you don't introduce any new information. There should be no leaps of faith in this chapter; only conclusions which are based firmly in your findings should be presented to your reader. It can be very tempting to allow your opinions to creep in at this point, after all you care an awful lot about this topic and you have spent considerable time and energy asking this question; you are bound to be passionate about the answer, but don't let that influence how you present your conclusions. Everything you say here must have emerged clearly from your analysis and be drawn from your evidence; any attempt to slip in person bias at this stage will weaken your research.

In qualitative research your conclusion is likely to be a working hypothesis based on the conceptual framework you have presented in your findings. In quantitative research it may be points in support of a hypothesis or points that clearly falsify a hypothesis. Again there is a need to resist temptation; be very clear to what extent the hypothesis is supported and be very wary of making claims that you have 'proven' anything. It is highly unlikely when dealing with the human condition that you have 'proven' anything. This in no way reduces the importance or impact of your findings; if anything it adds weight to them by highlighting that you really understand the nature of the research you have been engaged in.

Recommendations or suggested ways forward

Depending on the approach you have taken you may be in a position to put forward recommendations, but only if you have provided substantial evidence pointing to them. Don't feel as if you must present a long list of firm recommendations just because you presented conclusions that may suggest those recommendations. If your findings were highly time and context dependent then there is a limit to which you can make more universal recommendations; indeed that would not have been your goal in the first place. What you can do is to suggest ways forward. This is not taking the safe option, but making realistic claims about the potential application of your findings.

In this chapter you also have the opportunity to present those issues which you identified in your analysis but had to step away from as they were not central to your research question. You will want to suggest questions for further research and this is the place to do that. It is inevitable that you have identified other issues as you carried out your investigation. You did not have the resources available to pursue those issues but you know they need to be pursued, so share that knowledge.

Reflection and evaluation

All research is or should be a learning experience, a learning experience for the researcher and for the reader. You can enhance that experience by providing a critical review of your work and a reflection on the process and findings. Share your experience in an honest way; there is rarely such a thing as a perfect research study, there are always alternatives and there are always compromises along the way. By discussing these compromises you allow your reader to judge your findings based on the choices you made; it is often very difficult to evaluate yourself critically; reflective practice is not easy. A good way to prepare yourself for this is the researcher's diary; here you have discussed events as they occurred, defended choices and admitted shortcomings. Use the data in your diary to help you present an honest reflection on the research; you were the one who experienced it and therefore you are the one who can look at the outcome, examine the choices and think about what you could have done differently. There is a fine balance here between being overly critical and overly confident. This is usually the chapter that students find the most difficult, sometimes even painful. Try not to think of it as a discussion of failings; it is a celebration of success and the acknowledgment of learning. You have moved on as a researcher. For many of you there will have been a number of 'first times' for you in this study; you are sharing that and moving forward.

References and bibliography

This is usually all about expectations, standards and regulations; you must make yourself very familiar with those that apply to you. I ask for references at the end of every chapter of a dissertation with a full bibliography at the end. The reference list will include bibliographic details of all the work you directly referred to in the chapter; the bibliography will include all of these and list all the other sources which you consulted but did not refer to, in order to provide a comprehensive bibliography on the topic of your research. There is little point in me going into any detail here about the style for listing references as different rules apply in different institutions, for different journals and for different conferences. Never underestimate the value of your bibliography; you are providing people with a valuable source, and attention to detail is vital.

Appendices

Is can be tempting to use your appendices as a dumping ground for everything you wanted to include in your report but did not have room for; resist this temptation. There should be nothing in the appendices that is not directly referred to in the text of the report. If you have no reason to send your reader to look at an appendix then why is it there? At the very least there should be a copy of every research instrument used, whether a questionnaire, an interview schedule, a focus group guide, a context map for observation. What should not be there is a mountain of raw data. There is no need to include every completed questionnaire; that is raw data and as the researcher it is your responsibility to use that data and present findings; there is no need to share it with anyone after that stage. Remember any promises you made to respondents and honour those promises.

Summary

This chapter has mainly focused on the presentation of a research dissertation but the pattern and content of each section remains largely the same for most types of research reports. The emphasis may vary depending on the purpose of the report but you will have to decide (unless you have been given a specific remit) what to include and what to leave out. For most students the prospect of writing a dissertation is daunting; the word count alone can often make people feel the goal is unachievable, but this is not the case. Think of it in manageable chunks, essays which form chapters, chapters which form the whole. Practise writing; write often and share often until you find your voice and learn how to use it well. Every written task appears to be daunting the first time we do it but with practice, perseverance and a love of what you are doing you will get there in the end. After all, I got to the end of this book and there were times when I truly doubted that would ever be possible.

Suggested further reading

Bell, J. (1999) *Doing Your Research Project*, 3rd edn, Maidenhead, Open University Press, Chapter 13.

Coombs, H. (2001) *Research Using IT*, Basingstoke, Palgrave, Chapter 8.

Hart, C. (2005) *Doing Your Masters Dissertation*, London, Sage, Chapter 12.

PART 5

Glossary and references

Glossary of research terms

A priori: involving the investigation of a phenomenon by deduction without initial sensory experience.

Accuracy: a term used in survey research to refer to the match between the target population and the sample.

Attrition: a reduction in the number of participants during the course of a study. Any reduction in sample size will impact on the internal validity of the study.

Audit trail: the systematic presentation of material gathered within an interpretivist study that provides readers with a road map of the research process to follow and audit the researcher's thinking and conclusions about the data.

Bell curve: in frequency distribution statistics *normal distribution* is shaped like a bell; it is possible to see how far results deviate from the norm when placed against a bell curve.

Bias: any influence that distorts the results of a research study.

Bracketing: a process used by interpretivist researchers to identify their pre-conceived beliefs and opinions about the phenomenon under investigation in order to clarify how personal biases and experience might influence what is seen, heard and reported. These usually occur in memo writing.

Case study: the collection and presentation of detailed information about a particular participant, small group, organization or culture, frequently including the accounts of subjects themselves. A case study must be a functioning specific with definite boundaries.

Categorical variable: a variable with discrete values (e.g. a person's gender or a person's marital status, or the colour of a T-shirt).

Causal model: a model that represents a causal relationship between research variables.

Causal relationship: the relationship established that shows that an independent variable, and nothing else, causes a change in a dependent variable. The relationship will also demonstrate the extent to which the dependent variable has changed as a result of the independent variable.

Causality: the relation between cause and effect.

Central tendency: measures that indicate the middle or centre of a distribution. A measure of the typicality or centrality of a set of scores; the three main measures of central tendency are mean, median and mode.

Clinical trial: a large-scale experiment designed to test the effectiveness of a clinical treatment.

Coding: a procedure for transforming raw data into a standardized format for data analysis purposes. Coding qualitative data involves identifying recurrent words, concepts or themes. In quantitative research, coding usually involves attaching numerical values to categories or choices.

Confidence interval: an interval that identifies a range of values that includes the true population value of a particular characteristic at a specified probability level (usually 95%).

Confirmability: the degree to which research findings can be confirmed by triangulation of data source or data collection; the degree to which the research process can be audited.

Constant comparative method: a procedure used during grounded theory research whereby newly gathered data are continually compared with previously collected data in order to refine the development of theoretical categories. The process occurs in three stages: open coding, axial coding and selective coding.

Content analysis: a procedure for organizing narrative, qualitative data. This is traditionally focused on quantifying the narrative to apply standardized measurements to metrically defined units. These are then used to compare and characterize documents.

Context sensitivity: awareness by a qualitative researcher of the potential influence of factors such as values and beliefs on cultural behaviours within a given context.

Continuous variable: a variable that has fractional values with only artificial intervals such as height, weight and time, added along the continuum of measure.

Control group: a group in an experiment that is not treated with the independent variable in order to compare the treated group against a norm.

Core category: the central category that is used to integrate all the categories identified in grounded theory research.

Correlation: a statistical technique used to measure the association between pairs of interval variables. The range of correlation is from -1.00 to zero to $+1.00$.

Correlation coefficient: a measure of the degree of relationship between two variables. A correlation coefficient lies between $+1.0$ (indicating a perfect positive relationship), through 0 (indicating no relationship between two variables) to -1.0 (a perfect negative relationship).

Covariant: a product of the correlation of two related variables multiplied by their standard deviations.

Credibility: a researcher's ability to demonstrate that the object of a study is accurately identified and described, based on the way in which the study was conducted. Audit trails provide the necessary evidence.

Critical theory: social commentary examining and questioning the social status quo looking to bring about transformations in the commonly accepted social structures.

Data saturation: the point at which data collection can be terminated. Closure is arrived at when the information being gathered becomes repetitive and contains no new ideas, so the researcher can be reasonably confident that further data collection is unlikely to generate anything new.

Deductive reasoning: a logical process of developing specific predictions from general principles. This type of reasoning moves from the general to the particular.

Dependability: being able to account for changes in the design of the study as new knowledge emerges and the changing conditions surrounding that which is being studied.

Dependent variable: a research variable that is subject to treatment and is then measured for any effect the treatment has had on it.

Descriptive statistics: statistical methods used to describe or summarize data collected from the research sample (e.g. mean, median, mode, range or standard deviation and variance).

Deviation: the value of the distance between the mean and an observation in a given distribution.

Discrete variable: a variable that is measured in whole units, e.g. gender and siblings.

Emic perspective: a term used by ethnographers to refer to the insider's or native's view of his or her world (see also *Etic perspective*).

Empirical research: a process of systematic knowledge gathering through observations and questioning.

Epistemology: the nature of knowledge and the way in which we can acquire knowledge.

Ethics: the rules of behaviour recognized within a specific discipline or social group, a set of moral principles.

Ethnography: ethnographies study groups and/or cultures over a period of time. The goal of this type of research is to comprehend the particular group or culture through observer immersion into the culture or group. Research is completed through prolonged observation with the researcher immersed within the group for an extended period of time; it is similar to case study research in many ways, except that no direct questioning takes place. More detailed information is usually collected during the research than in case study investigation.

Ethnomethodology: a form of ethnography that studies activities of group members to see how they make sense of their surroundings. Systematic study of the ways in which people use social interaction to make sense of their situation and create their 'reality'. This research methodology, associated with sociology, focuses on how people understand their everyday activities.

Etic perspective: term used by ethnographers to refer to the outsider's view of the experiences of a specific cultural group (see also *Emic perspective*).

Experimental research: a research methodology used to establish cause-and-effect relationships between the independent and dependent variables by means of manipulation of variables, control and randomization. A true experiment involves the random allocation of participants to experimental and control groups, manipulation of the independent variable, and the introduction of a control group (for comparison purposes). Participants are assessed before and after the manipulation of the independent variable in order to assess its effect on the dependent variable (the outcome).

External validity: the extent to which the results of a study are generalizable to the wider population. It is dependent on nature and size of sample and the degree to which *Internal validity* can be demonstrated.

Extraneous variable: a variable that could potentially interfere with the relationship between independent and dependent variables, and needs to be controlled in some way.

Field notes: notes taken by researchers to record all events that occur 'in the field' and their interpretation of those observations.

Focus group: a discussion conducted with a small group of people to explore their ideas on a particular topic.

Frequency distribution: a visual display of numerical values, using either a graph or a chart to show the distribution of data within a dataset, ranging from the lowest to the highest and showing the number of times (frequency) each value occurs.

Generalizability: the extent to which research findings and conclusions from a study conducted on a sample population can be applied to the population as a whole.

Grounded theory: analysis that concentrates on theories that have emerged from investigating a particular phenomenon. Theories are grounded in observable experiences, but researchers add their own insight into why those experiences exist.

Hermeneutics: from the Greek [*hermeneutikos*] 'to interpret or explain'; the science and methodology of interpretation originally applied to biblical studies. Now also used as a term for dualistic cognitive theory, in which the researcher and the research subject are linked and the research becomes a product of that interaction.

Holistic perspective: approaching the whole phenomenon of the subject of the investigation, taking into account all factors which may influence it.

Hypothesis: a statement that predicts the relationship between the independent and dependent variables that are the focus of the investigation. This could be either a specific prediction about the nature and direction of the relationship between the independent and dependent variables, or one that does not specify these.

Independent variable: the variable that is assumed to cause or influence the dependent variable(s) or outcome. The independent variable is manipulated in experimental research to observe its effect on the dependent variable(s).

Inductive analysis: a form of analysis based on inductive reasoning; a researcher using inductive analysis starts with observation of the specific, then works up to the more general.

Inferential statistics: statistics that allow a researcher to make suggestions about whether relationships observed in a sample are likely to occur in the wider population from which that sample was drawn. Inferential statistics use mathematical processes to test hypotheses based on data gathered from a sample of the target population.

Informed consent: the process of securing voluntary participation of individuals in research, once they have been made fully aware of potential risks involved and what benefits are likely to be produced by the research.

Internal validity: in studies involving causal relationships, this relates to the rigour with which the study was conducted, including the design of the study, the care taken to conduct measurements, and what was and wasn't measured.

Interpretivism: sees the world as a construction of multiple realities; individuals each perceive their reality through their own unique understanding and experience. Interpretivist research focuses on individual experiences and lives.

Interval scale: when categories are ordered, there are equal intervals between points on the scale and there is a specific numerical distance between each level.

Interval variable: a variable that has all of the properties of nominal and ordinal variables with a specific numerical distance between each variation. These variables are comparable on three levels of measurement: the difference between variables (nominal measure); which is the greatest or smallest (the ordinal measure); and the distance between them (the interval measure).

Interviews: a data collection technique in which a researcher asks questions, usually face to face, of participants:

Structured interview: the interviewer asks the respondents the same questions using an interview schedule – a formal instrument that specifies the precise wording and ordering of all the questions to be asked of each respondent.

Unstructured interview: the researcher asks open-ended questions that give the respondent considerable freedom to talk freely on the topic and to influence the direction of the interview, since there is no predetermined plan about the specific information to be gathered from those being interviewed.

Likert scale: a method used to measure attitudes, which involves respondents indicating their degree of agreement or disagreement with a series of statements.

Matched T-test: a matched pairs T-test can be used to determine whether the scores of the same participants in a study differ under different conditions.

Mean: the average score within a data set distribution.

Mean deviation: a measure of variation that indicates the average deviation of scores in a distribution from the mean or central point in the dataset.

Median: the centre score in a distribution when those scores are arranged in ascending or descending order.

Meta-analysis: meaning 'an analysis of analysis', this is a statistical technique for combining and integrating the data derived from a number of studies undertaken on a specific topic.

Mode: the most frequent score in a distribution.

Narrative inquiry: a qualitative research approach based on a researcher's narrative account of the investigation.

Naturalistic inquiry: observational research of a group in its natural setting, now more common referred to as 'interpretivist' inquiry.

Nominal scale: a scale that does not actually measure anything, nominal implies 'name'; this is the lowest level of measurement that involves assigning data to categories which are mutually exclusive, but which lack any intrinsic order or have any defined relationship; examples include gender, the colour of a person's hair or eyes, or a book title.

Nominal variable: a variable determined by categories which cannot be ordered (see *Nominal scale* above).

Normal distribution: represented by the bell curve, normal distributions are symmetrical and affected only by random influences. The most frequently found scores are in the centre range, with cases becoming progressively rarer as we move to the greater and lesser extremes of the scores.

Objectivity: free from bias; value-free; observing a phenomenon without imposing any personal judgement on that which is being observed.

Ontology: to do with the nature and form of reality.

Ordinal scale: categories can be used to rank order a variable, but the intervals between categories are not equal or fixed (e.g. strongly agree, agree, neither agree nor disagree, disagree, strongly disagree).

Ordinal variable: a variable which can be ordered at specific data points but where the distance between data points cannot be determined; for example, letter grades such as 'A' and 'B'.

Paradigm: Kuhn (1970) defines a paradigm in two ways: first as the entire constellation of beliefs, values and techniques shared by a scientific community; second, as the procedures used to solve specific problems and take theories to their logical conclusion. Kuhn also suggests that paradigms function as maps or guides, dictating the kinds of problem that it is important to address, the kinds of theories or explanations that are regarded as acceptable, and the kinds of procedure that are used to tackle particular problems.

Parametric statistics: a type of inferential statistic that involves the estimation of at least one parameter. These tests can only be performed on either interval or ratio data and assume a normal distribution of scores.

Performance measures: a series of indicators presented in tangible form either qualitative or quantitative, that indicate if current performance is rational and cost effective. Performance measures can include a huge variety of organizational factors such as workload and output-to-cost ratios, transaction ratios, error rates, consumption rates, completion and back order rates, responsiveness rates and user satisfaction.

Phenomenology: a qualitative research approach which uses microanalysis to interpret group behaviour.

Population: the entire community under investigation.

Positive correlation: a relationship between two variables where higher values of one variable tend to be associated with higher values of the second variable.

Positivism: this paradigm assumes that human behaviour is determined by external stimuli and that it is possible to use the principles and methods traditionally employed by the natural scientist to observe and measure social phenomena.

Probability: the chance that a phenomenon has of occurring randomly. As a statistical measure, it shown as p (the 'p' factor).

Qualitative research: empirical research in which the researcher explores a phenomenon using textual, descriptive narrative rather than numerical data. Results are often transferable.

Quantitative research: empirical research in which the researcher explores relationships using numeric data. Results can often be generalized, though this is not always the case.

Quasi-experiment: the term generally used to describe research studies that attempt to examine variables but where no attempt is made to control those variables. Interpretation and transferability are often used to compensate for lack of control of variables.

Random sampling: process used in research to draw a sample of a population strictly by chance. The sample is said to be random because there is no regular or discernible pattern or order. Random sampling is used on the assumption that sufficiently large samples that are assigned randomly will exhibit a distribution comparable to that of the target population.

Randomization: used to allocate subjects to experimental and control groups.

Range: the difference between the highest and lowest scores in a distribution.

Reliability: the extent to which a measure, procedure or instrument produces the same result in repeated studies.

Research method: designs for undertaking the research activity such as case study, survey, experiment, ethnography and Delphi study.

Research methodology: different approaches to systematic inquiry developed within a particular paradigm with associated epistemological assumptions: interpretivist, positivist and postpositivist.

Research question: a clear statement in the form of a question of the specific issue that a researcher wishes to answer in order to address a research problem. A research problem is an issue that lends itself to systematic investigation through research.

Response rate: the actual percentage of questionnaires completed and returned.

Rigour: degree to which research methods are scrupulously and meticulously carried out in order to recognize important influences occurring in a experiment.

Sample: the actual research participants in a particular study. Choice of sampling technique will be determined by the research method. In studies that use inferential statistics to analyse results or that are designed to be generalizable, sample size is critical – generally the larger the number in the sample, the higher the likelihood of a representative distribution of the population.

> *Quota sampling*: sampling strategy where the researcher identifies the various strata of a population and ensures that all these strata are proportionately represented within the sample to increase its representativeness.

Snowball sampling: a non-probability sampling strategy whereby referrals from earlier participants are used to gather the required number of participants.

Theoretical sampling: the selection of individuals within a naturalistic research study, based on emerging findings as the study progresses, to ensure that key issues are adequately represented.

Sampling error: the degree to which the results from the sample deviate from those that would be obtained from the entire population, because of random error in the selection of respondent and the corresponding reduction in reliability.

Sampling frame: a listing that should include all those in the target population to be sampled.

Skewed distribution: any distribution which is not normal, that is not symmetrical along the x-axis.

Standard deviation: a measure of variation that indicates the typical distance between the scores of a distribution and the mean, calculated by taking the square root of the average of the squared deviations in a given distribution. It can be used to indicate the proportion of data within certain ranges of scale values when the distribution conforms closely to the normal curve.

Standard error: a value based on the size of the sample and the standard deviation of the distribution, indicating the range within which the mean of the population is likely to be away from the mean of the sample at a given level of probability.

Statistical inference: a procedure using the laws of probability to make inferences concerning the attributes of a population based on information gathered from a sample of that population.

Statistical significance: provided to give an indication of whether the results of analysis of data from a sample are unlikely to have been caused by chance at a specified level of probability (usually 0.05 or 0.01).

Survey: a research method used to gain specific information about either a particular group or a representative sample of it. Results are typically used to understand the attitudes, beliefs or knowledge of that particular group. Surveys are usually concerned with broad issues that are then used to describe a situation.

T-test: a T-test is used to determine if the scores of two groups differ on a single variable. For example, it could be used to determine whether information literacy levels differ between students in two classrooms.

Theoretical framework: the conceptual underpinning of a research study, which may be based on theory or on a specific conceptual model.

Theory: in its most general sense a theory describes or explains something. Often it is the answer to 'what', 'when', 'how' or 'why' questions.

Thick description: a rich and extensive set of details concerning methodology and context, provided in a research report.

Transferability: the ability to apply the results of a research study carried out in one context to the situation in another, similar context,

Triangulation: used in a research context to describe the use of a variety of data sources or techniques to examine a specific phenomenon, either simultaneously or sequentially, in order to produce a more accurate account of the phenomenon under investigation. This involves a combination of research techniques within a study; for example use of observation, interviews and focus groups all with the same participants. It could also be applied by using a single research technique on a variety of research subjects.

Trustworthiness: a term used to describe whether interpretivist research has been conducted in such a way that it gives you confidence in the findings.

Validity: the degree to which a study accurately reflects or assesses the specific research question. There are several different types of validity: *see* other entries in this glossary.

Variable: operational form of a concept; a characteristic that can counted, measured classified or ordered.

Variance: a measure of variation within a distribution determined by averaging the squared deviations from the mean of a distribution.

Variation: the dispersion of data points around the mean of a distribution.

References

Agar, M. (1996) *The Professional Stranger: an informal introduction to ethnography*, London, Academic Press.

Anderson, G. L. and Herr, K. (1999) The New Paradigm Wars: is there room for rigorous practitioner knowledge in schools and universities? *Educational Researcher*, **28** (5), 12-21, 40.

Atton, C. (1998) The Librarian as Ethnographer: notes towards a strategy for the exploitation of cultural collections, *Collection Building*, **17** (4), 154-58.

Badu, E. E. (2004) Academic Library Development in Ghana: top managers' perspectives, *African Journal of Library, Archives and Information Science*, **14** (2), 93-107.

Bailey, P., Cook, G., Glenn, S., Mitchell, A., Thynne, E. andWeatherhead, E. (2004) Distance Learning in Post-qualifying Nurse Education at Northumbria University: implications for the role of the library and library staff, *Health Information and Libraries Journal*, **21** (1), 66-9.

Bakowska, E. (2005) The Jagiellonian Library, Cracow: its history and recent developments, *Library Review,* **54** (3), 155-65.

Banwell, L., Coulson, G. and Pickard, A. (2003) Using the JUBILEE Toolkit to Bridge the Research-Practice Divide, *New Review of Information and Library Research*, **9** (1), 97-110.

Banwell, L. et al. (2005) *JUBILEE* (JISC User Behaviour in Information seeking: Longitudinal Evaluation of EIS), *Cycle 5 - Final Report*, Northumbria University, Information Management Research Institute/JISC.

Bell, J. (1999) *Doing your research project*, 3rd edn, Maidenhead, Open University Press.

Bensman, S. J. (2005) Urquhart's Law: probability and the management of scientific and journal collections, Part 1: The Law's Initial Formulation and Statistical Bases, *Science & Technology Libraries*, **26** (1), 31-68.

Bernard, H. R. (1994) *Research Methods in Anthropology: qualitative and quantitative approaches*, London, Sage.

Bertrand, I. and Hughes, P. (2005) *Media Research Methods: audiences, institutions and texts*, London, Palgrave McMillan.

Bingham, J. and Davies, G. (1992) *Systems Analysis*, Basingstoke, Macmillan.

Birley, G. and Moreland, N. (1998) *A Practical Guide to Academic Research*, London, Kogan Page.

Blandford, A., Connell, I. and Green, T. (2004) CASSM and Cognitive Walkthrough: usability issues with ticket vending machines, *Behaviour and Information Technology,* **23** (5), 307-20.

Blaxter, L., Dodd, K. and Tight, M. (1996) *How to Research*, Buckingham, Open University Press.

Blumer, H. (1937) Social Psychology. In Schmidt, E. P. (ed.), *Man and Society*, New York, Prentice-Hall.

Bohm, D. (1983) *Wholeness and the Implicated Order*, London, Ark.

Boud, D., Keogh, R. and Walker, D. (eds) (1985) *Reflection: turning experience into learning*, London, Kogan Page.

Bouthillier, F. (2000) The Meaning of Service: ambiguities and dilemmas for public library service providers, *Library and Information Science Research*, **22** (3), 243-72.

Bow, A. (1999) Ethnographic Techniques. In Williamson, K. (ed.), *Research Methods for Students and Professionals: information management and systems*, Wagga Wagga, Charles Sturt University, 247-61.

Bragg, W. H. (1932) Foreword. In Martin, T. (ed.), *Faraday's Diary: being the various philosophical notes of experimental investigation made by Michael Faraday during the years 1820-1862 and bequeathed by him to the Royal Institution of Great Britain*, 7 vols, London, G. Bell and Sons Ltd.

British Sociological Association (2002) *Statement of Ethical Practice*, www.britsoc.org.uk/about/ethic.htm.

Brookfield, S. D. (1995) *Becoming a Critically Reflective Teacher*, San Francisco, Jossey-Bass.

Bryman, A. (2000) *Qualitative Data Analysis: explorations with Nvivo*, Maidenhead, Open University Press.

Buchanan, E. (ed.) (2003) *Readings in Virtual, Research Ethics: issues and controversies*, New York, Ideal Group.

Budd, J. M. (2001) *Knowledge and Knowing in Library and Information Science: a philosophical framework*, New York, Scarecrow Press.

Burgess, R. G. (1981) Keeping a Research Diary, *Cambridge Journal of Education*, **11** (1), 75-83.

Burns, R. B. (2000) *Introduction to Research Methods*, 4th edn, London, Sage.

Busha, C. and Harper, S. P. (1980) *Research Methods in Librarianship: techniques and interpretations*, New York, Academic Press.

Caldwell, B. J. (1994) (rev edn) *Beyond Positivism: economic methodology in the twentieth century*, London, Routledge.

Cape, B. (2004) Gathering Opinion and Initiating Debate: the success of the Delphi Method in purely qualitative research, *Library and Information Research News*, **28** (89), 35-43.

Capel, S., Banwell, L., Reed, J. and Walton, G. (1998) *R&D Information in the NHS. Information Needs Assessment Phase 2 in the Northern and Yorkshire Region*, Newcastle upon Tyne, Department of Information and Library Management, University of Northumbria at Newcastle.

Capra, F. (2000) *The Tao of Physics: an exploration of the parallels between modern physics and eastern mysticism*, 4th edn, Boston, MA, Shambhala.

Carr, E. H. (1961) *What is History?* Harmondsworth, Penguin.

Carr, W. and Kemmis, S. (1986) *Becoming Critical: education, knowledge and action research*, London, Falmer.

Charmaz, K. (1995) Grounded Theory. In Smith, J. A., Harre, R. and Langenhove, L. V. (eds) *Rethinking Methods in Psychology*, London, Sage, 29–49.

Charmaz, K. (2006) *Constructing Grounded Theory: a practical guide through qualitative analysis*, London, Sage.

Choldin, M. T. (2005) Libraries in Continental Europe: the 40s and the 90s, *Journal of Documentation*, **61** (3), 356–61.

Colaizzi, P. F. (1978) Psychological Research as the Phenomenologist Views It. In Valle, R. and King M. (eds), *Existential-Phenomenological Alternatives for Psychology*, Oxford, Oxford Press.

Cole, B. and Harer, J. B. (2005) The Importance of the Stakeholder in Performance Measurement: critical processes and performance measures for assessing and improving academic library services and programs, *College & Research Libraries*, **66** (2), 149–70.

Coomber, R. (1997) Using the Internet for Survey Research, *Sociological Research Online*, **2** (2).

Coombs, H. (2001) *Research Using IT*, Basingstoke, Palgrave.

Cooper, H. (1998) *Synthesizing Research: a guide for literature reviews*, 3rd edn, London, Sage.

Corbetta, P. (2003) *Social Research: theory, method and techniques*, London, Sage.

Corti, L. (1993) Using Diaries in Social Research, *Social Research Update*, **2**, www.soc.surrey.ac.uk/sru/SRU2.html.

Council for American Survey Research Organisations (2002) *Code of Standards and Ethics for Survey Research*, www.casro.org/codofstandards.cfm.

Creaser, C. and White, S. (2005) Pay and Status: latest survey results, *Library and Information Update*, **4** (6), 40–3.

Creswell, J. W. (1998) *Qualitative Inquiry and Research Design: choosing among five traditions*, London, Sage.

Crumley, E. T. (2006) Exploring the Role of Librarians and Health Care Professionals Involved in Complementary and Alternative Medicine, *Journal of the Medical Library Association*, **94** (1), np.

Dalkey, N. and Helmer, O. (1963) An Experimental Application of the Delphi Method to the Use of Experts, *Management Science*, **9**, 458–67.

Deem, R. (1998) From Local To Global? The role of case study in policy-relevant educational research. Plenary address to the Centre for Educational

Development, Appraisal and Research Conference. In 'Case Study Research in Education', Warwick, University of Warwick, 26-37.

Denzin, N. K. (1978) *Sociological Methods*, Berkshire, McGraw-Hill.

Denzin, N. K. and Lincoln, Y. S. (eds) (1994) *Handbook of Qualitative Research*, London, Sage.

Dervin, B. (1997) Given a Context by Any Other Name: methodological tools for taming the unruly beast. In Vakkari, P., Savolainen, R. and Dervin, B. (eds), *Information Seeking in Context: proceedings of an international conference on research in information needs, seeking and use in different contexts, 14–16 August, 1996, Tampere, Finland*, London, Taylor Graham, 13-38.

De Vaus, D. (2002a) *Analyzing Social Science Data: 50 key problems in data analysis*, London, Sage.

De Vaus, D. (2002b) *Survey Research*, London, Sage.

Dexter, L. A. (1970) *Elite and Specialized Interviewing*, Evanston, ILL, Northwestern University Press.

Dey, I. (1993) *Qualitative Data Analysis: a user-friendly guide for social scientists*, London, Routledge.

Diamond, I. and Jefferies, J. (2001) *Beginning Statistics: an introduction for social scientists*, London, Sage.

Dmytriw, D. (2003), *Information Acquisition and Exchange Within Cryptozoological Virtual Communities*, unpublished dissertation, Northumbria University.

Einstein, A., and Infeld, L. (1938) *The Evolution of Physics*, New York, Simon and Schuster.

Ellis, D. (1989) A Behavioural Approach to Information Retrieval System Design, *Journal of Documentation*, **45** (3), 171-212.

Ellis, D. (1990) *New Horizons in Information Retrieval*, London, Library Association.

Ellis, D. (1993) The Information Seeking Patterns of Academic Researchers: a grounded theory approach, *Library Quarterly*, **63** (4), 469-86.

Ellis, D. (1996) *Progress and Problems in Information Retrieval*, London, Library Association.

Ellis, D., Cox, D. and Hall, K. (1993) A Comparison of the Information Seeking Patterns of Researchers in the Physical and Social Sciences, *Journal of Documentation*, **49** (4), 356-9.

Ellis, D. and Haugan, M. (1997) Modelling the Information Seeking Patterns of Engineers and Research Scientists in an Industrial Environment, *Journal of Documentation*, **53** (4), 384-403.

Ely, M. and Anzul, M. (1994) *Doing Qualitative Research: circles within circles*, London, Falmer Press.

Erickson, K. C. and Stull, D. D. (1997) *Doing Team Ethnography: warnings and advice*, Sage, Beverly Hills.

Erlandson, D. A., Harris, E. L., Skipper, B. L. and Allen, S. D. (1993) *Doing Naturalistic Inquiry: a guide to methods*, London, Sage.

Fetterman, D. (1989) *Ethnography: step by step*, London, Sage.

Feyerand, P. (1975) *Against Method*, London, New Left Review.

Field, A. and Hole, G. (2002) *How to Design and Report Experiments*, London, Sage.

Fife, W. (2005) *Doing Fieldwork: ethographic methods for research in developing countries and beyond*, Basingstoke, Palgrave Macmillan.

Filipenko, M. (2004) Constructing Knowledge About and With Informational Texts: implications for teacher–librarians working with young children, *School Libraries Worldwide*, **10** (1/2), (np).

Fink, A. (1998) *Conducting Research Literature Reviews: from paper to the internet*, London, Sage.

Fisher, A. (1993) *The Logic of Real Arguments*, Cambridge, Cambridge University Press.

Flick, U. (2002) *An Introduction to Qualitative Research*, 2nd edn, London, Sage.

Foddy, W. (1993) *Constructing Questions for Interviews and Questionnaires: theory and practice in social research*, Cambridge, Cambridge University Press.

Fontana, A. and Frey, J. (1994) Interviewing: the art of science. In Denzin, N. K. and Lincoln, Y. S. (eds), *Handbook of Qualitative Research*, London, Sage, 361–76.

Ford, J. (1975) *Paradigms and Fairytales: an introduction to the science of meanings*, London, Routledge and Kegan Paul.

Fowles, J. (1978) *Handbook of Futures Research*, Connecticut, Greenwood Press.

Freire, P. (1972) *Pedagogy of the Oppressed*, Harmondsworth, Penguin.

Garg, N., Haynes, S. R., Kannampallil, T. G. and Larson, L. L. (2005) Optimizing Anti-Terrorism Resource Allocation, *Journal of the American Society for Information Science and Technology*, **56** (3), 299–309.

Giorgi, A. (ed.) (1985) *Phenomenology and Psychological Research*, Pittsburgh, Duquesne University Press.

Glaser, B. (1992) *Emergence Versus Forcing: basics of grounded theory analysis*, Mill Valley, CA, Sociology Press.

Glaser, B. (1998) *Doing Grounded Theory: issues and discussion*, Mill Valley, CA, Sociology Press.

Glaser, B. G. (1978) *Theoretical Sensitivity*, Sociology Press.

Glaser, B. G. and Strauss, A. L. (1967) *The Discovery of Grounded Theory*, New York, Aldine.

Glesne, C. P. A. and Peshkin, A. (1992) *Becoming Qualitative Researchers*, New York, Longman.

Gorman, G. E. and Clayton, P. (2005) *Qualitative Research for the Information Professional: a practical handbook*, 2nd edn, London, Facet Publishing.

Gray, D. B. (2004) *Doing Research in the Real World*, London, Sage.

Greene, J. C. (1990) Three Views on the Nature and Role of Knowledge in Social Science. In Guba, E. (ed.), *The Paradigm Dialog*, London, Sage, 227–45.

Grills, S. (1998) On Being Partisan in Non-partisan Settings: field research among the politically committed. In Grills, S. (ed.) *Doing Ethnographic Research: fieldwork settings*, London, Sage, 76–93.

Guba, E. (ed.) (1990) *The Paradigm Dialog*, London, Sage.

Guba, E. G. and Lincoln, Y. S. (1989) *Fourth Generation Evaluation*, London, Sage.

Guba, E. G. and Lincoln, Y. S. (1994) Competing Paradigms in Qualitative Research. In Denzin, N. K. and Lincoln, Y. S. (eds), *Handbook of Qualitative Research*, London, Sage, 105–17.

Guba, E. G. and Lincoln, Y. S. (1998) Competing Paradigms in Qualitative Research. In Denzin, N. K. and Lincoln, Y. S. (eds), *The Landscape of Qualitative Research: theories and issues*, London, Sage, 195–220.

Gupta, U. G. and Clarke, R. E. (1996) Theory and Applications of the Delphi Techniques: a bibliography, *Technological Forecasting and Social Change*, **53**, 185–211.

Guttman, L. (1950) The Basis for Scalogram Analysis. In Stouffer, S. A. (ed.), *Measurement and Prediction*, Princeton, Princeton University Press.

Habermas, J. (1991) *The Structural Transformation of the Public Sphere: an inquiry into a category of bourgeois society*, trans. Thomas Burger with Frederick Lawrence, Cambridge, MA, MIT Press.

Hallcom, F. (ongoing) *An Urban Ethnographic of Latino Street Gangs*, www.csun.edu/~hcchs006/gang.html.

Halpern, E. (1983) *Auditing Naturalistic Inquiries: the development and application of a model*, PhD dissertation, Indiana University.

Hamel, J., Dufour, S. and Fortin, D. (1993) *Case Study Methods*, Newbury Park, CA, Sage Publications.

Hammersley, M. (1989) *The Dilemma of Qualitative Method: Herbert Blumer and the Chicago tradition*, London, Routledge.

Hammersley, M. (1990) *Reading Ethnographic Research: a critical guide*, London, Routledge.

Hammersley, M. (1992) *What's Wrong With Ethnography?* London, Routledge.

Hammersley, M. and Atkinson, P. (1995) *Ethnography: principles in practice*, London, Routledge.

Hart, C. (1998) *Doing a Literature Review: releasing the social science research imagination*, London, Sage.

Hart, C. (2001) *Doing a Literature Search: a comprehensive guide for the social sciences*, London, Sage.

Hart, C. (2005) *Doing Your Masters Dissertation*, London, Sage.

Hartley, R. J. and Booth, H. (2006) Users and Union Catalogues, *Journal of Librarianship and Information Science*, **38** (1), 7–20.

Harvey, R. (2000) Introduction. In Williamson, K. (ed.), *Research Methods for Students and Professionals: information management and systems*, Wagga Wagga, Charles Sturt University.

Heise, D. R. (1970) The Semantic Differential and Attitude Research. In Summers, G. F. (ed.), *Attitude Measurement*, Chicago, Rand McNally, 235–53, www.indiana.edu/~socpsy/papers/AttMeasure/attitude.htm.

Heisenberg, W. (1958) *Physics and Philosophy*, New York, Harper Row.

Helmer, O. and Rescher, N. (1959) On the Epistemology of the Inexact Sciences,

Management Science, **6** (1), October, 25-52.

Henry, G. (1990) *Practical Sampling*, London, Sage.

Herr, K. and Anderson, G. L. (2005) *The Action Research Dissertation: a guide for students and faculty*, London, Sage.

Hine, C. (2000) *Virtual Ethnography*, London, Sage.

Hjorland B. (2005) Empiricism, Rationalism and Positivism in Library and Information Science, *Journal of Documentation*, **61** (1), 130-55.

Holt, J. (1983) *How Children Learn*, London, Penguin.

Huart, J., Kolski, C. and Sagar, M. (2004) Evaluation of Multimedia Applications using Inspection Methods: the cognitive walkthrough case, *Interacting with Computers*, **16** (2), 183-215.

Internet Modern History Sourcebook, www.fordham.edu/halsall/mod/modsbook.html.

Janesick, V. J. (1994) The Dance of Qualitative Research. In Denzin, N. K. and Lincoln, Y. S. (eds), *The Landscape of Qualitative Research: theories and issues*, London, Sage, 209-19.

Jones, Q. (1997) Virtual Communities, Virtual Settlements and Cyber-archaeology: a theoretical outline, *Journal of Computer Mediated Communications*, **3** (3), http://jcmc.indiana.edu/vol3/issue3/jones.html.

Kendall, M. (2005) Tackling Student Referencing Errors Through an Online Tutorial, *Aslib Proceedings*, **57** (2), 131-45.

Kerlin, B. (2002) *NUD.IST4 Classic Guide*, http://kerlins.net/bobbi/research/nudist/.

King, S. A. (1996) Researching Internet Communities: proposed ethical guidelines for the reporting of results, *The Information Society*, **12** (2), 119-28.

Kinnear, P. R. and Gray, C. D. (2004) *SPSS Made Simple*, Hove, Psychology Press.

Kottak, C. P. (2005) *Window on Humanity: a concise introduction to general anthropology*, McGraw Hill, New York.

Kreuger, R.A. (1988) *Focus Groups: a practical guide for applied research*, London, Sage.

Kuhn, T. S (1970) *The Structure of Scientific Revolutions*, Chicago, Chicago University Press.

Kumar, R. (1999) *Research Methodology: a step-by-step guide for beginners*, London, Sage.

Kvale, S (1996) *InterViews: an introduction to qualitative interviewing*, London, Sage.

Lal, V. (2005) Much Ado About Something: the new malaise of world history, *Radical History Review*, 91, 124-30.

Lazar, D. (1998) Selected Issues in the Philosophy of Social Science. In Seale C. (ed.), *Researching Society and Culture*, London, Sage, 8-22.

Lewin, K. (1948) *Resolving Social Conflicts; selected papers on group dynamics*, London, Harper and Row, 1948.

Likert, R. (1932) *A Technique for the Measurement of Attitudes*, New York, Columbia University Press.

Lincoln, Y. S. and Guba, E. G. (1985) *Naturalistic Inquiry*, London, Sage.

Linstone, H. A. and Turoff, M. (eds) (2002) *The Delphi Method: techniques and applications*, www.is.njit.edu/pubs/delphibook/.

Lobenthal, J. (2004) *Tallulah!: the life and times of a leading lady*, New York, Regan Books.

Ludwig, L. and Starr, S. (2005) Library as a Place: results of a Delphi study, *Journal of the Medical Library Association*, **93** (3), (np).

Malinowski, B. (1922) *Argonauts of the Western Pacific*, London, Routledge and Kegan Paul.

Mann, C. and Stewart, F. (2000) *Internet Communication and Qualitative Research: a handbook for researching online*, London, Sage.

Marshall, C. and Rossman, G. B. (1989) *Designing Qualitative Research*, 2nd edn, 1995, London, Sage.

Marvasti, A. B. (2004) *Qualitative Research in Sociology*, London, Sage.

Marwick, A. (2001) *The New Nature of History: knowledge, evidence, language*, Basingstoke, Palgrave Macmillan.

Mason, J. (2002) *Qualitative Researching*, London, Sage.

Maykut, P. and Morehouse, R. (1994) *Beginning Qualitative Research: a philosophic and practical guide*, London, Farmer Press.

McNicol, S. (2004) Is Research an Untapped Resource in the Library and Information Profession? *Journal of Libarianship and Information Science*, **36** (3), 119-26.

Mead, M. (1960) *Coming of Age in Samoa: a psychological study of primitive youth for western civilisation*, New York, Mentor.

Melia, K. (1996) Rediscovering Glaser, *Qualitative Health Research*, **6** (3), 368-75.

Melia, K. M. (1997) Producing 'Plausible Stories': interviewing student nurses. In Miller, G. and Dingwall, R. (eds), *Context and Method in Qualitative Research*, London, Sage, 26-36.

Mellon, C. A. (1990) *Naturalistic Inquiry for Library Science: methods and applications for research, evaluation and teaching*, London, Greenwood.

Mertens, D. M. (2005) *Research and Evaluation in Education and Psychology*, London, Sage.

Mezirow, J. (1991) *Transformative Dimensions of Adult Learning*, Oxford, Jossey-Bass.

Miles, M. B. and Huberman, A. M. (1988) Drawing Valid Meaning From Qualitative Data: towards a shared craft. In Fetterman, D. M. (ed.), *Qualitative Approaches to Evaluation in Education: the silent scientific revolution*, New York, Praeger, 222-44.

Miles, M. B. and Huberman, A. M. (1994) *Qualitative Data Analysis: a sourcebook of new methods*, 2nd edn, London, Sage.

Miller, G. (1997) Introduction. In Miller, G. and Dingwall, R. (eds), *Context and Method in Qualitative Research*, London, Sage, 27-36.

Minichiello, V., Aroni, R., Timewell, E. and Alexander, L. (1995) *In-depth Interviewing*, 2nd edn, Sydney, Longman.

Mitchell, R. G. and Charmaz, K. (1998) Telling Tales and Writing Stories: postmodernist visions and realist images in ethnographic writing. In Grills, S. (ed.), *Doing Ethnographic Research: fieldwork settings*, London, Sage, 228-47.

Morgan, D. (1993) *Successful Focus Groups: advancing the state of the art*, London, Sage.

Morgan, D. L., and Kreuger, R. A. (1998) *The Focus Group Kit*, London, Sage.

Morse, J. M. (1994a) Designing Funded Qualitative Research. In Denzin, N. K. and Lincoln, Y. S. (eds), *The Landscape of Qualitative Research: theories and issues*, London, Sage, 220-36.

Morse J. M. (1994b) 'Emerging from the Data': the cognitive processes of analysis in qualitative inquiry. In Morse, J. M. (ed.), *Critical Issues in Qualitative Research Methods*, London, Sage, 23-43.

Morse, J. M. (1997) *Completing a Qualitative Project: details and dialogue*, London, Sage.

Muddiman, D. (2005) A New History of ASLIB 1924-1950, *Journal of Documentation*, **61** (3), 402-28.

National Archives, www.nationalarchives.gov.uk/default.htm.

Nielsen, J. (1993) *Usability Engineering*, Boston, MA, Academic Press.

Nielsen, J. (1994) *How to Conduct a Heuristic Evaluation*, www.useit.com/papers/heuristic/heuristic_evaluation.html.

Nuvolari, A. (2005) Open Source Software Development: some historical perspectives, *First Monday*, **10** (10), (October), http://firstmonday.org/issues/issue10_10/nuvolari/index.html.

Oppenheim, A. (1992) *Questionnaire Design, Interviewing and Attitude Measurement*, London, Pinter.

Osgood, C. E., Suci, G. J. and Tannenbaum, P. H. (1957) *Measurents of Meaning*, Urbana, IL, Illinois University Press.

Othman, R. (2004) An Applied Ethnographic Methods for Evaluation Retrieval Features, *Electronic Library*, **22** (5), 425-32.

Outhwaite, W. (1987) *New Philosophies of Social Science: realism, hermeneutics and critical theory*, London, Macmillan Education.

Pallant, J. (2005) *SPSS Survival Manual*, 2nd edn, Maidenhead, Open University Press.

Paterno, F. (2000) *Model-based Design and Evaluation of Interface Applications*, London, Springer Verlag.

Patton, M. Q. (1987) *How to Use Qualitative Methods in Evaluation*, London, Sage.

Patton, M. Q. (1988) Paradigms and Pragmatism. In Fetterman, D. M. (ed.), *Qualitative Approaches to Evaluation in Education: the silent scientific revolution*, London, Praeger, 116-37.

Patton, M. Q. (2002) *Qualitative Research and Evaluation Methods*, London, Sage.

Pavlov, I. P. (1927) *Conditioned Reflexes*, Oxford, Oxford University Press.

Payne, P. (1990) Sampling and Recruiting Respondents. In Slater, M. (ed.), *Research Methods in Library and Information Studies*, London, Library Association, 22-43.

Pearl, J. (2002) *Causality: models, reasoning and inference*, Cambridge, Cambridge University Press.

Pickard, A. J. (1998) The Impact of Access to Electronic and Digital Information

Resources on Learning Opportunities for Young People: a grounded theory approach, *Information Research*, **4** (2), http://informationr.net/ir/4-2/isic/pickard.html.

Pickard, A. J. (2002) *Access to Electronic Information Resources: their role in the provision of learning opportunities to young people. A constructivist inquiry*, PhD thesis, Northumbria University.

Pickard, A. (2004) Young People and the Internet: accessing internet-based electronic information resources, *Update*, **3** (1), (January), 32–4.

Pickard, A. (2005) The Role of Effective Intervention in Promoting the Value of EIS in the Learning Process, *Performance Measurement and Metrics*, **6** (3), 172–82.

Pickard, A. and Dixon, P. (2004) The Applicability of Constructivist User Studies: how can constructivist inquiry inform service providers and systems designers? *Information Research*, **9** (3), paper 175, http://InformationR.net/ir/9-3/paper175.html.

Pike, K. L. (1954) *Language in Relation to a Unified Theory of the Structure of Human Behavior*, Glendale, CA, Summer Institute of Linguistics.

Popper, K. (1963) *The Open Society and its Enemies*, London, Routledge.

Powell R. A., Single H. M. and Lloyd K. R. (1996) Focus Groups in Mental Health Research: enhancing the validity of user and provider questionnaires, *International Journal of Social Psychology*, **42** (3), 193–206.

Preece, J., Rodgers, Y. and Sharpe, H. (2002) *Interaction Design: beyond human-computer interaction*, New York, Wiley & Sons.

Prior, L. (2003) *Using Documents in Social Research*, London, Sage.

Punch, K. (1998) *Introduction to Social Research: quantitative and qualitative approaches*, London, Sage.

Punch, K. (2003) *Survey Research: the basics*, London, Sage.

Punch, M. (1994) Politics and Ethics in Qualitiative Research. In Denzin, N. K. and Lincoln, Y. S. (eds), *Handbook of Qualitative Research*, London, Sage, 83–97.

Rael, P. (2004) *Reading, Writing and Researching for History: a guide for college students*, http://academic.bowdoin.edu/WritingGuides/.

Rafaeli, S. (1996) How Do You Get a Hundred Strangers to Agree? Computer-mediated communication and collaboration. In Harrison, T. M. and Stephens, T. D. (eds), *Computer Networking and Scholarly Communication in the Twenty-First-Century University*, Albany, NY, State University of New York Press, 115–36.

Rheingold, H. (1993) *The Virtual Community: homesteading on the electronic frontier*, London, Sage.

Ritchie, A. and Genoni, P. (2002) Group Mentoring and Professionalism: a programme evaluation, *Library Management*, **23** (1/2), 68–78.

Ritchie, J. and Lewis, J. (2003) *Qualitative Research Practice: a guide for social science students and researchers*, London, Sage.

Robson, C. (1997) *Real World Research: a resource for social scientists and practitioner-researchers*, Oxford, Blackwell.

Rossman, G. B. and Rallis, S. F. (1998) *Learning in the Field: an introduction to qualitative research*, London, Sage.

Rowley, J. (2004) Researching People and Organizations, *Library Management*, **25** (4/5), 208-14.

Rudestam, K. E. and Newton, R. R. (2001) *Surviving Your Dissertation: a comprehensive guide to content and process*, 2nd edn, London, Sage.

Sapsford, R. J. (1999) *Survey Research*, London, Sage.

Schatzman, L. and Strauss, A. (1973) *Field Research: strategies for a natural sociology*, Englewood Cliffs, Prentice Hall.

Schinke, S. P. and Gilchrist, L. (1993) Ethics in Research. In Grinnell, R. M. (ed.), *Social Work, Research and Evaluation*, 4th edn, Illinois, Peacock, 80-92.

Schön, D. (1991) *The Reflective Practitioner: how professionals think in action*, Aldershot, Avebury.

Schwartz, M. T. (1997) The Eyes of our Ancestors have a Message: studio photographs at Fort Sumner, New Mexico, 1866, *Visual Anthropology*, **10** (1), 17-47.

Schwartz, P. and Ogilvy, J. (1979) *The Emergent Paradigm: changing patterns of thought and belief*, Analytical Report 7, Values and Lifestyles Program, Menlo Park, CA, SRI International.

Seale, C. (ed.) (1998) *Researching Society and Culture*, London, Sage.

Seale, C. (ed.) (2004) *Social Research Methods: a reader*, London, Routledge.

Selden, L. (2005) On Grounded Theory - With Some Malice, *Journal of Documentation*, **61** (1), 114-29.

Shen, E. and Liang, C. C. (2000) Research of Interactive Exhibition Design for the Web-based Virtual Reality Museum, *Journal of Educational Media and Library Sciences*, **37** (3), 275-98.

Silverman, D. (2000) *Doing Qualitative Research: a practical handbook*, London, Sage.

Skinner, B. F. (1987) *Upon Further Reflection*, London, Prentice-Hall.

Skodal-Wilson, H. and Ambler-Hutchinson, S. (1996) Methodological Mistakes in Grounded Theory, *Nursing Research*, **45** (2), 122-24.

Slater, M. (ed.) (1990) *Research Methods in Library and Information Studies*, London, Library Association.

Smith, J. K. (1990) Alternative Research Paradigms and the Problem of Criteria. In Guba, E. (ed.), *The Paradigm Dialog*, London, Sage, 167-87.

Smith, M. J. (1998) *Social Science in Question*, London, Sage.

Somekh, B. (2006) *Action Research: a methodology for change and development*, Maidenhead, Open University Press.

Spradley, J. (1979) *The Ethnographic Interview*, New York, Holt, Rhinehart & Winston.

Stake, R. E. (1994) Case Studies. In Denzin, N. K. and Lincoln, Y. S. (eds) *Handbook of Qualitative Research*, London, Sage, 236-47.

Stake, R. E. (1995) *The Art of Case Study Research*, London, Sage.

Stake, R. E. (2003) Case Studies. In Denzin, N. K. and Lincoln, Y. S. (eds) *Strategies of Qualitative Inquiry*, 2nd edn, London, Sage, 134–64.

Stenhouse, L. (1984) Library Access, Library Use, and User Education in Academic Sixth Forms: an autobiographical account. In Burgess, R. G. (ed.), *The Research Process in Educational Settings: ten case studies*, London, Falmer Press.

Stephen, P. and Hornby, S. (1997) *Simple Statistics for Library and Information Professionals*, London, Library Association.

Stewart, D. W. and Shamdasani, P. N. (1990) *Focus Groups: theory and practice*, London, Sage.

Strauss, A. and Corbin, J. (1990) *Basics of Qualitative Research: grounded theory procedures and techniques,* London, Sage.

Strauss, A. and Corbin, J. (1994) Grounded Theory Methodology: an overview. In Denzin, N. K. and Lincoln, Y. S. (eds), *Handbook of Qualitative Research*, London, Sage, 273–85.

Strauss, A. and Corbin, J. (1998) *Basics of Qualitative Research: techniques and procedures for developing grounded theory*, London, Sage.

Strauss, A. L. (1987) *Qualitative Data Analysis for Social Scientisits*, Cambridge, Cambridge University Press.

Stringer, E. T. (1996) *Action Research: a handbook for practitioners*, London, Sage.

Stringer, E. T. (1999) *Action Research: a handbook for practitioners*, 2nd edn, London, Sage.

Swingewood, A. (2000) *A Short History of Sociological Thought*, 3rd edn, London, Macmillan.

Tabatabai, D. and Shore, B. M. (2005) How Experts and Novices Search the Web, *Library and Information Science Research,* **27** (2), 222–48.

Tagg, S. K. (1985) Life Story Interviews and Their Interpretation. In Brenner, M., Brown, J. and Canter, D. *The Research Interview: uses and approaches*, New York, Academic Press.

Tellis, W. (1997) Introduction to Case Study, *The Qualitative Report*, **3** (2), www.nova.edu/ssss/QR/QR3-2/tellis1.html.

Thurstone, L. L. and Chave, E. J. (1929) *The Measurement of Attitudes*, Chicago, Chicago University Press.

Tosh, J. (2002) *The Pursuit of History: aims, methods and new directions in the study of modern history*, 3rd edn, London, Longman.

Toulmin, S. (1958) *The Uses of Argument*, Cambridge, Cambridge University Press.

Travers, M. (2001) *Qualitative Research Through Case Studies*, London, Sage.

Trochim, W. (2005) *Research Methods: the concise knowledge base*, Ohio, Atomicdog.

Tucker, K. H. (1998) *Anthony Giddens and Modern Social Theory*, London, Sage.

Turkle, S. (1995) *Life in the Screen: identity in the age of the internet*, New York, McGraw-Hill.

Turoff, M. and Hiltz, S. R. (1997) *Computer based Delphi Processes*, http://eies.njit.edu/~turoff/Papers/delphi3.html#AI.

US National Archives and Records Administration, www.archives.gov/.

Vidich, A. J. and Lyman, S. M. (1994) Qualitative Methods: their history in sociology and anthropology. In Denzin, N. K. and Lincoln, Y. S. (eds), *The Landscape of Qualitative Research: theories and issues,* London, Sage, 23-59.

Walsh, D. (1998) Doing Ethnography. In Seale, C. (ed.), *Researching Society and Culture,* London, Sage, 217-32.

Warren, A. and Dearnley, J. (2005) Data Protection Legislation in the United Kingdom: from development to statute 1969-84, *Information, Communication & Society,* **8** (2), 238-63.

Warren, C. A. B. and Hackney, J. K. (2000) *Gender Issues in Ethnography,* 2nd edn, London, Sage.

Wharton, C., Rieman, J., Lewis, C. and Polson, P. (1994) The Cognitive Walkthrough: a practitioner's guide. In Nielsen, J. and Mack, R. L. (eds), *Usability Inspection Methods,* New York, John Wiley and Sons.

White, K. J. and Sutcliffe, R. F. E. (2006) Applying Incremental Tree Induction to Retrieval from Manuals and Medical Texts, *Journal of the American Society for Information Science and Technology,* **57** (5), 588-600.

Wilcox, K. (1982) Ethnography as a Methodology and its Application to the Study of Schooling: a review. In Spindler, G. (ed.), *Doing the Ethnography of Schooling,* New York, CBS Publishing, 456-88.

Williams, R. C. (2003) *The Historian's Toolbox: a student's guide to the theory and craft of history,* Armonk, NY, M. E. Sharpe.

Wilson, T. D. (1994) Information Needs and Uses: fifty years of progress? In Vickery, B., *Fifty Years of Information Progress: a journal of documentation annual review,* London, Aslib, 15-51.

Wilson, V. (1997) Focus Groups: a useful qualitative method for educational research?, *British Educational Research Journal,* **23** (2), 209-24.

Wolcott, H. F. (1990) On Seeking and Rejecting: validity in qualitative research. In Preshkin, A. and Eisner, E. W. (eds), *Qualitative Inquiry in Education: the continuing debate,* New York, Teachers College Press, 121-52.

Wolcott, H. F. (1999) *Ethnography: a way of seeing,* Walnut Place, CA, AltaMira Press.

World Archives, www.hartford-hwp.com/archives/index.html.

World Wide Web Consortium (W3C) (1999) *Web Content Accessibility Guidelines 1.0,* W3C, www.w3.org/TR/1999/WAI-WEBCONTENT-19990505/.

Woundenberg, F. (1991) An Evaluation of Delphi, *Technological Forecasting and Social Change,* **40** (2), 131-50.

Yin, R. K. (2002) *Case Study Research: design and methods,* 3rd edn, London, Sage.

Zuber-Skerritt, O. (ed.) (1996) *New Directions in Action Research,* London, Falmer.

Index